The Native Tourist
Mass Tourism within Developing Countries

Edited by

Krishna B Ghimire

EARTHSCAN

Earthscan Publications Limited, London and Sterling, VA

First published in the UK and USA in 2001 by
Earthscan Publications Ltd

ISBN: 1 85383 804 7 paperback
        1 85383 803 9 hardback

Typesetting by JS Typesetting, Wellingborough, Northants
Printed and bound by Biddles Ltd, Guildford and King's Lynn
Cover design by Declan Buckley
Cover photograph © Panos Pictures/Dermot Tatlow

For a full list of publications please contact:

Earthscan Publications Ltd
120 Pentonville Road
London, N1 9JN, UK
Tel: +44 (0)20 7278 0433
Fax: +44 (0)20 7278 1142
Email: earthinfo@earthscan.co.uk
http://www.earthscan.co.uk

22883 Quicksilver Drive, Sterling, VA 20166–2012, USA

A catalogue record for this book is available from the British Library

Library of Congress Cataloging-in-Publication Data

The native tourist : mass tourism within developing countries / edited by Krishna
Ghimire.
      p. cm.
   Includes bibliographical references (p.).
   ISBN 1-85383-803-9 (cloth) — ISBN 1-85383-804-7 (pbk.)
      1. Tourism—Developing countries. I. Ghimire Krishna.

   G155.D44 N38 2001
   338.4'791091724—dc21

                                                                          2001023273

Earthscan is an editorially independent subsidiary of Kogan Page Ltd and publishes in
association with WWF-UK and the International Institute for Environment and
Development

This book is printed on elemental chlorine-free paper

Contents

List of Tables and Figures

Tables

Figures

Contributors

David Barkin

Professor
Universidad Autónoma Metropolitana/
   Unidad Xochimilco
Apartado 23–181
16000 Xochimilco
D.F.
Mexico

David Bezic

Researcher
Thailand Development Research Institute
565 Soi Ramkhamhaeng 39
Wangthonglang Bangkapi District
Bangkok 10310
Thailand

Antonio C Diegues

Professor
Universidad de São Paulo – Cidade Universitaria
Rua de Anfiteatro
181, Colméia
Favo 6
Cp 05508-000 SP
Brazil

Krishna B Ghimire

Project Leader
United Nations Research Institute for Social
   Development
Palais des Nations
1211-Geneva 10
Switzerland

Mingsarn Kaosa-ard

Vice-president
Thailand Development Research Institute
556 Soi Ramkhamhaeng 39
Wangthonglang Bangkapi District
Bangkok 10310
Thailand

Eddie Koch

Journalist
Daily Mail and *The Guardian*
PO Box 32362
Braamfontein
Johannesburg 2001
South Africa

Zhou Li

Professor
Rural Development Institute
Chinese Academy of Social Sciences
5 Jianguomennei Dajie
Beijing 100732
China

Peter John Massyn

Co-director
MAFISA
28 Tyrone Avenue
Parkview 2193
South Africa

Abdul Raufu Mustapha

Lecturer and Course Director
Oxford University
Queen Elizabeth House
21 St Giles
Oxford OX1 3LA
United Kingdom

Nina Rao

Reader and Head of Department
Department of Tourism
College of Vocational Studies
University of Delhi
Delhi 7
India

KT Suresh

Director
Equitable Tourism Options
198, 2nd Cross
Church Road
New Thippasandra
Bangalore 560075
India

Suzanne White   Researcher
Thailand Development Research Institute
565 Soi Ramkhamhaeng 39
Wangthonglang Bangkapi District
Bangkok 10310, Thailand

Acronyms and Abbreviations

ABRESI	Associação Brasileira de Gastronomia, Hospitalidade e Turismo
ACTSA	Action for Southern Africa
AMACUP	Asociación Mexicana de Arte y Cultura Popular, A.C.
ANC	African National Congress
ASEAN	Association of South-East Asian Nations
ATBTC	Abubakar Tafawa Balewa Tourist Complex (Nigeria)
ATTO	Association of Thai Tour Operators
BJP	Bharatiya Janata Party (India)
BNDES	Bank for Socio-Economic Development (Brazil)
BOI	Board of Investment (Thailand)
BOP	balance of payments
CBN	Central Bank of Nigeria
CNC	National Peasant Confederation (Mexico)
CNUMAD	Conferencia de las Naciones Unidas sobre el Medio Ambiente y el Desarrollo (Brazil)
COMBRATUR	Brazilian Commission for Tourism
COSATU	Congress of South African Trade Unions
CPC	Communist Party of China
CSS	Center for Spirituality and Sustainability (South Africa)
DACST	Department of Arts, Culture, Science and Technology (South Africa)
DEAT	Department of Environmental Affairs and Tourism (South Africa)
DOT	Department of Transport (South Africa)
DTI	Department of Trade and Industry
ECOWAS	Economic Community of West African States
EIA	environmental impact assessment
EMBRATUR	Brazilian Enterprise for Tourism
ESCAP	Economic and Social Commission for Asia and the Pacific
FHRAI	Federation of Hotel and Restaurant Associations of India
FINAM	Investment Funds for Amazonia
FUNGETUR	General Fund for Tourism Development (Brazil)
GDP	gross domestic product
GEAR	Growth Employment and Reconstruction (South Africa)

GI	general infantry
GNP	gross national product
HRD	human resource development
IATO	Indian Association of Tour Operators
IBAMA	Brazilian Institute for Environment Protection
IDB	Inter-American Development Bank
IDCO	Infrastructural Development Corporation of Orissa Ltd (India)
ILO	International Labour Organization
IMSS	Mexican Social Security Institute
INAH	National Institute of Anthropology and History (Mexico)
INEGI	National Statistics Bureau (Mexico)
INTACH	Indian National Trust for Culture and Heritage
ITDC	India Tourism Development Corporation
KZN	KwaZulu-Natal (South Africa)
LAPC	Land Agricultural Policy Centre (South Africa)
LSSG	Living Standards Super Group (South Africa)
LTC	Leave Travel Concession (India)
Mercosur	Mercado Común del Cono Sur
NAFTA	North American Free Trade Agreement
NAP	National Action Plan (India)
NGO	non-governmental organization
NIC	newly industrialized country
NTDC	Nigerian Tourism Development Corporation
OECF	Overseas Economic Cooperation Fund of Japan
PATA	Pacific Asia Travel Association
PLANTUR	National Plan for Tourism (Brazil)
PRODETUR	Projeto de Desenvolvimento do Turismo (Brazil)
PT	Partido dos Trabalhadores (Brazil)
R&R	rest and recreation
RCI	Research Center Imarat (India)
RDP	Reconstruction and Development Programme (South Africa)
RETOSA	Regional Tourism Organization of Southern Africa
RMB	Chinese currency
SAP	Structural Adjustment Program
SAR	South African Railways
SATOUR	South African Tourism Board
SAARC	South Asian Association for Regional Cooperation
SADC	Southern Africa Development Community
SALDRU	South African Labour and Development Research Unit
SANCO	South African National Civic Organization
SDIs	spatial development initiatives

SEBRAE	Serviço Brasileiro de Apoio às Micro e Pequenas Empresas
SEMFs	strategic environmental management frameworks
STA	special tourism area (India)
SUDENE	Superintendency for the Development of the Northeast (Brazil)
TAAI	Travel Agents Association of India
TAP	Tourism Awareness Programme (India)
TAT	Tourism Authority of Thailand
TDRI	Thailand Development Research Institute
TNC	transnational corporation
TNT	National Policy for Tourism (Brazil)
TOT	Tourism Organization of Thailand
UNDP	United Nations Development Programme
UNESCO	United Nations Educational, Scientific and Cultural Organization
UNRISD	United Nations Research Institute for Social Development
VFRs	visiting friends and relatives
WTO	World Tourism Organization
WTTC	World Travel and Tourism Council

Chapter 1

The Growth of National and Regional Tourism in Developing Countries: An Overview

Krishna B Ghimire

Background[1]

Past trends in the expansion of tourism and the prognosis for continued growth have been favourably received by the business community and governments. Over 560 million people travelled abroad in 1995 with an estimated tourist expenditure of US$350 billion (WTO, 1997a, pp2 and 7), and projections for the year 2010 estimate 937 million international tourists. This makes tourism a very appealing strategy for promoting economic activity and growth (WTO, 1995a, p35). However, existing tourism policies in developing countries have tended to concentrate overwhelmingly on expanding international tourist arrivals from the North and have frequently ignored both the benefits and problems of the emerging phenomenon of mass tourism involving domestic and regional visitors.

The importance of domestic and regional tourism in developing countries has grown in recent years. Regional travel patterns, based on the data provided by the World Tourism Organization (WTO), suggest a substantial tourism flow in the respective regions. In 1998, about 55 per cent of tourists in the Association of South-East Asian Nations (ASEAN) countries came from the Asian and Pacific developing countries. Some 73 per cent of the visitors to the Southern African Development Community (SADC) region originated from Africa. In the case of the Mercado Común del Cono Sur (Mercosur), visitors from Latin America constituted over 70 per cent of regional arrivals. Indeed, not only is the number of tourists from developing countries in the region high, but WTO forecasts suggest a sustained growth on intraregional travel in developing countries in the coming years (WTO, 2000, pp11–803; WTO, 1997b, pp10–15).

The number of domestic tourists, as some authorities estimate, may soon be as much as ten times greater than current international tourist arrivals (WTO, 1995a, p1). It is not clear whether this estimate includes domestic tourism in both the South and the North. Nevertheless, the information collected for this book clearly shows a rapidly rising trend in domestic tourism in developing countries. For example, in the mid-1990s, India, South Africa and Brazil had 135, 12 and 96 million domestic tourists respectively (based on tourist nights). China had an even higher number of national tourists. Current domestic tourism patterns and expected growth will be discussed later in this chapter, but one point worth making here is that in almost all developing countries the number of nationals travelling for leisure is considerably higher than the number of international tourist arrivals. In 1994, India, South Africa and Brazil received only 1.88, 3.66 and 1.70 million foreign tourists respectively (WTO, 1996, p12).

Despite rapid growth – and many potential and impending problems – information on domestic and regional tourism in developing countries is currently very obscure. Even countries with a significant increase in the number of nationals travelling within their own country, such as the nations of South-East Asia, lack reliable statistics on the number of people involved, let alone on tourist behaviours, impacts and possible remedies.

As the dominant official concept of tourism in developing countries focuses on receiving wealthy foreign visitors from the industrialized North, most governments have put significant effort into promoting international tourism, neglecting the potentials – as well as the problems – related to mass tourism involving domestic and regional tourists. In almost all developing countries, domestic tourism development is generally taking place without any systematic government planning. When a significant number of people begin to travel for leisure within their own country, they demand facilities and services. Governments have tended to cope with this process in an ad hoc manner, with tourism policies being formulated in a completely unplanned fashion. When investments from the private sector are made in this sector, they remain highly sectoral and short-term and are often motivated by quick profit-making.

The 'Northern bias' is not only reflected in government tourism policies, but also in the writing on tourism. The bulk of past social science enquiry has been concerned mainly with the socio-economic effects of tourism in the North or involving Northern tourists in the South.[2] Little knowledge exists on Southern tourists. Although a great deal of research has been carried out on the impact of tourism on national economies and cultures, and more recently on the environment, few studies focus systematically on the different social groups that interact in the context of Southern national and regional tourism, or on the wider socio-political structures and processes that very often determine who ultimately benefits or loses from tourism. Tourism studies rarely separate the respective impacts of national and international tourism. The type and extent of tourism impacts can greatly differ depending not only on the total number of visitors involved, but also on their destinations, social origins and leisure expectations, as well as on the type of political and economic systems in the country.

Although the major international organizations working in the area of tourism, such as the WTO and the United Nations Educational, Scientific and Cultural Organization (UNESCO), commonly acknowledge the import-ance of domestic tourism, their contribution to increasing knowledge and postulating appropriate planning measures in this area is extremely limited.[3] Interestingly enough, this is not very different from the major tourism non-governmental organizations (NGOs) as well. For example, Tourism Concern, a major activist and policy-oriented NGO, does not mention this phenomenon in its strategic document, and the Ecumenical Coalition on Third World Tourism, which brings together numerous developing world NGOs working in the field of tourism, has not considered Southern domestic and regional tourism to be important enough to include it in its mandate and proposed activities.[4]

Why should this be so? The answer is not evident. One plausible explanation may be that domestic and regional tourists have a lower spending capacity compared to Northern tourists; thus, the domestic and regional tourism sectors may be seen as less interesting for tourism investment and planning. However, globally, as we shall see later, national and regional tourists seem to be generating far more income than Western tourists in all the developing countries analysed in this book. It is also possible that tourism research and publications are more market-driven, commissioned by tourism investors and governments, thus resulting in little independent or deep reflection covering these new groups of tourists. Most of the NGOs, on the other hand, are barely able to handle the work related to the lobbying, advocacy and documentation involving Northern tourists. The development of national and regional tourism demands a further burden on their work and resources. Some of them may also be lacking imaginative thinking and future appraisals. In any event, most of them are based in the Northern countries and react primarily to their government's tourist policies or specific travel patterns involving their nationals. The existing tourism literature and planning, on the whole, see a 'tourist' as being automatically a 'Northerner', with leisure activity being his or her privileged practice.

A serious approach to domestic tourism needs an operational definition that will allow both those who work in the industry and those who study tourism as an economic, social and cultural phenomenon to collect accurate data and accordingly provide sound analysis and policy guidelines. The WTO has defined a 'domestic tourist' as:

any person residing in a country, who travels to a place within the country outside his/her usual environment, for a period not exceeding 12 months and whose main purpose of visit is other than the exercise of an activity remunerated from within the place visited (WTO, 1993).

For a person to be qualified as a 'tourist', the minimum stay-away should be longer than 24 hours, otherwise the WTO considers that person a 'same-day visitor'. The WTO has also specified that the journey of a domestic tourist could involve the following purposes: a) leisure, recreation and holidays; b) visiting friends and relatives; c) business and professional; d) health treatment; e) religion/pilgrimages; and f) other (ibid).

The problem with this definition is that it is so broad that it encompasses any possible purpose that a person might have to leave his/her home and, in consequence, anybody travelling inside his/her country for more than 24 hours could be seen as a 'domestic tourist'. Business, visits to relatives and friends, pilgrimages and other religious forms of tourism, for instance, are all traditional motivations for travel that have always been present in any society. What is currently more outstanding and attracts the attention of this study, in particular, is the growth in the number of nationals of developing countries who travel exclusively for leisure purposes. Tourism is a multifaceted phenomenon and tourists often combine different purposes when travelling. But these intrinsic characteristics of tourism still leave us with the same question: who should be considered a domestic tourist?

Diegues in Chapter 3 argues that the WTO definition makes it impossible to quantify the number of passengers travelling exclusively for leisure purposes, as the definition includes so many other purposes of travel. The data available from Brazil, for example, are mostly based on the number of passengers embarking and disembarking at airports in a given year. This results in very inaccurate figures, as there is a greater number of domestic and regional tourists who travel by bus or by car, and who are not being taken into account. Rao and Suresh in Chapter 8 also refer to problems of definition related to tourism. The definition of a domestic tourist in India also includes people travelling for pleasure, pilgrimage, religious and social functions, business conferences and meetings, study and health. It excludes those who do not use commercial facilities when visiting friends and relatives or when attending social or religious functions. The collection of often unreliable data due to such broad definitions results in inadequate planning, insufficient facilities and deficient services, among other things.

With respect to regional tourism, the WTO combines both 'overseas' and 'regional' tourists in the same definition of 'international tourists'. 'Regional tourists' are those who come from distinct neighbouring regions, such as South-East Asia, Southern Africa, Central America and South America. Besides geographical proximity, the countries in a given region may share many similar historical developments, ecological characteristics, standards of living, socio-economic structures, culture and population composition. Regarding the problems arising from the definition of 'regional' tourists, Pleumaron states that:

> *Official data concerning visitor arrivals and purpose of travel need to be treated with great caution as they tend to blur the division between tourist and non-tourist practices. For instance, today's world is characterized by vast migration movements, and it seems common that people seeking work in foreign countries are travelling on tourist visas. People frequently crossing borders to neighbouring countries for all kinds of purposes may be registered as tourists each time they pass the checkpoints* (Pleumaron, 1997).

The inconsistencies and weaknesses in the definitions of domestic and regional tourism are the result of a lack of in-depth studies in the field, and the absence of a careful assessment of this growing phenomenon in formal tourism planning. The fact that domestic tourists do not cross borders represents another difficulty in the process of quantifying the amount of nationals travelling within their own country.

A core issue is under what circumstances can the emerging national and regional tourism in the South contribute to sustainable development. In this regard, the core question is: would national and regional tourism represent 'self-reliance' and become an economic dynamo for the country (as in theory it should be less sensitive to international political instability and economic stagnation, less detrimental to the country's balance of payments, less 'leaky' and able to create substantial income and employment)? From the point of view of the local populations affected by tourism, what ultimately matters is whether their livelihoods are protected and new ones created, leading to improved living conditions. An interrelated question is: which groups benefit and which are marginalized? Similarly, what is the ability of the state to intervene on behalf of the latter? How are local cultures and social cohesion influenced and how do they interact? Similarly, how is local ecology affected, especially as domestic and regional tourists involve a relatively large number of people requiring substantial accommodation, transport, recreational facilities, etc?

Thus, the chief aim of this book has been to increase knowledge and debate concerning the socio-economic, cultural, political and environmental implications emerging from the rise in domestic and regional tourism in developing countries. More specifically, the study has attempted to collect and examine the available information on the nature, magnitude and various impacts of domestic and regional tourism in different socio-economic and environmental contexts on diverse social groups, as well as any concrete policy measures that have been undertaken. The analysis of the principal policy issues is especially important as national and regional tourism involve a large number of people, thereby presenting a challenge to the concept of socio-ecologically sustainable tourism; and controlling tourists' movements is logically difficult and politically unfeasible.

What is the best way to tackle the growing number of domestic and regional tourists in developing countries and what are their consequent impacts? Domestic tourism is now being incorporated in a few government development plans, but it is usually promoted for the sake of preventing the outflow of foreign currency from the country. And should regional tourism receive special and differentiated attention in comparison to international tourism? It is clear that in certain respects the behaviour of a 'regional tourist' differs from that of the average international tourist, thus necessitating different policy measures. For example, he or she may be satisfied with less luxurious accommodation and be more aware of the local cultural norms than tourists coming from Europe or North America. In some cases, the opposite could also be true, especially when the majority of the regional and national tourists originate mainly from the privileged classes engaged in lavish consumption activities (see Ghimire, 1997, p5). In other cases, the growth in regional tourism may only reinforce the existing regional power relations and inequalities. For instance, some scholars argue that the recent increase in Indian tourists going to Nepal may actually exacerbate the unequal economic and political relations that exist between the two countries, with the Indian economy, business and travel sector mainly benefiting in the process (Aditya and Shrestha, 1998).

International, regional and domestic tourism are in some ways different faces of the same phenomenon in that they all involve leisure travel and many associated socio-economic relations and exchanges. They also have their particularities, problems and possible benefits. International tourism has always been seen by governments, the business community and international funding agencies as an effective tool for economic development. North–South tourism has evolved for several decades. Intraregional and domestic travel within the Southern countries is now a growing phenomenon that has expanded in the last few years thanks to the improvement of socio-economic conditions of certain sections of the population, the proliferation of workers' rights, such as paid holidays, and the expansion in the transport system. In addition to this, a very rapid globalization process involving the strong influence of Western mass media, education systems and lifestyles in the South has helped to promote the Northern-style consumerism and leisure travel. To look only at international tourism, therefore, could mean not only to overlook the full scope of tourism potential involving domestic and regional tourism, but also to ignore problems arising from its spontaneous growth.

This book represents a first attempt to elucidate some of the main issues concerning this largely ignored and neglected phenomenon. The different chapters originate mostly from a review of secondary material and a few basic official statistics. This being said, the different authors have also sought to compile the information through their own sources and work. The main purpose of the study has been to raise critical questions rather than to provide complete answers, while inviting academics, students, government officials and those directly involved in the tourism industry to analyse and engage in more in-depth studies in the future.

This introductory chapter has the objective of summarizing the principal questions, concepts and processes related to the rise in national and regional mass tourism in developing countries. It will seek to highlight the historical trends in domestic tourism development, the current extent and growth trends of domestic and regional tourism, tourist groups and motivations, the associated impacts and the crucial issues related to tourism planning and public policies. In Chapter 2, Barkin highlights the development in domestic tourism in Mexico, especially the tendency of the successive governments to invest only in international tourism development, neglecting the potential internal market. The author remarks on the destructive character of the present tourism development model for the least developed sites favoured by nationals. The possibilities for 'social tourism' and grass-roots initiatives for community-based tourism as instruments to promote decentralized development are also discussed. In Chapter 3, based largely on a case study in the north-eastern region of Brazil, Diegues demonstrates how the negative impacts of tourism can be offset by actively integrating local communities into tourism development. Despite the growing importance of domestic and regional tourism in the country, it has only recently been the subject of debate and discussion. The chapter points to the need for more adequate statistics and analyses on these issues. The growing economic role of domestic tourism in China is the focus of Chapter 4 by Ghimire and Li. It indicates that the domestic tourism market in the country is enormous, due to the lifting of restrictions on travel within the country, the introduction of the five-day working week and an increasing disposable income among certain categories of the population. However, the sheer size of the domestic tourism sector creates novel environmental and cultural challenges; and, in particular, its possible impacts on local livelihoods and cultures have not been carefully considered. In Chapter 5, Kaosa-ard et al analyse current inconsistencies in national tourism policies in Thailand. They expose how present tourist development policies focus solely on increasing demand. In reality, however, in several areas the number of tourists may already be beyond the environmental carrying-capacity, with severe consequences for local communities. The growth of domestic and regional tourism will only exacerbate this problem unless this issue is addressed by the government's tourism policies. In Chapter 6, Koch and Massyn address the 'boom' of domestic and regional tourism in post-apartheid South Africa. They raise questions about the ability of governmental domestic tourism policies to serve as a vehicle for national reconciliation, and income and employment generation, since the government is heavily dependent on multinational investment capital and tourism promotion. Chapter 7 by Mustapha analyses the socio-economic situations and political upheavals that have impeded the take-off of the Nigerian tourism industry, despite the many tourist resources that the country possesses. In Chapter 8, Rao and Suresh describe the growth in the domestic tourism sector in India and the tensions it is creating between urban lifestyles and village traditions, as well as the trade-offs involved in increasing economic revenue and promoting culturally and environmentally friendly tourism policies. The authors argue for a more sustainable form of tourism through awareness-raising activities for tourists, residents and policy-makers, and the increased participation of local groups in defining tourism.

The Evolution of National Tourism in Developing Countries

Before discussing the current growth trends in domestic tourism, the main tourist groups involved and the resultant impacts, it is instructive to look briefly into the evolution patterns of domestic tourism in developing countries. It should help us to understand when and how national tourism began to expand in most contexts, especially in the case study countries. This should also help us to find out if the trends in developing countries are similar to those of developed countries.

Travelling for pilgrimages, health treatment or paying visits to friends and relatives are common features of tourism in almost every society. In developing countries, religious tourism is often the primary motive for travelling, which is combined with other purposes such as a holiday. Religious tourism may involve the periodic movement of a large number of people. For instance, in India 20 million people visited 150 well-known holy sites in 1988 (Rinschede, 1992, p52); in Mexico, 'fiestas' or religious festivals attract a great number of visitors to small towns throughout the year (Barkin, Chapter 2). What is important is perhaps the indirect contribution of the religious events to the tourist development of an area. In Thailand, for example, the mere restoration of an ancient temple attracts a great number of Thais and propels food, souvenir and lottery stalls in the nearby premises, or stimulates the organization of fairs and festivals (Cohen, 1992, p39). Travel involving some elements of Western-style leisure and holiday-taking patterns is also quite old among certain social groups in Southern countries. Changing summer and winter residences, and undertaking hunting or sports expeditions were common practices among the dominant Asian aristocracies, even prior to Western influence in the region (Ghimire, 1997, p12). However, mass domestic tourism motivated exclusively for leisure purposes is a more recent phenomenon related mostly to economic growth and the consequent expansion of the urban middle classes. This is also the result of the rapid spread of Western-style consumerism and leisure ethic, as noted above.

In Latin America, domestic tourism developed earlier than in Asian or African countries. This was due in part to the region's earlier accelerated integration into the global economy resulting in a higher level of social stratification with a small (but substantially large in terms of the total number of population) number of the middle and upper classes enjoying a standard of living quite comparable to their counterparts in Europe and North America. In Argentina and Chile the sector had already developed before the Second World War; and it had become a notable feature in Mexico and Brazil by the 1960s. From the 1970s onwards, domestic tourism became a common phenomenon in many other Latin American countries. Regional economic differences and the desire of tourists for exploring new locations provided a great deal of impetus to cross-country travel, such as Argentineans visiting Brazil.

What were the very ingredients that led to this evolution? In Brazil, for example, as Diegues points out in Chapter 3, domestic tourism first started in the 1940s and 1950s with the expansion of the urban industrial working and middle classes, especially in the south-eastern part of the country. The recognition and consolidation of labour rights, such as annual vacations, also contributed to the process. In the 1960s, tourist numbers grew due to the setting up of the first car-making industries and the rapid construction of road networks. In the 1970s, the domestic tourist sector was boosted thanks to the growth in the urban middle classes; a higher participation of women in the labour market; an increasing number of families owning a car; the amelioration of highways and communication systems; the proliferation of travel agencies offering competitive prices; publicity; rapid urbanization; the expansion of the construction sector; and the rising popularity of weekend houses in coastal and mountain areas.

In Mexico, on the other hand, as Barkin shows in Chapter 2, domestic travel has traditionally been oriented towards reinforcing strong family and community ties. Visits to friends and relatives are usually timed to coincide with the celebration of the day honouring a local patron saint or the traditional celebration of local and regional fairs, as well as the Easter and Christmas seasons. These factors, combined with the growth in leisure travel, have resulted in a considerable expansion in domestic tourism. It was estimated that in 1994 as many as 40 per cent of the country's population travelled away from home.

In India, leisure travel is a more recent occurrence. Traditionally, the main purposes of travel were pilgrimage and visits to fairs and festivals for commercial or religious purposes. Rao and Suresh, in Chapter 8, divide Indian tourist development into three phases: traditional (pilgrimage, fairs and festivals); historical (leisure and pleasure activities of the nobility); and the colonial period in which the British attempted to recreate the ways of holidaying that they were familiar with at home. Many hill areas were turned into tourist sites and sports and adventure activities (eg hunting) were promoted. However, it was only in the post-colonial era (starting in 1947) that domestic and regional travel and tourism activities began to receive attention within the government's development planning. The introduction of paid holidays encouraged Indians to travel beyond their home environment. In the 1950s, hill stations, such as Simla or Darjeeling, became popular holiday destinations for the privileged urban middle classes. And, in recent years, coastal areas have also attracted Indian tourists, prompting the development of hotels, beach resorts and recreational centres. Until the 1960s, the domestic sector developed spontaneously, and it was only in the 1980s that it started to receive more attention on the part of the government.

In Thailand too the majority of travel was limited to religious pilgrimage to Buddhist temples and holy places, involving merit-making activities. As described in Chapter 5, this pattern changed by the early 1980s, when Thailand's economic growth accelerated and higher incomes favoured domestic travel for leisure purposes. In Thailand today all major tourist destinations and attractions (whether they be forest parks, beaches, highlands or historical monuments) are heavily frequented by Thais, generally outnumbering foreign tourists.

In China, as elaborated in Chapter 4, domestic tourism has expanded at an extraordinary rate since travel restrictions were removed in the 1980s. The government's economic liberalization policies produced increased socio-economic stratification, with a small privileged group having considerable spending capacity. In addition, workers' higher salaries and the introduction of a five-day working system allowed a larger number of people to take holidays, prompting some to travel long distances, including to neighbouring countries.

In Africa, South Africa in particular has experienced a significant growth in domestic travel since the end of apartheid. Traditionally, as Koch and Massyn suggest in Chapter 6, the domestic tourist market was dominated by the white population who enjoyed the highest levels of wealth, mobility and access to amenities. The dismantling of restrictions on access to tourist attractions and facilities, as well as the growing prosperity among some sections of the black, coloured (mixed-race) and Indian populations, have led to a remarkable expansion in domestic travel in the 1990s. As we shall see later, its overall economic contribution to the nation as well as to the local level is now highly appreciated in the government's present tourism policy.

Another African country which has seen growth in domestic tourism is Nigeria. With a large population, the economic expansion and end of the civil war in the 1960s and 1970s made leisure travel available to a great number of middle-class Nigerians. However, as Mustapha indicates in Chapter 7, the economic crisis that took hold of the country since the 1980s and 1990s has changed the situation somewhat and, at present, most middle-class professionals, who previously were able to take holidays abroad, are now barely able to travel in Nigeria. The end of the war also resulted in campaigns to encourage the Nigerian population to take holidays within the country, partly with the aim of saving foreign exchange, but also promoting national awareness and cohesion.

Domestic and regional travel within the privileged circles of politicians, business people and the urban middle class have grown steadily in Zimbabwe, Botswana, Kenya, Morocco, Algeria, Tunisia and Egypt. Frequently, leisure travel in these countries involves short trips combined with other activities, but during the school holidays and festival times many go on longer vacations (Ghimire, 1997, p14). In Egypt, the expansion in domestic travel has given a great deal of stimulus to economic investment and the development of tourist resorts in the Mediterranean and Red Sea coastal areas.

As observed in the case studies, religious tourism and visits to friends and relatives have played an important role in propelling initial leisure travel and even today constitute an important motivation for travel when combined with leisure purposes. But many other factors have come to play an important role in the recent expansion of domestic and regional tourism. If one looks back at the European experience, the development of national and regional mass tourism was the result of such factors as the strong desire to travel among the urban population, an expanding national economy, the rapid development in transport, increased workers' benefits – including paid holidays – accompanied by increased tourist facilities and publicity (Ghimire, 1997). As seen above, many of these aspects are commonly discernible in most developing countries. In particular, the concept of leisure seems to be tied intimately with the increased acceptance of Western-style liberal thinking on democracy, education, market economy and the cultural processes of globalization. This has helped on the whole to produce a highly favourable perception on recreational travel, thereby creating an urge to travel even among the lower income population groups (especially in urban areas).

The Current Extent and Growth Trends in Domestic Tourism

Domestic mass tourism constitutes an already large and growing industry in several developing countries. However, it is not possible to determine the exact number of people participating in leisure travel. Domestic tourism is a very heterogeneous and informal phenomenon. For instance, unlike international tourists, domestic tourists do not cross borders or require visas, and the owners of accommodation generally do not keep accurate registers on national and regional visitors.

The WTO has stated the need for a comprehensive and uniform system to collect statistics on domestic tourism (1995b, p3). This recommendation is guided by its belief that, as previously mentioned, domestic tourist movements outnumber international tourist arrivals, as well as their perceived economic benefits. However, the WTO has yet to develop a satisfactory method of data collection. It suggests in its technical manual three different ways of 'counting' domestic tourists: tourist nights in tourist establishments; tourist visits to specific sites; and tourist in-country trips. All three techniques have several limitations. For example, the number of tourist nights does not take into consideration those tourists who travel in caravans, or stay in less formal types of accommodation than hotels (eg camping, pensiones, rooms rented in family homes, dharmsalas, school lodges, etc). On the other hand, this formula may result in the overenumeration of tourists staying in hotels since a visitor who will be passing several nights in one given hotel could potentially be counted as being many. The number of visits to specific tourist sites is useful to estimate the volume of visitors to certain destinations, but may not be representative of the entire country. Many of the tourist gatherings are frequently seasonal or a periodic phenomenon. They may also be favoured by one or another ethnic or religious group. Likewise, the problem concerning the number of in-country trips is that they might not be valid for long periods of time or for the country as a whole. More importantly, people may travel away from home for a variety of purposes other than leisure travel. Some of this travel may even include regular commuting to work or joining the family over a weekend.

This problem is reflected in the data used in the country case studies included in this book. In the case of Brazil, the number of Brazilian tourists disembarking at national airports is used as being the most accurate representation on domestic tourists as mentioned above. Considering that most domestic tourists in the country travel by road, this figure leaves a large number of people unaccounted for. China's government Statistics Bureau combines air-travel data with traffic volume on highways and railways. All this combined amounted to 639 million trips in 1996. This high figure could just as well include Chinese people travelling for non-tourist purposes. No comprehensive, reliable nation-wide domestic tourism figure exists in India. The estimate of 135 million domestic tourists cited in the study is based on projections made after a 1995 survey of 22 tourist destinations. The Mexican Secretary of Tourism offers both the number of check-ins and tourist nights, while South Africa's South African Tourism Board (SATOUR) chose the number of domestic trips. The calculation of Thai domestic tourists, based on both the number of domestic trips and tourist nights, is an estimate of the Thai Development Research Institute. Finally, Nigeria has information only on the number of domestic and international visitors to specific tourist sites. From this, it is clear that there is a critical need for a widely accepted data collection system on domestic tourism.

In spite of the deficiencies explained above, it is possible to appreciate the magnitude of domestic tourism to a certain extent. The figures in Table 1.1 and Table 1.2 show that domestic tourism in the developing world experienced a significant growth between 1991 and 1996. Except for the Middle East region, in which the number of tourist nights spent by nationals in hotels and similar establishments diminished, the amount increased in all the other regions: 21 per cent in Africa; 35.5 per cent in Latin America; 11.6 per cent in the East

Table 1.1 *Domestic tourist nights in hotels and similar establishments in developing countries, by region*

Region	1991	1996
Africa	17,266	21,897
Latin America	110,040	170,555
East Asia/Pacific*	490,477	555,109
South Asia	4659	13,025
Middle East	2182	1766
Total	624,624	762,352

Note: *Australia and New Zealand are not included
Source: World Tourism Organization, 1998

Table 1.2 *Domestic tourist nights in hotels and similar establishments in selected countries*

Country	1992	1996
Brazil	57,870	95,752
China	134,465	195,288
India	87,200	135,000[a]
Mexico	37,254	42,604
South Africa	9304	12,100
Thailand[b]	97,000	139,000

Note: a These figures represent 1991 and 1995 respectively. Source: Chapter 8
       b Source: Chapter 5
Source: World Tourism Organization, 1998. The study by the WTO included 88 countries

Asia/Pacific region, and 64 per cent in South Asia. Domestic tourism grew by 18 per cent in the South as a whole (Table 1.1).

If the growth pattern is analysed in the case study countries for which the information is available, the increase is even more remarkable (see Table 1.2). For example, between 1992 and 1996, Brazil, China and Thailand experienced growth in domestic travel by 39.5 per cent, 31 per cent and 30 per cent respectively. India saw a remarkable rise of over 38 per cent. Similarly, South Africa realized 23 per cent growth, and domestic tourism in Mexico increased by nearly 13 per cent.

By taking a look at the number of international and domestic tourists visiting popular tourist destinations, such as Agra and the Taj Mahal in India, the city of Chiang Mai in Thailand and the Yankari National Park in Nigeria, it is evident that the number of nationals visiting those sites greatly outnumber foreign visitors. The Indian tourists visiting Agra represent five times the number of foreigners; while it is approximately three times for both Yankari and Chiangmai (Table 1.3). In the case of Brazil's Ceará and Jiuzhaigou of China, this proportion is even more striking.

Table 1.3 *Number of domestic and international tourists visiting a specific site in selected countries*

Site/country	No of domestic tourists	No of international tourists
Ceará/Brazil[a]	373,180	17,013
Jiuzhaigou/China[b]	270,000	400
Agra/India[c]	7,000,000	1,400,000
Yankari Nat Park/Nigeria[d]	8401	2470
Chiang Mai/Thailand[e]	4,006,000	1,431,000

Sources: a PRODETUR Recife, 1993: figures for 1992. b State Statistics Bureau, *China Statistics Yearbook*: figures for 1992. c *Economic Times*, 11 May 1997: figures for 1996. d NTDC (personal communication): figures for 1996. e Chapter 5: estimates for the year 2003

Regional tourism does not present as many difficulties as domestic tourism in terms of quantification. Most governments tend to keep data on travellers coming from regional countries, except those who do not require travel documents. Intraregional travel in 1992 accounted for 73 per cent of total tourist arrivals in East Asia and the Pacific region. They increased by 32 million from 1990 at an average growth rate of 12.5 per cent a year. For the region's developing countries, intraregional tourism grew from 74 per cent in 1980 to 87 per cent in 1990 (WTO, 1994a, pxii). For example, approximately 78 per cent of outbound Thai nationals travelled in East Asia in 1996. In 1994, 32 per cent of international tourists to Thailand came from East Asia (Kaosa-ard et al, 1997 [first draft], p20). In 1990, 74 per cent of tourist arrivals in the Americas (including both North and Latin) were from the region, increasing by almost 13 million since 1987 at an average growth rate of 4.8 per cent a year. In Brazil, 55 per cent of international tourists came from neighbouring countries. Latin America is also the main tourist-receptor for Brazilians travelling abroad (Chapter 3). In the case of Africa, in 1990, 60 per cent of arrivals recorded by residents of the region's countries were intraregional, almost double the 38 per cent recorded in 1980. For instance, Africa was the most favoured destination for South African outbound tourists in 1992; and, within the region, Namibia, Zimbabwe and Botswana were the three top destinations (WTO, 1994b, p38). In 1995, regional tourists to South Africa constituted 75 per cent of all international arrivals (Koch, 1998 [first draft], p5). In the case of Nigeria, despite the low number of international – and regional – tourist arrivals, 37 per cent of tourists in 1990 came from the Economic Community of West African States (ECOWAS) (Chapter 7). In the Middle East and South Asia, 34 and 31 per cent of the visitors respectively came from these regions (WTO, 1995a, p9). Factors that seem to encourage intraregional travel are regional, political and economic integration, specific tourist attractions (cooler climates, wildlife, tourist infrastructure, cheaper hotels, shopping prospects etc) and the favourable relations and perceptions of the nationals of one country in respect to another. The importance of regional or Southern tourism appears especially evident when it is compared with the number of tourists coming from developed countries. For example, WTO data suggest that in 1998 within ASEAN, SADC and the Mercosur blocs, Northern tourists comprised only 39, 23 and 24 per cent respectively (WTO, 2000, pp11–803).

Tourist Groups and Motivations

Which are the principal tourist groups engaged in national and regional leisure travel? This is a vital question, as the future growth in this kind of activity would largely depend upon which groups are actually participating or aspiring to do so. It is clear that up until recently leisure travel in developing countries was the exclusive privilege of the upper classes. These groups are quite comparable to their counterparts in the North in their leisure interests, consumption patterns and, in some cases, income levels. However, for mass tourism to develop as in the North, it is evident that there would be a need for the participation of the bulk of the national population. The central argument of the book is that this process is already occurring on a significant scale in many developing countries.

Most Southern tourists are essentially urbanites. But urban and rural societies are becoming increasingly mixed, with rural societies growing expeditiously urbanized in their physical infrastructure as well as in their consumption behaviour. What is especially noteworthy is that the urban population itself is growing so rapidly that an accelerated growth in national and regional mass tourism is more or less certain. For the present moment, there exist considerable differences between urban and rural travellers in terms of the rate of their participation, destination and motivations. For example, the majority of urban dwellers capable of travelling may seek to enjoy the greenery, fresh air and 'simple' village life, while tourists originating from rural areas may prefer to see the cities and historical monuments.

In general, those who travel exclusively for leisure purposes in the South are the relatively higher income groups. They are usually professionals, businessmen and bureaucrats, followed by urban workers with some stable disposable income. In China, for instance, this sector is mainly composed of government officials, technical personnel, businessmen and private entrepreneurs of urban origin with a level of education above junior middle school. Businessmen and private entrepreneurs are the big spenders in the domestic tourist market (Chapter 4). Before the end of apartheid in the early 1990s, the South African domestic market was clearly dominated by the white population. Now, this sector also encompasses the more accommodated segments of urban origin, the higher income and tertiary or university-educated black people who were formerly relegated by the regime (Chapter 6).

In countries where national tourism is well developed, after the proliferation of labour rights in the 1950s and 1960s, such as Mexico, Argentina or Brazil, travel for holiday or leisure purposes was also made available to the working class. For instance, in Argentina, many trade unions or affiliated mutualist organizations own hotels or guest-houses in popular tourist destinations where workers can take holidays at lower prices than in private establishments, and are usually able to pay in monthly instalments for their week at the beach or in the mountains. Unfortunately, structural adjustment, the trade unions' gradual loss of power and harsher economic conditions for the working class are making holiday travel again the privilege of a few. In Mexico, the facilities destined to cater for this type of tourism were very popular with family groups and those organizing conferences and business meetings from the late 1960s onwards. But, currently, they are operating at half their capacity due to the decline in government budgets and the commitment to privatize many parts of the social security system (Chapter 2).

It is clear that low-income workers and other less privileged population groups would seek to combine their travel with various other purposes, including visits to friends and relatives, health treatment and participation in fairs and religious festivals. As noted earlier, religious tourism (ie pilgrimage and visits to holy places) is a chief motivation for travel in the developing world. In Brazil or Mexico, Thailand or India, to participate in religious festivals is an old practice that is now combined with other less traditional activities, such as visiting cultural or historical sites. Domestic travel for Mexicans not only reassures family ties, but also community organization, as it is greatly related to assisting in the celebration honouring a local patron saint or a regional fair in the home-town. In India, pilgrimages to the sacred Ganges, or fairs like the Durga Puja in Bengal, attract innumerable amounts of people.

Visits to friends and relatives are also an important reason for travelling. In many countries, individuals who migrated from poorer to more affluent regions of their countries often return to visit their families. This is the case, for example, of people from northern Thailand travelling to and from Bangkok, or from the north of Brazil going to the more industrialized and richer south-eastern region. After the economic crisis in Nigeria in the mid-1980s, most Nigerians today, except for a small portion of the population, can only afford day-trips or visits to friends and relatives. Before the economic crisis, middle-class Nigerians were keen travellers both abroad and in their country (Chapter 7). It is also true that extended families widely dispersed throughout the country made these visits a deep-rooted tradition. In South Africa, 'emerging' national tourists also tend to stay with friends and relatives during their short trips as their spending power is rather low (Chapter 6).

Although an increasing phenomenon, business travellers usually constitute a small amount of the population in these countries, but comprise a group that tends to have very high expectations regarding services and facilities, thereby leading to the rapid development of tourism infrastructure. Some of them are actually instrumental in this evolution.

In all the countries studied, nature-related activities seem to be growing in importance. Especially among the young, natural scenery is top of the list in terms of preference and motivation for travel. In Thailand urban dwellers tend to flock to national parks over the weekend to get away from the cities' pollution and noise (Chapter 5; see also Ghimire, 1991). For Indians travelling exclusively for leisure purposes, their main interest is sightseeing, although 'adventure' sports and trekking are also a growing focus of attention (Chapter 7). In China, the main interest of urban domestic tourists is natural scenery, although many are also interested in seeing different parts of the country, historical monuments and local cultures (Chapter 4). In Brazil and South Africa, beaches near urban centres are overcrowded, especially over the weekend. The high concentration of people in nearby beaches with the accompanying problem of waste disposal and pollution has made many visitors turn to the countryside and national parks (Chapters 3 and 6). Clearly, the motivations of Southern national and regional tourists are diverse and constantly changing. A better understanding of this helps us to conceive the possible socio-economic and ecological impacts. This aspect is considered in the following section.

The Impact of Domestic and Regional Mass Tourism

Determining the actual as well as the potential impacts of domestic and regional tourism is more complicated than it might appear on the surface. A large number of actors and institutions that have an interest in promoting tourism tend to show the tourism-related impacts in a more or less preconceived manner. As in the case of international tourism, the economic benefits of domestic and regional tourism are highlighted by the government and business groups, while minimizing the negative outcomes. The study on the economic role of national tourists in China (Chapter 4) describes how the domestic tourism sector in the country has been seen exclusively from the positive side, stressing its capacity to strengthen regional economies and alleviate rural poverty. The potential of domestic and regional tourism in stimulating economic growth in and around the tourist sites should be recognized, especially as this sector on the whole is labour-intensive and tourists may spend more money locally. But such gains become less relevant in the long run if they are not accompanied by appropriate income distribution measures. They may also be short-lived in the absence of adequate visitor facilities, or due to the degradation of scenic spots through excessive construction or careless waste disposal. It is indispensable that tourism-related local socio-economic indicators and effects are continually monitored. Unfortunately, most of the tourism impact studies remain only occasional and partial.

For the bulk of tourism studies, what seems to really matter is the aggregate amount of income generated from tourism. However, much of this may never reach the actual tourist sites and local communities. More importantly, there is a vast difference among various socio-professional groups in terms of their ability to participate in this sector and share the ensuing benefits. And there is the question of how the associated costs are actually endured by different groups.

In some ways, the development of national and regional tourism in itself is the result of a growing social differentiation: firstly, between the urban and rural populations, and secondly, with the rise of the middle classes usually bringing considerable penury among the mass of the population. The recent expansion in domestic tourism in China, for example, is clearly the result of a rapid rise of a large middle class with a considerable spending capacity, although the country's sustained economic growth has also allowed the lower-middle classes to participate in leisure travel. This aspect is by no means unique to China. Indeed, in Brazil, Mexico and South Africa, those who could afford to travel initially were the political elites and business people, and many tourist facilities were developed mainly to satisfy their expectations.

The process of social differentiation is frequently further reinforced because of the lack of sufficient attention to the potential damage in planning specific tourism projects. For example, in the case of India, Rao and Suresh point out that investments and growth in the construction sector due to domestic tourism development have induced inflation of real-estate costs and changes in land ownership (Chapter 8). No institutional or financial measures have been taken to control these negative outcomes. A growing social differentiation that the tourism projects generally provoke is also reducing community solidarity to confront many such undesirable effects.

A social group approach is necessary in examining the impacts of national and regional tourism, as the various groups face the consequences of tourism quite differently. The poorer and weaker social groups especially suffer. Also, as tourism is generally related to the exploration of isolated areas and ethnic lifestyles, traditional communities are frequently the target. At times, the potential tourism sites are cleared of original inhabitants to make the area look desolate and free of human activities. An example of this is Thailand's Kao Yai national park area, where 98.5 per cent of the visitors are Thai, where local villagers have been deprived of their traditional right to use the forest and other natural resources, and where the government has failed to provide economically viable alternatives (Chapter 5). In Brazil, along the coast from south of São Paulo to the north-east towns such as Recife, artisan fishermen and peasants are expropriated from their land, water and beach areas in order to satisfy the ambitions of middle-class city-dwellers and tourism investors to construct holiday homes and recreational facilities; many of these people are forced to migrate to urban slums while some become seasonal housekeepers receiving a small salary from the owner (Chapter 3).

Domestic and regional tourism activities, as with international tourism, are usually based on existing unequal, exploitative relationships. The abuse of children in tourism activities, such as in small tourism business, hotels and restaurants in the entertainment sector, the production and sale of handicrafts and child prostitution, are common practices in many tourist destinations (Plüss, 1999; Black, 1995). Estimates suggest that children and young people under 18 years of age constitute 10 to 15 per cent of the tourism industry's labour force (see Plüss, ibid, p1). It is difficult to establish how many of them work exclusively for the domestic and regional tourism sectors. Nevertheless, the growth in national and regional tourism can only exacerbate the situation. This is especially so as these sectors are more labour-intensive, and Southern national and regional tourists may also not find it exceptional that the children are working in the tourism industry as they already do in agriculture, manufacturing or domestic work.

Sex tourism attracts a great deal of attention in tourism literature. It is usually connected to international tourism, and the behaviour of nationals is widely overlooked by the researchers and organizations dealing with this issue and the authorities at tourist destinations. Even though 'sex tourism' might not be the main purpose of travel for male domestic tourists, they also participate in the sex trade, and prostitution has proliferated in sites as diverse as temples in Thailand and India to beach resorts in Indonesia. For instance, in Pangandaran – a popular beach destination for domestic tourists in Indonesia – prostitutes from West and Central Java flee to the village to work in the local brothels during the tourist peak-season. The clientele of the brothels is domestic (Wilkinson and Pratiwi, 1995, p295). In Brazil, drug abuse in the host communities has also risen with the increase in the number of tourists. Youth groups are especially vulnerable to drug taking. Alcoholism has also increased, in part due to tourism.

The traditional role of women has also undergone changes where domestic tourist development has occurred. For example, in Pangandaran (Indonesia), it has been noticed that, with the affluence of tourists, women started to produce handicrafts to sell as souvenirs or set up food stalls within the informal sector. They had in some cases gained more importance and independence in the household economy as money-earners. However, the work burden on women had also increased as they still had to carry out their domestic and farm duties (ibid, p296). Another direct consequence found in some Indian villages (Chapter 8) is the transformation of the cottage industry where women occupy a central position. Items that were once produced for everyday use are now made and sold as souvenirs. Women are also abandoning their traditional materials for non-local, mass-produced goods sold at markets.

Harvey et al (1995, p353) remark that gender issues in tourism development are important as rapid changes in family life and rural lifestyles may push women into poverty, domestic problems, or into double-duty with work and family responsibilities. For instance, as women start to perform a more economically active role during the peak season, if both parents are involved in tourism activities, patterns in child-rearing are affected. Usually, grandparents, relatives or older children tend to look after the young children; or else they are brought to the stalls or other business. This results in the young children's involvement in selling and making handicrafts or helping their parents to sell food at their stalls (Wilkinson and Pratiwi, 1995, p293). In India, the harassment of women in some hill stations is a phenomenon increasingly associated with the rise in the number of incoming domestic tourists (Chapter 8).

In terms of cultural changes induced by tourism, the most evident consequence is the use (or rather misuse) of traditional cultural practices to attract visitors to a destination, adapting performances, customs, festivals to please the tourists. This has been the case of many Chinese and Indian villages frequented by tourists (Chapters 4 and 8). Concerning the protection of cultural patrimony, Rao and Suresh argue in Chapter 8 that many historical sites, such as palaces and forts, are restored and transformed into hotels to cater for both domestic and international tourists, not always properly depicting the lifestyle of the period they intend to represent. In Mexico, the foreign-oriented tourist development model supported by the government has allowed private investors to develop resorts on the edges of archaeological ruins, creating opportunities for the theft of pre-Columbian treasures, or threatening the physical integrity of the monuments (Chapter 2).

On the environmental front, the picture at times is quite alarming. The movement of large numbers of people to areas without adequate infrastructure to cater for tourist needs causes not only environmental degradation, but also serious health hazards for both local people and visitors. A common environmental problem is the lack of proper waste disposal in villages and towns, but there are many other problems. In India, tourism development is accompanied by air pollution produced by car exhausts, and both solid waste and plastic bags spread around sanctuaries, lakes, hill stations and monuments (Chapter 8). In Mexico, popular events like fairs and festivals generate massive volumes of wastes that local systems are incapable of handling, creating health hazards in the absence of appropriate public sanitary facilities. Even hotels that cater for domestic tourists and that are not connected to sewage systems with water-treatment plants resort instead to discharges into the local rivers or underground aquifers. This threatens the quality of the water supply and the safety of the agricultural production that depends on these water supplies (Chapter 2). In Brazil, environmental degradation in the north-east province of Ceará is a direct result of the expansion in both the international and domestic tourism sectors. Large portions of the coastline are undergoing rapid erosion due to the construction of hotels and tourist houses on dunes. Even the local people have been forced to build their houses on state-owned dunes and mangroves, as they were expelled from their lands. Ecological regulations are reinforced less in this region and the local communities are also not well organized to oppose environmental degradation (Chapter 3). In China, there is a complete lack of awareness campaigns, regarding the chaotic and uncontrolled exploitation of tourist resources. Domestic tourists tend to prefer lower prices rather than a protected environment (Chapter 4).

To comprehend fully the different socio-cultural, economic as well as political impacts (both positive and negative) of Southern national and regional tourism, as well as the possible means to correct the negative ones, more site-specific studies (extended over a longer period of time) are needed. The scope of this has been to provide an overview of this situation. Nevertheless, the different chapters do indicate a few crucial trends that need to be acknowledged. What is quite clear is that Southern national and regional tourism is involving a large number of people and many of them are keenly adopting the Western consumeristic leisure attitudes and behaviours that have not been benign to the local culture, economy and environment. Many impending impacts are thus evident, unless appropriate policy measures are taken. This logically leads us to question the public policy measures in this area.

Domestic and Regional Tourism Planning and Policies

The declaration that followed the 1980 World Conference on Tourism held in Manila expressed the importance of domestic tourism in diversifying the national economy. It also described domestic tourism as a means to secure everyone's right to holidays, to know his/her own country, as well as to reaffirm national conscience and solidarity. The declaration also stated that 'social tourism' should be regarded as a prime objective to be achieved by every country in order to provide its less favoured nationals with the right to rest (WTO, 1995b, p1). Twenty years have passed since this declaration, but very little has changed in the way of integrating these aspects into formal tourism and wider economic and social provisioning policies. Most governments are primarily keen to promote international tourism.

There exist few consistent public policies on domestic and regional tourism. An even fewer number of countries have sought to elaborate, implement and reinforce legislation relating to domestic and regional tourism. Most tourist sites retain no long-term project planning. Public policies are frequently chaotic when it comes to the development of infrastructure, tourism facilities and tourist products. Training and marketing are generally neglected. Employment policies often remain very vague, at times totally unrealistic, and tourism workers' rights are seldom protected. The role of different actors, such as the local communities, business people and the authorities, is never defined. There is a total lack of proper policies on income distribution; as such, much of the ensuing income and benefits is reaped mainly by the more powerful and wealthier sections of the population or by outside investors. The collection of relevant statistics, the carrying out of independent research, the evaluation and monitoring of tourism trends and government projects are conspicuously absent in most domestic and regional tourism policy measures.

All the country studies included in this book affirm this general policy neglect on national and regional tourism. In Mexico, there is a systematic bias in public policy-making to provide for the needs of foreign tourists or national wealthy groups, potential customers of the four- and five-star mega-projects. There has also been a government withdrawal from the promotion of social tourism targeting popular classes. Currently, facilities that used to cater for the less privileged classes are operating at half their capacity due to a decline in government budgets and the privatization process. Community initiatives for tourist development need to confront frequently with the government's indifference, the opposition of powerful local property-owning groups, and the lack of adequate working capital, managerial skills and training. This results in a high rate of failure of the community enterprises.

In Brazil, since 1991, a National Plan for Tourism has been elaborated with the goal to foster international and domestic tourist flows, to develop tourist poles with adequate infrastructure according to the particular regional characteristics, to create employment and income, and to encourage investments from the private sector. The plan seeks to encourage the Brazilian mass to travel at weekends. It is also attempting to promote low-price hotels and special travel arrangements. However, the government has little financial means of its own and the private sector is keen to invest only in short-term, high profit-making projects. Joint ventures between the government and the private sector often create social tensions, as the latter tends to expropriate land or buy it from local population groups under unfair conditions to carry out their tourism investment projects. In spite of the government's aim of creating employment, the fact that most of the local population is not skilled or trained to initiate and manage tourism business further reinforces the existing social marginalization. Municipalities that have been given more responsibilities in recent years lack resources and are not well equipped to implement tourism development activities (Chapter 3).

In China, domestic tourism has expanded spontaneously due to the popular demand for travel and interest on the part of travel groups that needed to tap into the Chinese tourists as foreign tourists drastically declined in the aftermath of the Tiananmen Square incident in the late 1980s. The government's reaction to the domestic tourism sector was only in response to this demand, and most of the public investment has gone to the development of infrastructure, including civil aviation, highways, railroads and water transportation. Since 1993, a number of government agencies have been involved in conducting market research with the view to setting up more structured price competition, the development of tourist products for 'ordinary' people, and the improvement of the quality of tourist services. They have also sought to up-grade public security and sanitary facilities at tourist destinations, and to encourage enterprises to practise sustainable use of tourism resources (Chapter 4). However, tourism policies in China are formulated in a very centralized manner at the ministerial level and their actual implementation is low at the local and regional level. Analytical research and evaluation of the recurring phenomena and negative impacts of tourism are especially lacking.

In Thailand, the government's domestic tourism has been dictated in large part by its interest in reducing foreign exchange outflow by outbound Thai travellers. Current policies, as described in government documents, stress the improvement of infrastructure, amenities and access to sites, and the expansion of tourism to remote areas to facilitate a more equitable income distribution across the regions; the conservation and renovation of cultural sites and natural features; to foster national identity and to nourish public participation in activities related to the development of tourism (Chapter 5). However, in reality, very few of these aspects are integrated in the government's ongoing tourism planning; most of the recent policy measures are still geared towards encouraging foreign tourists.

In 1996, South Africa elaborated a detailed domestic and regional tourism policy aimed at spawning investments, creating new services, stimulating other sectors of the economy, strengthening rural communities, generating foreign exchange and creating employment. It suggests that the government should practise responsible tourism, promoting tourist products in rural communities and less developed areas, transferring skills and technologies to residents, and promoting joint ventures with local partners and communities. Regional tourism within Southern Africa is seen as a vital and integral component of wider regional cooperation. The government is also trying to improve links between the tourism sector and other related industries, such as transport and communications, and the environment and land management (Chapter 6). But with most of these measures at the initial stage of conceptualization and pre-testing, so far little has actually been implemented.

In Nigeria, throughout the 1980s, although domestic tourism was seen as a powerful nationalistic ideology, the government decided to prioritize international development. In 1990, the government policy on tourism set the following goals: to increase the inflow of foreign exchange through the promotion of international tourism; to encourage the even development of tourism-based ventures in all parts of the country; to accelerate rural–urban integration through infrastructural provisions for rural tourist sites; to foster national unity through the promotion of domestic tourism; to encourage private sector participation in tourism development, and to preserve national cultural and historical monuments (Chapter 7). There has only been lukewarm support of domestic tourism, if not a total retreat. There have been little concrete policy measures or achievements. On the other hand, it has increased bureaucratization without any improvements in management efficiency in the coordinating government institutions.

In India, domestic tourism has grown spontaneously since the 1950s, when the state decided to invest in domestic tourist services and infrastructure using both national and local, private and public funds. This has led to a greater segmentation of the domestic tourist market and the emergence of new products and destinations. In the 1980s, domestic tourism development was recognized as a viable instrument for national integration and economic development. This led the government to increase financial investments in tourism-related services. However, many tourist sites visited by domestic tourists continued to lack basic infrastructure and facilities. At the same time, poorer urban and rural people, especially tribal communities, are increasingly dispossessed of their land and other resources that are vital for their subsistence. In the 1990s, however, economic reforms have shifted away from this approach, focusing mostly on 'first-class' tourists and the international market (Chapter 8).

What is clear from the above is that most developing countries are just beginning to develop policy measures that are designed to tackle the growth in domestic and regional tourism. Very few of these policies are actually being implemented. There are few or no mechanisms to monitor their outcomes. On the whole, the government's policy measures are oriented towards achieving accelerated economic growth, usually through the participation of the private sector. The private sector, on the other hand, has remained keen to invest in short-term projects that offer hefty profits with little care to labour rights, cultural protection and the sustainability of natural resources (unless they begin to affect actual or perceived profits). Governments are not able to develop an effective policy mechanism to ensure that the private sector pays the taxes due, let alone control their undesirable activities. Whether one considers economic, social, environmental or cultural aspects, the ensuing negative impacts of domestic and regional tourism are scarcely handled in government policies. No effective policy measures have been introduced to control prostitution, child labour, drug and alcohol taking in domestic tourists' sites. There is especially a critical policy need to inform domestic tourists, as with international tourists, to minimize the impacts of globalization in the consumption of food and services, lifestyles and aspirations.

Conclusions

The main conclusion is that the emerging national and regional mass tourism in developing countries is a subject of keen interest for critical reflection and policy-making. The sheer number of people who are involved in leisure travel is in itself a clear indication of the magnitude of the phenomenon. Given the present urbanization trends and the influence of the Western leisure ethic, the demand for travel by the mass of the Southern population is most likely to grow. Against this background, irrespective of major economic or political crises, domestic and regional tourism is likely to develop, but obviously it will grow more slowly when such crises occur and persist. A continued expansion in the modern communications and transport systems would allow people to discover most parts of their countries with less and less time and effort. Furthermore, increased regional interactions, especially involving the creation of regional co-operation bodies such as ASEAN, SADC, Mercosur and the South Asian Association for Regional Cooperation (SAARC), and the easing of travel and currency restrictions, would further facilitate leisure travel in the South.

Inasmuch as the Southern national and regional tourism are 'inevitable', could they be made a better option for sustainable socio-economic development than the North–South tourism has been so far? The question is valid, especially as national and regional tourism are just beginning to expand in many of the developing countries, and there is a certain level of experience already gained from international tourism to attempt to minimize the negative consequences. Public policies and site-specific tourism planning have thus the possibility of being more adaptive and imaginative. But this may just be wishful thinking, given the government bias to the development of tourism infrastructure and facilities for richer, Northern tourists, and its inability to regulate the market forces.

Different chapters have indicated a few prospects of domestic and regional tourism in promoting a more sustainable type of socio-economic development in and around the major tourist destinations. In theory, small-scale, locally managed tourism projects should reflect better community values; they should also help to direct the resultant economic benefits towards the interests and most urgent needs of the local population. Culturally, the tension between the host community and tourists could be better assimilated. This has been the case of the Museum of Popular Culture in Mexico City, where the works of local communities are exhibited to strengthen local artisan and environmental management practices. In Rhodes village, Eastern Cape, South Africa, local residents have opened their homes to tourists (national and international combined) and this has encouraged them to live according to their traditions, from housework to primary healthcare based on the use of a local herb. In Icapui and Cascavel, state of Ceará, Brazil, where the traditional communities in coastal areas, with the support of NGOs and the Church, organized the establishment of lodges and small traditional restaurants, the impacts on their livelihoods have been especially positive, allowing them to maintain to a certain extent their former lifestyles. It also allowed the artisan fishermen to sell their produce to local tourist lodges and restaurants. Examples such as these can be found in many locations and countries.

Unfortunately, all these community efforts generally find little support, if not opposition, from the tourism officials, international experts or interested investors, as the latter groups have their own agendas. For example, more visible projects involving expensive hotel and recreational facilities are commonly preferred by the government, bilateral and multilateral investors and business groups. Local communities that want to develop small-scale initiatives lack not only financial resources to begin the tourism schemes, but they also have difficulties in meeting the high-level managerial capacity that is required in tourism projects. They have little knowledge of the tourism market and tourists (including national and regional) tend to be more demanding in terms of the range and quality of the products sought. Tourism development imposes entirely new institutions and working methods, simply excluding many local communities.

On the other hand, many of the negative outcomes generated by tourism projects are shared more widely, even by those who have little to do with tourism. Some of the consequences commonly mentioned in the different chapters include the dispossession of local people from their agricultural land, traditional fishing areas, forests, rangelands, etc. Cultural pollution and environmental degradation are also commonly referred to. Some level of social differentiation is also taking place. Similarly, tourism in general has not helped to alter the political status quo and power relations, despite the fact that many politically agile urban youths are arriving in the countryside. Little information is available on these evolving political situations; the dominant tourism leisure ethic essentially conveys an 'apolitical' message, stressing repose and melancholy.

In addition to the political aspect of national and regional tourism, data are lacking on the many basic economic cost-benefit figures (which tourism experts in general have been keen to develop), investment patterns and groups, the impacts on local employment and income generation, the community's institutional, financial and managerial capacity, tourist groups and their behaviour, as well as many aspects relating to the protection of cultural heritage. Apart from this, analytical rigour and incisiveness (which many of the tourism studies and writings critically lack) are greatly needed for a deeper understanding of the phenomenon and potential impacts and policy measures that are required to correct the pernicious consequences of domestic and regional tourism.

The role of different actors with a stake in domestic and regional tourism needs to be understood especially. The external institutions, such as the government, national business groups, transnational corporations (TNCs), bilateral donor agencies and international financial institutions that have consistently emphasized the positive economic role of tourism, are generally satisfied with showing global national or international employment and income figures, with little care in finding out how these benefits are being translated at the local level and correcting the shortcomings. Under what circumstances can these groups be influenced and pressured so that the local interest becomes more reflected in the tourism planning process? And what are the roles of NGOs and a host of other civil society organizations beside being a useful protester? In particular, what are the prospects of their being an effective interlocutor between the local population groups and the powerful outside actors, as well as proposing concrete tourism initiatives and projects that are supportive of local livelihoods, culture and the environment?

Naturally, the local population groups affected by tourism themselves are the most evident actors, which too are scarcely homogeneous in their composition and interest. Tourism projects should aim at managing this tension and improving local livelihood systems. They should seek to promote education and public awareness. Cultural diversity and human dignity should be ameliorated, not undermined. It is clear that tourism alone can never change the existing social deprivation and inequalities, but it can be a useful tool if enough care is given to prioritize local interests. Unfortunately, on the basis of the information that this work has been able to collect and analyse, it can be said that this is far from being achieved. For many local population groups, ensuring an improved agricultural production and wage labouring (including the off-farm), combined with access to education, health and enhanced social provisioning, is more significant than the meagre seasonal income that some of them might be able to generate through tourism. What seems to be especially important is that the concerned population groups are made aware of the different potentials and problems associated with national and regional tourism. It may help if the tourists too are made conscious of their actions and behaviour.

Notes

1   I am grateful to Mariana Mozdzer, who has helped me to search and synthesize a vast amount of available literature on tourism and provided me with many useful ideas and comments for the preparation of this chapter. I am also grateful to Anita Tombez for the bibliographical control and systematization of the document. Besides a review of secondary literature, the information used in this chapter is derived from the various country overview papers included as chapters in this book. Furthermore, the chapter draws on an earlier paper by myself (Ghimire, 1997), as well as my personal exposure to a few tourist locations frequented by Southern national and regional tourists.

2   For example, a rapid survey of the issues from 1985 until 1995 of the *Annals of Tourism Research* – a leading tourism journal – showed that there were

no articles specifically focusing on domestic tourism. By taking a look at the index of contents there was not one title that reflected a study on domestic tourism in developing countries. Thirty issues of *Tourism Management*, another important journal, were also reviewed from 1990 until 1995 and found only one title specifically analysing domestic tourism in the UK (Vol 13, No 1, 1992, pp85–90).

3   An Internet survey of the World Tourism Organization (http://www.world-tourism.org) showed that by March 1998 the list of the organization's publications on the site included only one publication that referred to domestic tourism (ie, 'Collection of Domestic Tourism Statistics' – Technical Manual No 3). The list of 'Meetings and Seminars' did not have any events specifically addressing questions of domestic tourism. Similarly, the UNESCO site (http://www.unesco.org), dated March 1998, included mostly information related to the cultural aspects of tourism as well as issues of heritage, but nothing was found specifically on domestic tourism.

4   This was confirmed in writing by both NGOs when consulted by the author for verification.

References

Aditya, A and S Shrestha (1998) *Indian Tourists in Nepal*, a draft report, UNRISD, Geneva

Black, M (1995) *In the Twilight Zone: Child Workers in the Hotel, Tourism and Catering Industry*, ILO, Geneva

Cohen, E (1992) 'Pilgrimage Centers: Concentric and Excentric', *Annals of Tourism Research*, USA, vol 19, pp33–50

Economic Times (1997) 11 May

Ghimire, K (1991) *Parks and People: Livelihood Issues in National Parks Management in Thailand and Madagascar*, Discussion Paper No 29, UNRISD, Geneva

Ghimire, K (1997) *Emerging Mass Tourism in the South*, Discussion Paper No 85, UNRISD, Geneva

Harvey, M, J Hunt and C Harris (1995) 'Gender and Community Tourism Dependence Level', *Annals of Tourism Research*, USA, vol 22, no 2, pp349–366

Kaosa-ard, M et al (1997) First draft of the chapter prepared for this volume

Koch, E (1998) First draft of the chapter prepared for this volume

Pleumaron, A (1997) *Political Economy of Regional Tourism Development and Environmental Change in the Mekong Sub-region*, UNRISD draft report, Geneva

Plüss, C (1999) *Quick Money – Easy Money? A Report on Child Labour in Tourism*, Swiss Agency for Development and Co-operation, Berne

PRODETUR (1993) *Programa de ação para o Desenvolvimento do Turismo – no Nordeste PRODETUR, Recife*

Rinschede, G (1992) 'Forms of Religious Tourism', *Annals of Tourism Research*, USA, vol 19, pp51–67

State Statistics Bureau (1992) *China Statistics Yearbook*, Beijing

Wilkinson, P and W Pratiwi (1995) 'Gender and Tourism in an Indonesian Village', *Annals of Tourism Research*, USA, vol 22, no 2, pp283–299

WTO (1993) *Recommendations on Tourism Statistics*, Madrid

WTO (1994a) *Global Tourism Forecasts to the Year 2000 and Beyond: East Asia/ Pacific*, Madrid

WTO (1994b) *Global Tourism Forecasts to the Year 2000 and Beyond: Africa*, Madrid

WTO (1995a) *Global Tourism Forecasts to the Year 2000 and Beyond: The World*, vol 1, Madrid

WTO (1995b) *Manual Técnico No 3: Recopilación de las Estadísticas de Turism Interno*, Madrid

WTO (1996) *Yearbook of Tourism Statistics*, Madrid

WTO (1997a) *Yearbook of Tourism Statistics*, vol 1, Madrid.

WTO (1997b) *Tourism 2020 Vision: Executive Summary*, Madrid

WTO (1998) Personal communication (2 September 1998) with Mr Enzo Paci, Chief, Statistics, Economics and Market Research

WTO (2000) *Yearbook of Tourism Statistics*, vols 1 and 2, 52nd edition, Madrid

Chapter 2

Strengthening Domestic Tourism in Mexico: Challenges and Opportunities

David Barkin

Tourism: the industry without smokestacks. The industry is considered by many people to be a virtually costless generator of employment and well-being that offers seemingly limitless opportunities for 'real' economic development for countless communities away from the centres of global industry and financial power. Mexican governments, one after another, have focused almost exclusively on international tourism, assuming it to be a sort of cornucopia, a bottomless well. In this chapter, after we examine the contribution that Mexicans make to their country's tourist industry, we attempt to identify official policies that might stimulate this domestic tourism. We then focus on the present state of 'social' or mass tourism, including some examples of this local activity, and reflect on its potential for stimulating community development. This analysis is a point of departure for making some recommendations that might transform domestic tourism into an effective tool for rural sustainable development in many parts of the country.

Introduction: The Tourism Industry

Foreign tourists have been flocking to Mexico for more than half a century. During the past three decades the government has begun to take a different attitude towards this bonanza, a source of wealth that is ready to be more fully exploited. The government promoted mega-projects to stimulate tourist activity in five new centres: Cancun, Los Cabos, Ixtapa, Huatulco and Loreto; designed to attract foreign visitors, they were built with a combination of generous financial incentives and private international capital, often in joint ventures with local entrepreneurs. Traditional destinations such as Acapulco, Veracruz and Puerto Vallarta continue to attract domestic tourism and smaller flows of international tourists. As tourist traffic grew, however, official declarations made the sector appear even more grandiose, transforming cross-border traffic into international tourism, inflating traditional tourist receipts by adding border spending to the total; further distorting our understanding of the phenomenon is the practice of including Mexicans residing in the US who come home to visit family or participate in village festivities in the total tourist flow. International figures rank Mexico seventh worldwide in the number of visitors, with more than 21 million in 1997, but only 16th in income (with total revenues estimated at almost US$7 billion, some US$3.5 billion more than what Mexicans are reported to spend on their international travels), as average expenditures are much lower than elsewhere. 'Removing these people from statistics gives a more realistic picture of how many "authentic" tourists visited the country – between 7.5 million and 8.5 million, spending roughly US$550 per stay' (Chi Chase, 1998). (Day travellers to the border areas account for most of these visitors per year, some 12.4 million people in 1996, but spend only about $640 million gross; another 69 million people came for very short stays, either in the border region or from cruise ships, spending an estimated $1.6 thousand million in 1996.)

There are about 1.7 million people employed by the restaurant and hotel sector, out of a total labour force of more than 33 million (1994 Economic Census); the government estimates that there are another 4.3 million paid jobs generated indirectly by these establishments. The National Businessmen's Council for Tourism estimates, more realistically, that the industry effectively employs about 550,000 people (Consejo Nacional Empresarial Turístico, 1996). Tourism is much more than these service sectors and the figures underestimate its importance in the national economy. Since the figure does not include the services of workers in transport and guide services, or the housing services involved with condominiums, time shares and other less formal arrangements, the significance of tourism may be as much as twice as great as suggested by the employment figure cited above. In many poorer rural regions in particular, where people offer services to tourists on a part-time basis, or as part of a broader strategy of developing a diversified productive structure, tourist visits may have a significant impact on local livelihoods.

Another way to attempt to quantify the magnitude of tourist activity in Mexico is by examining hotel facilities and occupancy. Although the hotel occupancy statistics are incapable of separating out their guests by tourists and other types of travellers, we get some indication of the magnitude of the flows by noting that there were more than 43 million 'check-ins' at hotels in 1995, of which about 64 per cent were in major tourist centres (Table 2.1). Save

1994, occupancy rates were fairly stable at about 52–54 per cent of total capacity nationally; there were notable exceptions in the most luxurious five-star hotels (about 60 per cent) and in the more expensive destinations in each of the three categories of tourist destinations: beach, large cities and provincial. About three-quarters of hotel patrons were Mexican, with the remaining people coming from other countries; the proportion fell from 81 per cent in 1986, probably reflecting the accelerated growth of the sale of package tours to Mexico and, more recently, the deepening economic crisis following the devaluation of December 1994 that forced many Mexicans to cancel travel plans, both locally and internationally. The data also confirm that foreigners stay longer during their hotel stays in Mexico than does the local population.

The Mexican Traveller

The Mexican people do a great deal of travelling. From the information available about domestic tourism in Mexico, based on the quarterly survey of tourist activity that has been applied irregularly since 1994 by the National Statistics Bureau (INEGI), we gather that more than 40 per cent of the population says it travels away from home.[1] Although a valuable source of information, the survey is not generally used by the private sector for its own planning. Since the data are collected from a probabilistic sample of the national population, the results are available only in proportional terms, and can only offer a rough estimate of the phenomena examined in the questionnaire; furthermore, the raw data are not available to researchers so that we might run our own comparisons of the various series. For example, the information that was made available to us from these surveys does not allow us to quantify the relative flows going to domestic destinations and those going abroad. We learned that about 22 per cent of the population leave home each year, staying away for at least one night, while another 18 per cent of the population make day trips; based on a population of about 93 million people, this would suggest that more than 20 million people make at least one overnight trip a year, a number equal to the flows coming from abroad, including visiting Mexican nationals and border travellers. The overnight travellers are predominantly young (between 15 and 34 years of age); about half of the university-educated people travel, as do those in the upper income groups. There are significant differences among occupational groups, with high-level personnel, predominantly in public service, and educators travelling substantially more than others.

From other questions in the survey we learn that domestic travel is predominantly family oriented. Almost half of the people who spend at least a night away from home visit family; however, the survey cannot distinguish between those going to visit family and those who take part in regional fairs or religious events, a common form of relaxation for Mexican families. This is in contrast

to international travel by Mexicans, which is primarily motivated \
pleasure (40–45 per cent) rather than family visits (30–35 per cent). 1.
most important reason for domestic travel is for vacation or pleasure \
per cent). When travelling within the country, Mexicans overwhelmingly
with family or friends (60 per cent) rather than in hotels or motels (25 per
cent). Reinforcing the impression from this information, we find that these
travellers are widely dispersed, reflecting the significance of historical patterns
of extended family relationships in determining destinations, rather than the
distribution of urban settlements that developed during recent decades. Finally,
in spite of the fact that most better-off Mexicans travel a disproportionate
amount, the majority of voyages are by interurban bus (55 per cent), with private
vehicles representing a second option (35–40 per cent); this is an indicator of
the highly skewed distribution of income in Mexico, with more than three-
quarters of the population earning less than what is officially considered to be
the poverty level, thus finding it necessary to use public transportation. In
contrast, more than 40 per cent of Mexican travellers going abroad drive their
own cars, with a similar proportion using commercial airlines, reflecting the
wealth of this small segment of international travellers or their proximity to
the northern border with the US; less than 10 per cent of the population leave
the country, substantially fewer than the number travelling within the country.
As a result of the family-oriented character of domestic travel, the expenditure
data show that local travel costs are relatively low: in contrast to the US$550
per person per trip that foreigners are said to spend in Mexico, Mexicans report
spending only about US$250 per trip, or less than $15 per person/night within
the country. Comparable figures for Mexicans going abroad are about $1400
per trip and $50 per person per night.

In contrast to widely dispersed patterns of domestic travel, services provided
by the tourist industry are highly concentrated in a few regions. A spatial analysis
of the industry, based on the 1994 census data, shows that only 103 of the
more than 2000 counties in the country report more than 1300 people working
in this sector. These localities have 63 per cent of the service establishments for
tourism, occupy more than three-quarters of the people in the sector and account
for about 85 per cent of total tourist revenues (de Sicilia Muñoz and López,
1998, p5). Tourism in Mexico is typically divided into three separate categories:
interior, border and beach destinations. When using this classification, we find
the concentration of services even more striking: the three largest metropolitan
areas (Mexico City, Monterrey, and Guadalajara) account for 30 per cent of
employment, 27 per cent of the businesses, and 39 per cent of income. Nine
important beach destinations (Cancun, Acapulco, Puerto Vallarta, Veracruz,
Ixtapa, Mazatlan, Los Cabos, Manzanillo, and Cozumel) account for another
12 per cent of employment and 17 per cent of revenues. The five most significant
colonial cities in economic terms (Puebla, Merida, Morelia, Oaxaca, and Tuxtla
Gutierrez) account for 5 per cent of the people and 4 per cent of sector revenues.

Table 2.1 Indicators of tourism in Mexico

	1986	1987	1988	1989	1990	1991	1992	1993	1994	1995	1996
International tourism											
Total visitors to Mexico[1] (000s)	12,258.0	14,361.2	14,140.1	14,964.1	17,171.7	16,066.7	17,146.3	16,440.0	17,182.0	20,162.0	21,428.0
Numbers of tourists[2] (000s)											
To Mexico	4625.0	5407.2	5692.1	6186.1	6392.7	6371.7	6352.3	6625.0	7135.0	7784.0	8981.7
From Mexico	6389.5	5264.7	7965.2	7316.9	7357.2	7712.9	11,226.0	10,184.8	12,029.0	8450.0	9000.8
Expenditure (millions of dollars)											
In Mexico (by visitors)	3025.7	3545.4	4048.1	4821.8	5526.4	5960.0	6084.8	6167.0	6363.0	6164.0	6894.0
In Mexico (by tourists)	2116.7	2593.4	2902.2	3387.5	3933.8	4339.3	4471.1	4564.1	4854.0	4689.5	5288.9
Abroad (by Mexicans)	787.2	888.2	1322.8	1749.8	2171.5	2149.5	2541.6	2416.6	2445.0	1240.4	1536.4
Average expenditure (dollars/tourist)											
In Mexico	387.4	420.6	447.0	477.5	532.0	593.8	608.9	606.7	596.2	520.7	517.5
Abroad (by Mexicans)	251.1	272.1	329.7	399.9	448.1	450.2	444.5	433.6	386.4	276.4	297.5
Mexican hotel activity											
Total number of check-ins (000s)							42,193.0	40,948.4	41,262.7	43,164.0	
Activity in tourist centres											
No of tourist check-ins (000s)	19,921.0	21,280.0	20,802.5	21,377.4	22,259.6	22,403.0	22,187.5	21,976.0	22,077.2	27,483.0	29,430.7
Mexicans	81%	77%	78%	79%	78%	77%	77%	76%	77%	76%	75%
Foreigners	19%	23%	22%	21%	22%	23%	23%	24%	23%	24%	25%
No of tourist-nights (000s)	48,923.4	53,181.4	52,337.8	53,384.4	56,358.9	57,460.3	57,079.6	55,138.5	55,134.9	66,154.1	70,695.5
Mexicans	69%	64%	65%	66%	65%	65%	65%	64%	64%	62%	60%
Foreigners	31%	36%	35%	34%	35%	35%	35%	36%	36%	38%	40%
Regional distribution											
Beach resorts	45%	47%	44%	46%	49%	51%	52%	54%	54%	46%	47%
Big city tourists	24%	23%	25%	22%	22%	21%	20%	19%	19%	31%	29%
Provincial centres	32%	30%	31%	31%	29%	28%	28%	28%	27%	22%	24%

Cultural visitors (000s)											
Mexicans								10,785.6	11,675.1	13,074.0	12,817.4
Foreigners								3141.7	3092.3	3174.3	3734.3
Spas and vacation centres[3]											
Spas: Morelos and Michoacan	1886.1	2708.8	2373.6	2485.9	2553.2	2179.9	2687.2	3140.7	2035.8	2216.5	2111.5
IMSS: vacation centres	2359.2	2,198.2	2277.9	2731.0	2701.2	2514.0	2111.5	2325.0	1737.7	1382.1	1264.4
Financing of tourist investments											
Tourist Promotion Trust Fund (000)[4]		14,000	32,892	25,709	2,500	25,201	12,494	41,049			
Private investment generated (000)[5]		62,950	96,099	120,044	6,042	64,680	44,121	79,904			
National Foreign Trade Bank[6]	94,176	187,589	195,346	254,436	704,205	821,955	532,941	798,794			
Tourist Promotion Trust Fund (000)[7]		179,624	378,929	270,067	227,034	181,285	159,389	41,480			
Private investment generated (000)[8]		448,755	1,105,672	606,542	630,082	443,764	242,770	9,217			

Notes: 1 Foreign visitors to Mexico, including people who visit border area for less than 72 hours
2 Refers to people who stay in the border area more than 72 hours or 24 hours in the interior
3 Thousands
4 In thousands of dollars
5 In thousands of dollars
6 In thousands of dollars
7 In thousands of pesos
8 In thousands of pesos

The seven most important border cities account for 6 per cent of both national tourist sector employment and revenues.

Thus, in strictly quantitative terms, we see a very different picture than the national tourist authorities would have us imagine. The Tourist Ministry defines a 'tourist' as 'a person who lives abroad, crosses the border and spends at least one night in the country' (Chi Chase, 1998). Although foreign tourism in Mexico is a major generator of foreign exchange in gross terms, census data indicate that most sectoral employment and income is not generated in the regions where the mega-projects have been promoted in recent years. (NB: There is ample evidence to suggest that net earnings from foreign tourism to beach areas is substantially lower because of the heavy import component of expenditures there, and the high fees and commissions charged by tour organizations and service providers for this segment of the market.) Spontaneous (small group and individual) foreign tourism and domestic travel account for considerably more employment and revenue than organized beach tourism, and probably has a far more widely distributed economic impact. This type of tourism generally has a higher multiplier effect in terms of both employment and income because it uses fewer imported products; requires less payments abroad for licences, royalties, franchises, and profit; and employs less sophisticated technologies that frequently require more intensive use of labour with lower skill levels. In this context, then, it is extraordinarily important to examine the potential for domestic tourism in Mexico and the nature of official policies in this regard.

Present Government Policies towards Domestic Tourism

There is a widespread neglect of the potential of domestic mass tourism. A careful review of official documents and interviews with key participants in the tourist industry, and even in the academic centres preparing professionals, reveal a disdain for domestic tourism. With a few notable exceptions, such as hoteliers in the less famous or popular centres of cultural and historical significance, little attention is devoted to attracting or servicing any but the most affluent of Mexico's tourists.

The neglect of mass tourism within the country is compounded by a systematic bias in public policy-making to provide for the needs of the most wealthy groups. As with most public policy formulation in Mexico during the past 15 years, the emphasis on encouraging private investment with infrastructure investments and attractive credit facilities has been combined with the privatization of publicly held properties that created attractive opportunities for four- and five-star tourist developments in the beach resorts and adjoining regions; financing for these mega-projects (Table 2.1) is quite generous, in contrast to the absence of any special programmes in other parts of the country. Domestic tourism is generally only considered to the extent that these clients are oriented towards these properties. The bias against 'popular' tourism is further reinforced by another characteristic of public policy formulation in Mexico with regard to tourism: the people appointed to ministerial rank at both the national and state levels are frequently named for their political connections rather than for their knowledge of the sector; even in those instances where they have experience in the area, their programmes usually are designed to further their personal investments and to create new personal opportunities, and are rarely oriented towards an overall plan for balanced development that takes into account environmental considerations and the needs of the various social groups. The conflict between the individual gain of the titular head of tourist agencies and the design of facilities or the development of regional programmes is obvious in an analysis of virtually every tourist development programme in the country in which the government plays a role. At the state level, personal interests dominate public decision-making.

Interestingly enough, however, this was not always the case. The Mexican Social Security Institute (IMSS) devoted considerable resources to developing a number of important facilities for 'social' or 'popular' tourism, as it is called in Mexico. The first of these relatively large-scale facilities was constructed in 1968 in Oaxtepec, Morelos, as part of the installations for the Winter Olympics held in the country. This installation includes 408 hotel rooms of different categories (ranging from traditional hotels to hostels) as well as camp grounds and areas for day visitors. At its height in the early 1980s, Oaxtepec received as many as 2.5 million people per year, most of whom were day visitors. In 1982, two other, much smaller facilities (145 and 45 rooms respectively) were opened; these are also in areas close to Mexico City. A fourth vacation centre was opened in 1987 with 188 rooms. All of these facilities have proved very popular with family groups and with domestic groups interested in organizing business and professional meetings. From a peak of more than 2.5 million visitors a year in 1989, the four centres are now serving only about half that number as a result of a decline in government budgets, and the commitment to privatize many parts of the social security system (see Table 2.1 on vacation centres).

Another official programme to promote tourism was initiated by the National Peasant Confederation (CNC), as part of an effort to stimulate rural development in the mid-1970s. In this programme, a large number of small investments were made to stimulate local initiatives designed to reduce dependence on primary production. Among the almost 200,000 projects that were initiated, several hundred were designed to provide services for tourists; although there is no reliable information about these projects, 150 of them are still in operation (16 hotels, 3 hostels, 20 mobile home parks, 65 swimming resorts, 26 amusement parks and 20 restaurants). Most of the earlier projects failed for lack of adequate working capital and administrative systems that ensured continuity as the communal officers were rotated. Even today, in spite of these problems, rural communities are considering more than 1000 different projects that have passed a preliminary evaluation of technical viability (based on internal documents from the Department of Tourist Development of the CNC).

The IMSS and the CNC are part of the National Council for Social Tourism. This coordinating body, convened at the initiative of the Federal Ministry of Tourism, is the official organization responsible for promoting mass domestic tourism in Mexico. It brings together representatives of the 'popular sectors' (organizations representing working people in industry and agriculture, the young and the old), as well as those from the Chambers of Commerce in sectors offering tourist services (hotels, spas, resorts, transportation, infra-structure, tourist agencies and guides), along with the government agencies offering these services (toll roads and archaeological sites) and community development departments. Unfortunately, in our efforts to find out more about the specific projects that were being organized by each of the 21 organizations that participate in the Council, we found that the titular heads of each of them dismissed this consultative group as a poorly organized and ineffective mechanism that created more obstacles than benefits for the participating organizations. When we delved further, we found that very little in the way of real investment was taking place because of the lack of resources and the absence of support from the official bodies charged with stimulating social tourism.

Aggravating the problem of bureaucratic ineffectiveness is the lack of resources to support entrepreneurial activities oriented towards 'social tourism'. The high rate of failure among peasant enterprises reflects a more generalized problem among small enterprises and the inability of official promotional programmes to address the specific causes of business failure. Independent evaluations of these community development and small business efforts generally point to three common problems these enterprises face: 1) the lack of working capital to finance the whole production cycle, including marketing, sales and financing; 2) the lack of effective administrative and information systems to identify bottlenecks, points of inefficiency and problems of quality control; and 3) the absence of marketing capabilities and an understanding of its importance. Although the government has emphasized the growing installation capacity to provide training in both public and private schools of tourism, these centres almost always cater to the profiles supplied by transnational service providers rather than to community-based or 'social' tourism; nature, ecological or adventure tourism is on the curriculum of only one school – the National Polytechnic Institute.

Social Tourism as an Instrument for National Development

In spite of the absence of any concerted policy, travel by Mexicans is an important stimulus to local development in many parts of Mexico. Official Mexican policy continues to be very hostile for rural communities: while price policies and technical assistance programmes have been unfavourable for more than a quarter of a century, in recent years the onslaught has intensified, as illustrated by the 1991 declaration of the Under-Secretary of Agriculture that it was his (*sic*) intention to remove one-half of the population from rural Mexico in the following five years. That one-third of Mexico's population continues to live in rural areas and produce about one-third of the country's basic maize requirements, in spite of an official commitment to discourage such production, is a reflection of a deep-seated commitment by important segments of rural communities to defend themselves and their traditions at any cost.

This spontaneous programme to defend their communities is very important. We estimate that there is an annual transfer from outside these communities of more than US$10,000 million, amounting to an injection of more than 40 per cent of the value of rural production. About half of these resources comes from migrants who have gone abroad (primarily to the US), either temporarily (by far the largest part) or permanently; the other half comes from remittances from community members who are working in other parts of Mexico itself, generally in urban service employment, construction or as agricultural day labourers (Barkin, forthcoming). While Mexican authorities consider the visits of Mexicans coming from the US as international tourism, it seems more appropriate to analyse them as one important form of a domestic variety, pointing to a significant avenue for future development.

Unfortunately, very little of these massive resource transfers is used to diversify the productive base or to create new productive enterprises in the communities. Many analysts lament this wasted opportunity, criticizing the migrants for their penchant for conspicuous consumption; they often purchase expensive consumer durables or finance luxurious celebrations for family or community events, rather than using these funds to build new businesses. More recent research suggests, however, that there are major institutional and political obstacles in many parts of the country that condemn many successful initiatives, even before they get off the ground; local political leaders often appropriate the ideas and even the investments themselves when they prove to be successful, or corrupt practices destroy such enterprises to prevent upstarts from changing the local balance of political or economic power. If some of these resources are to be mobilized to overcome the extreme polarization that characterizes Mexican society, it will be necessary to create mechanisms to protect the new ventures from these barriers. One significant and unusual development suggesting the potential for this type of investment was the initiative of a former governor of the state of Zacatecas actually to encourage the development of 'home-town clubs' among migrants in areas with large concentrations of migrants, like the Los Angeles, California, area; they responded to this encouragement by collecting money for public infrastructure in embellishing the town plaza or improving local roads. One wealthy group of expatriates joined with the governor in refurbishing and transforming the shell of a colonial building into a five-star hotel. Similar efforts in other regions, however, have been frustrated by political and bureaucratic obstacles and outright corruption.

As the survey data show, domestic travel is primarily oriented towards reinforcing the strong family ties that persist, in spite of the virulent process of modernization. It would be erroneous, however, to create an important distinction between family ties and community organization. A great deal of anthropological and cultural research demonstrates that these visits are timed to coincide with the celebration of the day honouring a local patron saint or the traditional celebration of local or regional fairs; this 'fiesta' complex, as it is sometimes called in the anthropology literature, is a fundamental part of social organization in rural and small-time Mexico, and the occasion for a significant part of domestic travel. Of course, another grouping of family visits occurs during the Easter and Christmas seasons; summertime is less important an occasion for travel because breadwinners rarely have lengthy vacations. Thus, family and pleasure visits are highly correlated with other events that reinforce community cohesiveness and the local economy, even when the local productive activities might not appear to be sufficient to support the population. This particular character of travel in Mexico must be an important element in thinking about a programme to promote domestic tourism.

Interestingly enough, these community-based activities are also magnets for promoting visits by other people. The most important of these occasions are the regional fairs, some of which are assuming national (and even international) prominence, as local entrepreneurs join with governmental authorities to promote them. The San Marcos Fair in Aguascalientes dates back to the last century; the celebration of the Guelaguetza (a dance ceremony of indigenous origin) in Oaxaca has been popularized and widely promoted, the food fairs around the production of mole (a widely appreciated indigenous sauce based on a combination of several chiles, herbs, cacao and peanuts) in indigenous communities in the Mexico City area, the celebration of the spring equinox at the Mayan pyramids in Yucatán, the rites of spring at Papantla on the Gulf coast, the Day of the Dead in early November in Michoacan, and the massive religious mobilizations honouring the Virgin of Guadalupe at the shrine in Mexico City, to which millions come, are but a few of the most important. Regional differences lend unique cultural significance to rodeos and feast days throughout the country. Most of the local fairs and community celebrations, however, take place without assistance or interest from the state or federal governments.

Local merchant groups and government organizations have joined to create new events of a cultural and commercial significance. The Cervantine Festival in Guanajuato is now 25 years old, bringing to this town rich in colonial architecture and university culture a large variety of Mexican and international musical, choreographic and theatrical talent that attracts more visitors than the region is capable of accommodating. Agroindustrial interests in the central plateau have been successful in creating a commercial and cultural fair that attracts visitors from way beyond the region; similarly, cultural or historical events in other provincial centres are being used as an occasion to attract visitors by garnering sponsorship from local or national merchants who then promote these events more widely. In Mexico City, specialized book fairs are now being organized by publishers, thus diversifying the offerings traditionally sponsored by the universities.

Unfortunately, as with most other aspects of Mexican society, in spite of involving significant proportions of the country, the financial benefits from these widely dispersed events are generally highly concentrated in a small coterie of wealthy groups on a regional and national level. Since Mexico's business community is even more highly polarized than its highly skewed income distribution, most of the small-scale local merchants find themselves without sufficient resources to finance the scale of production and the inventories that would be needed to take advantage of the highly concentrated pattern of sales that occur during these special events. These ordinary market factors are compounded by the political influence that the wealthier merchants command, effectively consolidating their monopoly control in many local and regional markets, in addition to their high market shares in national markets.

Furthermore, because of the lack of adequate infrastructure and the poverty of many of the merchants and many of the people attending these events, these very popular events are often environmental disasters, not just generating massive volumes of wastes that local systems are incapable of handling, but sometimes, as in the case of the pilgrimage to the Guadalupe Shrine in Mexico City in mid-December, creating public health hazards as millions of people flock to a small area where no public sanitary facilities are available to permit the visitors to deal with their basic needs appropriately. Less evident, but no less worrisome, is the fact that virtually none of the resort facilities or hotels that receive domestic tourists are connected to sewage systems with water-treatment plants, resorting instead to discharges into local rivers or underground aquifers, contaminating water supplies and threatening the quality and safety of agricultural production that depends on these water supplies. These structural obstacles to environmental responsibility are compounded by a lack of information and education that prepares the visitors to act responsibly. Rising crime is also a growing concern at these events.

Community Initiatives

In the face of governmental indifference or outright opposition to local efforts, however, there are notable examples of communities who are stimulating tourism as part of their efforts to promote local development. One important case that takes advantage of the available infrastructure to divert existing tourists from traditional destinations is the coalition of 16 villages that organized a project – 'Community Museums in the State of Oaxaca' – to offer ecological and cultural tours to twelve different villages;[2] the tours include visits to museums, to little known natural and archaeological sites, to see healers at work and artisans making candles, fireworks and breads, as well as more commonly visited trades such as weavers, stone carvers and potters. Villagers explain the many products they obtain from their environment: collecting materials for natural dyes and for healing; the planting of the majestic maguey plants to supply ingredients to make pulque (a pre-Columbian form of beer) or the much stronger mezcal; harvesting cinnamon bark, ginger root, coffee; raising animals to provide wool and milk for their highly regarded cheese. They have shaped 12 museums that illustrate many colourful and unusual aspects of their history and culture, such as the extensive documental and monumental history, the treasure of medicinal knowledge and practice that is still alive, the artistic and culinary skills that developed apace with production skills that led to a highly developed technical division of labour. This experience is important, not only because it has been successful in attracting both local and foreign visitors to the beautiful city of Oaxaca, but also because it has strengthened the resolve of these communities to work together for their own welfare, rather than depend on state and federal institutions that generally have been unsuccessful when attempting such projects. Of particular note is their outreach, now available on the World Wide Web (Morales, 1997).

Another promising local effort coalesced around a community's concern to protect a geothermal geyser in Michoacan. In this case, a local governing board (patronato), composed of local citizens, worked selflessly for years to provide a minimum of maintenance and to make minor investments to attract more visitors from within the region and to improve the quality of their stay. Years of negotiation with different authorities to improve the site proved fruitless. When the state tourism agency intervened at last, with an inflated budget, it overcharged the patronato for minor improvements that effectively forestalled a more ambitious local development scheme being considered by the community. This project – in collaboration with a local university – would have transformed the area into a regional tourist and recreational facility for the large-scale mass domestic tourist market. This case offers stark testimony of a common pattern in Mexico of direct government intervention to thwart grass-roots initiatives that might spark an autonomous process of local development.

In other cases, outside groups sometimes have been successful in assisting local groups in taking the first steps towards a form of promoting community tourism. Although these outsiders almost always focus on foreign tourists as a more lucrative market, and one to which they often have privileged access, the projects often have an unexpected effect of attracting local tourists to a region that they might not otherwise visit. Various projects associated with the incorporation of local communities into efforts to protect several varieties of giant marine turtles, an endangered species with protected status, have included tourist promotion efforts; among the more notable of these is the conversion of a former slaughterhouse into a museum, and the construction of beachfront facilities operated by people from the local community to generate alternative livelihoods from protecting rather than hunting them. Unfortunately, the momentary success of these two projects does not weaken the broader criticism of the turtle programme offered in the next section.

The Possibilities and Limits of Social Tourism in Mexico

Many rural communities and local NGOs are actively engaged in developing their own alternatives to traditional tourist destinations and activities. While official policy seems to be oblivious to the importance of 'social tourism' as an instrument to promote decentralized development, new initiatives are being proposed and implemented throughout the country. In this section we examine some of these ventures as part of a discussion of an alternative model that might be more conducive to the country's needs and to those of its people.

There is a growing literature about grass-roots efforts to promote tourism.[3] Local communities are trying to attract visitors sensitive to, and interested in, their cultural heritage, their natural beauty, and their contribution to protecting biodiversity. Spontaneous outside efforts to support these initiatives, or to stimulate them, are increasingly common. Communities are becoming dissatisfied with the way in which the national park system is managed, or the arbitrary way in which biosphere reserves are created, without reference to local leaders; they are also dissatisfied about the scarcity of resources or the privileges accorded private capital at the expense of local communities. This is particularly glaring in the case of the 'ecology' theme park of X'caret on the new Mexican Riviera, carved out of rainforest lands owned by Mayan communities who have no participation in the project, except as menial labourers. Peasant efforts to defend their homeland and their right to the autonomous management of a rich cultural and natural heritage in North America's largest remaining rain forest (Chimalapas) by developing a sustainable resource management programme, including a 'sustainable' ecotourist component, have met with concerted opposition. Local

landlords and politicians are fearful of the new model that will probably be effective enough to wrest control of the region from these traditional autocrats.

An Example of Mass Domestic Tourism without Development

Although there are numerous examples of dedicated local efforts to protect resources and create facilities to receive tourists, as part of a diversified sustainable development programme, most of them are plagued by the same problems that have condemned well-intentioned projects to failure in the past. Lack of working capital, administrative systems, marketing channels and managerial skills combine with the lack of participation of local people and organizations to thwart the most promising of projects. A good example is provided by the case of the monarch butterfly that overwinters in Mexico each year and attracts more than 200,000 Mexican visitors during its four-month stay (eg Chapela and Barkin, 1995). Even though a proven demand exists to see this spectacular attraction, the local communities have been unable to consolidate a programme to provide tourist services and complementary activities to generate employment and income opportunities that would permit them to initiate a programme of regional development.

The Monarch Butterfly Project is instructive because it illustrates both the promise and the pitfalls of community-based tourism programmes. Since becoming a major sightseeing attraction in the mid-1980s, the biosphere reserve created to protect the region visited by the Lepidoptera has been increasingly plagued by conflict. In essence, more than 50,000 people living in the region were upset by developments that excluded them from continuing to work on and exploit their own lands, without offering them any productive alternatives. Aggravating the problem, one community in the region was singled out for privileged treatment by a businessmen's group (Monarca, AC) that obtained a concession to operate in the reserve, and received the first international grant for its management from the World Wide Fund for Nature. Fewer than 100 people from this community were employed as watchmen and to provide transportation and guide services, while others were permitted to operate a few makeshift stands offering souvenirs and light meals. Most of the tourists, however, were advised to bring their own food because there were only minimal facilities in the region. Tourists stayed only a few hours, trekking into the midst of the thick carpet of butterflies, with little regard for the objects of their admiration or for other tourists; there was never any reason for them to consider the plight of the human residents of the area or the special aspects of their local cultures. Tourist agencies from Mexico City or other nearby points of origin heightened tensions by operating their own programmes, bringing in their own guides and meals, and carrying their clients out as fast as possible to continue on their tightly programmed journeys; the State Tourism Office further compounds the problem, promoting these same tourist agencies and hotel accommodations in the capital city, rather than working to upgrade and publicize facilities in the area of the reserve.

Ironically, as the spectacular phenomenon of the nesting butterfly became better known and more visitors arrived, tensions mounted. Outside groups and interests irrupted in the area, staking a privileged claim on fast solutions to local problems. Ecologists went so far as to propose buying the local peasants' lands and moving them out as the only viable way to protect the butterfly's habitat, without, of course, any consideration of what thousands of families might do instead, or their impact on other regions if forced to migrate. As individuals, many of the local managers of the state and federal agencies responsible for operating the reserve were cognizant of the contradictions. However, their lack of authority, skills or resources to propose realistic alternatives made them the target of acerbic attacks from within the regions and they were charged with incompetence or corruption from outside.

With the expansion of the North American Free Trade Agreement (NAFTA), the region was transformed into a political maelstrom. The monarch (*Dannaus plexippus*) was adopted as the symbol of the process of integration and environmental concern by the environment ministries in all three countries, along with pious declarations of concern for the well-being of all involved. The international Model Forests Project selected the region for special attention and the North American Commission on Environment Cooperation convened an international symposium to confront the challenge. Aside from a number of small community-run projects that siphon off tourists from the principal sites, no credible alternative has emerged for this region because of the short-sightedness of the planning and implementation process.

With so much international attention, years of experience with conflict, and hoards of 'experts' offering their frequently contradictory and almost invariably unrealistic solutions, it is little wonder that the communities are incredulous. Few peasants can afford to take the risks and make the sacrifices required to participate in the long-term process of building new enterprises and reconstructing the diversified resource-based productive structure that would be required in order to be able to incorporate fruitfully this short-term avalanche of tourists into the region; the outside agencies are rarely willing even to consider the broad range of complementary, non-tourist related projects that would be essential for the tourist programme to be viable. Although all agree that any viable alternative will have to consider the needs of people in several dozen communities, few are cognizant of its cost, given the years of neglect and destruction that the communities have suffered. Orthodox models of local development have proved inoperative because the region is ill-equipped to compete with nearby areas to generate productive modern employment opportunities, and because of the lack of infrastructure and a population struggling to maintain its traditional forms of social organization and production.

There are groups attempting to promote an alternative plan for a more balanced programme of year-round tourism based on a diversified regional resource management scheme, including recreational installations, agroindustrial production, and a broad-based programme of local investment in small-scale enterprises. They face considerable political opposition from local power hierarchies who understand that such a proposal might erode their continued political control of the region's natural and human resource base.

Problems of Scale and Bureaucracy

Failures like that of the butterfly reserve are further compounded by problems of scale. Many community-based programmes are designed to receive small groups of visitors who have been carefully informed of the fragile nature of the ecosystems that they will be visiting, and the need for sensitivity on the part of the 'intruders'. As a result, they are correctly positioning themselves for a select market of ecotourism, based on very small groups and individually tailored visitor programmes; for small organizations and isolated communities, this solution is quite acceptable, but does not address the broader problem of developing a national capability to meet the needs for leisure time travel and recreation of an urban-based working class population, or for the daunting challenges of regional development. This potential market is important not only because it offers the possibility of a desperately needed service; if an investment were made to create installations to receive large domestic tourist groups from workers in the industry and the service sectors, it could begin to address some serious problems that Mexico must solve: the need to create a consciousness about environmental problems and the possibilities of rural communities to participate in the solution of these same problems, while also raising their own quality of life. We have learned that these projects are very difficult to initiate and sustain: they require sustained effort during an often long gestation period; they require attention to details that the service providers themselves sometimes cannot understand and eventually find alienating; finally, they require the communities to accept postponing the enjoyment of the benefits, as there is a great need to pay off loans and reinvest the proceeds.

Some examples of these initiatives illustrate this potential and the problems. As mentioned above, many sites along Mexico's 13,000 kilometres of shoreline are historically important breeding areas for several species of giant marine turtles, most of which have been placed on the worldwide list of endangered species. Local environmental and university groups have worked successfully for many years with coastal populations to inculcate a culture of protection and conservation in the communities. School trips and volunteer groups are organized to support these local efforts and to build facilities to receive tourists, offering local cuisine and some familiarization with local culture and language. Many of these efforts have proved disappointing or have failed, as natural disasters (Hurricane Paulina in Autumn 1997 is one case) combine with international investors seeking these prime beach-front parcels (as the example of the Melia chain in Quintana Roo in spring 1998) to frustrate or vitiate community efforts. Similarly, community efforts to attract tourists by building bungalows and other facilities are often hampered by official regulations shaped by wealthy, urban standards of quality and development; such is the case of the imaginative and very productive efforts in the Yucatán peninsula to organize communities to offer cultural and recreational activities that would raise local incomes and strengthen community organization. University-based efforts, some of which are in biosphere reserves, are incipient examples of well thought out programmes that offer visitors informative and relaxing opportunities to learn to appreciate the country's extraordinary natural heritage; unfortunately, in many cases these projects lack experienced administrative staff and systems, with a consequent lack of continuity in management and maintenance. In other cases, inadequate compensation schemes fail to provide sufficient incentives and income to assure continuing interest on the part of the operations staff responsible for day-to-day operations (Chapela and Barkin, 1995).

An Exception: Archaeological and Cultural Visits

Mexico has a great deal of experience with mass domestic tourism, although it is not part of the model in the minds of tourism officials; refer to Table 2.1 for an idea of the magnitude of this type of activity in Mexico. The National Institute of Anthropology and History (INAH) is responsible for managing the several dozen archaeological sites that have been opened to visitors to examine the wonders of pre-Columbian societies. The museums and 'ruins' receive millions of visitors each year, many in large group tours assembled by commercial operators or by educational, workplace or social organizations. Many of these excursions are successful experiences and contribute to enriching popular understanding of their rich heritage; in most cases, however, these visits cannot offer any appreciation of the continuity of these cultures or the process of transformation into present-day vibrant communities because the communities do not have the capability to receive the visitors, to explain the ways in which they organize production today, the way in which their culture has contributed to a rich culinary tradition and to an eclectic understanding of the interplay between herbal remedies and modern medicine, or the way in which traditional authorities or organizations still play an important role in local society. Even more troublesome, the INAH is unable to develop any constructive links with the surrounding communities. As a result, there are frequently important conflicts between the demands for protecting the historical and cultural heritage on the one hand, and those of local merchants and residents on the other, who are bent on encroaching on the protected areas for personal gain; the outright invasion of the areas surrounding the site at Mitla and the

gradual spread of urban development at Monte Alban, both in Oaxaca, are particularly egregious cases in point (Robles Garcia, 1996). In the exceptional case of the pyramid at Tulum on the Caribbean coast, where the nearby agrarian community (ejido) has gone to great lengths to develop a mutually advantageous programme of activities, highly regarded by tourists and professionals alike, government officials do nothing to promote the effort.

There are, however, numerous examples of expert professionals transforming their traditional activities into innovative opportunities for tourists from home and abroad. The Museum of Popular Culture (in Mexico City) is a showplace operated by the INAH, exhibiting the fruits of its work with local communities to strengthen and diversify local artisan and environmental management practices, transforming them into income-generating activities. In this area, when the government cut back this activity, an NGO, Asociación Mexicana de Arte y Cultura Popular AC (AMACUP),[4] stepped into the breach, continuing and expanding the official programme with international foundation support. There is great scope for expanding and enriching this portfolio of offerings, but public penury and an obsolete conceptual and administrative apparatus would require major innovations in public institutions and in entrepreneurial thinking before the foreign-oriented beach tourist model can be supplemented with new creative opportunities that would diversify and increase domestic tourist opportunities and spark local development. Unfortunately, the INAH does not have either the resources or the authority to impede developments on the edges of its sites and there are innumerable 'horror stories' of commercial developments encroaching on the 'ruins', destroying the majesty of the original settings, creating opportunities for the theft of parts of the pre-Columbian treasures, or actually threatening the physical integrity of the monuments; two such examples in the Mexico City area in recent years (at the royal city of Teotihuacan and the first ceremonial centre in the valley, Cuicuilco) revealed the difficulties of impeding real-estate developers from abusing their wealth and power to appropriate the benefits of these sites.

An Innovative Programme to Encourage Tourism and Promote Development

One interesting project, currently being implemented in the area of the 'Bays of Huatulco', offers an excellent example of an alternative vision. In this case, the large-scale international model of beach tourism had created obstacles to its own development as a result of inadequate planning and poor management by the National Tourist Development Fund. An aquifer that was expected to supply 25 five-star hotels quickly proved insufficient; the water shortage currently impedes the construction programme of more than a dozen projects that were in advanced stages of implementation. A local environmental group, Centro de Soporte Ecológico, proposed a new model for regional resource management in which 32 communities in the surrounding region, with 65,000 people belonging to several ethnic groups, would participate in a programme of watershed reconstruction and management to assure more reliable and abundant supplies of water in exchange for guarantees for their own livelihoods, through the diversification of their productive base, improving the productivity of existing crops, introducing new agricultural and livestock products, and the emplacement of a new ecotourism business owned and operated by the communities, but financed by the hotels. At a later stage, plans are being discussed for creating a wildlife reserve for photographic and conservation purposes, while nurseries for endemic but threatened plants and trees are sprouting up in many communities (Barkin and Pailles, 1998).

The key to the success of this project is the effective participation of all sectors of society (Barkin, 1998). The project brought together representatives from the indigenous communities and the transnational hotel industry to implement a mutually beneficial regional resource management programme; in turn, they persuaded local, state and federal agencies of its viability and wisdom. The local NGO was aided by the abject failure of the authorities to confront the impending threat of severe water shortages and declining tourism. The proposed approach to the regional problem offers an opportunity to generate attractive opportunities for the communities to strengthen their local organs for decision-making by creating productive employment for members who would otherwise have been forced to leave. Unlike the example of the monarch, the series of proposed projects are programmed to offer a continual flow of tangible results and a growing demand for workers. At the same time, the proposal explicitly supports community efforts to strengthen traditional systems of production and environmental management that are already attracting visitors who are interested in learning about the environment, while enjoying a vacation in the bungalows and camp grounds that are being constructed for the guests. Some of the chores of environmental management are now financed by the hotels as they demonstrably contribute to recharging the underground aquifers on the coast; these functions had been abandoned as national policy and international markets are discriminating against products produced by poor peasants. Even in its early stages, the project offers a creative example of a collaborative development programme in which all participants will be beneficiaries.

The Search for Alternatives

Throughout the country, people committed to developing local communities are searching for ways to diversify local economies by introducing new productive alternatives, including tourist activities. It is interesting to observe that in many of these spontaneous examples of local initiatives, the innovators understand the importance of integrating tourism into a more balanced programme of productive development. In a forest community in Oaxaca, Ixtlan de Juarez, a local NGO sparked local enthusiasm for sustainable forestry programmes by supporting a local effort to build a small hotel for technicians and tourists visiting the project and offering classes in environmental education. A family in Delicias, Chihuahua, refurbished a 19th-century hacienda shell as a hotel and restaurant-bar, taking advantage of a municipal initiative to open a palaeontology museum to show off the local finds of prehistoric remains of various species of large mammals and reptiles (dinosaurs), and further enriched the local offering by rehabilitating an old river boat to accommodate groups for short cruises, all at accessible prices for Mexican visitors.

On the Yucatán peninsula, there is a growing realization of the limitations of the dominant model of exclusive beach-oriented international tourism. Critics of the highly publicized and well-financed collaboration among the five Central American nations, known as Maya-World, are concerned about the environmental destruction and social dislocation that it is occasioning among native populations. Furthermore, with the changes in social organization, new problems are emerging or anticipated as the tropical forests and ecosystems are rapidly being destroyed or degraded. In response, creative programmes like the Maya Echo Project in the area just south of Cancun can serve as an example of how even small-scale efforts can have a dramatic impact in protecting a community and its area of influence, while accommodating increasing numbers of visitors. In this case a group of foreigners joined forces with community members to design a development programme that would be attractive for tourists. They raised enough funds from outside sources and from selling tours and local craft products to purchase sewing-machines and then develop a steam bath to complement the 'exhilarating' experience of swimming in the sinkholes that naturally emerge from the underground rivers on the peninsula. Their evolving relationship, begun in the early 1990s, illustrates the perseverance and commitment required to forge a different development path. The project began when the organizers offered local women from the indigenous community the opportunity to make blouses and other cotton goods for visitors to a nearby botanical garden; the initial success sparked the interest of the men, who suggested bringing tourists to swim in their cenote, as it is called, which is continually fed by underground water that maintains the water clear and chilly. The visitors learn about the chicle trade (a gum derived from a native tree) and other traditional productive activities while enjoying the local cuisine; the community's response has been to 'reinvent' and expand their participation of 'traditional' products (indigenous maize and chicle) and to reconsider disappearing models of home construction, as they realize how much they are appreciated by the outsiders, including people from other parts of Mexico (in sharp contrast to the scorn heaped on these activities by local ne'er-do-wells) (Locke, 1997).

A series of studies in the southernmost state of Chiapas extend and deepen the lessons from other parts. On the one hand, we find that community tourist activities can be an important tool to spur development efforts and strengthen local efforts to improve environmental management practices (Nigh and Ochoa, 1997). But they also reveal the difficulty of implementing even the most well-intentioned and designed of projects: with contentious and paternalistic political systems and development models instilling distrust and individualism through-out the society, the purposeful collective action required for a successful community project requires tenacious leaders and constant support to build an organizational capability and 'social capital'; this bundle of attributes, the building-block of grass-roots development, consists of the political and social skills required for a community to implement a collective project of development (Kersten, 1997). This community approach to development could be important in providing a decentralized panoply of recreational and cultural offerings that are well suited for the travel patterns of the Mexican population: individualistic and spontaneous family-centred voyages in public transportation.

The Dilemma

The commercial and social service organizations that presently offer large-scale tourism services in Mexico reinforce traditional models for the provision of such services. They share the vision that the best (most profitable) way to provide for these groups is through large-scale operators organized according to an international model based on large hotels, managed by transnational providers or their national counterparts. This vision excludes rural producers as potential providers of low-cost large-scale facilities for a new type of tourist service designed specifically for a market oriented explicitly to 'social' or working-class and middle-sector tourists, including public schoolchildren and senior citizens. A different approach would not focus on the fragile ecosystems that are so popular among rural development advocates today, but rather would direct their attention to installations that could accommodate large groups in camping, dormitory, or cabin arrangements, with a combination of local service provision for recreational activities and meals, with economical self-service capabilities; one uniquely appropriate example of this is the large dormitory and other facilities located in the Popocatepetl National Park, a favourite attraction for day travel and climbers in the Mexico City area. Destinations might be designed to facilitate visits to existing centres of attraction (including the INAH sites), as well as the development of new programmes that combine tourism and recreation with social service, related to programmes of reforestation and other tasks of environmental management. This alternative approach would have the added advantage of contributing to reversing some of the problems of environmental deterioration occasioned by these same rural communities for lack of income and employment opportunities (Barkin, 1998).

Conclusions and Recommendations

At present, it is unlikely that government tourism policy will recognize the potential of domestic mass tourism as a mechanism to promote rural development. Nor is the government prepared to consider as a priority in its own right, or as an instrument for environmental management and social well-being, the provision of services to meet the needs for diversion and relaxation of the large majority of urban denizens who cannot aspire to visit the tourist developments on which the government is focusing. Such neglect of a valuable, productive and low-cost instrument is likely as long as public policy is driven by the service providers who are organized along the models of the large-scale tour operators who focus their efforts in the most profitable and easiest segments of the market.

This existing model is an environmentally destructive model and one that contributes to further social polarization. Ironically, it does not even seem to generate the volume of employment and the net earnings of foreign exchange that its promoters claim. There are too many leakages in the system and too much technology used to really deliver the local development benefits that are promised. We are not suggesting that the government should abandon this pattern of development, but rather that there is a need for a critical reconsideration of the advisability of continuing with the substantial subsidies for credit and infrastructure that this strategy now requires. There is also an urgent need for an evaluation of the social and environmental impacts of this model of service provision.

The several examples that illustrate the alternative model examined in this chapter offer an important counterweight with considerable benefits for rural communities and the Mexican working class. In this way it would contribute substantially to breaking down some of the obstacles to building a more balanced national society. A programme of mass social tourism would open a new model for decentralized development that would respond to the urgent needs of present-day society. Well organized, it could be financed much more readily than the international model and offers more employment and an inexpensive way to improve the quality of life for both consumers and providers.

It is clear that an initiative for developing a capacity to service domestic mass tourism would be an imaginative and inexpensive way to promote rural sustainable development in some selected areas of Mexico. The knowledge, skills and capacity exist to implement such a programme. Given the current character of government policies, it would be unreasonable to expect a public sector programme, but with the capacities already in the hands of many communities and intermediate level organizations, such a programme might be promoted by the social sector itself.

The principal finding of this review of the domestic tourism scene in Mexico is that this neglected sector offers great promises for future development.

But the analysis confirms a crucial lesson learned in Mexico and elsewhere: these small-scale rural sustainable initiatives must not be stand-alone projects, but rather should be fully integrated into a broader programme of regional development. Thus, if domestic mass tourism is to emerge in Mexico as part of a strategy for local development and environmental management, it will have to come from the organizations representing the 'popular' sectors of the population and the receiving communities themselves. Therefore, if there were to be any public sector action in this area, the most productive policy would be one to facilitate initiatives by NGOs and intermediate level community organizations that are already in place.

For the foreseeable future, official efforts will be channelled into promoting private sector investment in foreign tourism in beach-front locations. With regard to domestic mass tourism, an important first step would be to develop an alliance of public institutions working to study and promote local initiatives, systematizing existing information and making it available for local promoters looking for ways to diversify their offerings in coordination with local communities and grass-roots development organizations. A research agenda must contribute to this effort by highlighting the promises and difficulties of this sector, and channelling resources into the evaluation of existing initiatives.

Notes

1   The data from the survey are too incomplete to warrant including any systematization in this report. Although the information is generally consistent over time, the presentation of the data available for this project does not lend itself to easy tabular presentation.
2   Email: muscoax@antequera.com
3   Two excellent sources are: 1) *El Planeta Plática*, an electronic newsletter that deals with ecotourism and related issues in the Americas; and 2) a comprehensive guidebook that mentions many of these efforts (see Mader, 1998).
4   E-mail:amacup@mail.internet.mx.

References

Barkin, David (forthcoming) 'Overcoming the neoliberal paradigm: Sustainable popular development', *Journal of Development Studies*

Barkin, David (1998) *Wealth, Poverty and Sustainable Development*, Editorial Jus and Centro de Ecología y Desarrollo, Mexico

Barkin, David and Carlos Pailles (1998) 'Water as an instrument for sustainable regional development', *Arid Lands Newsletter*, no 44, November. http://ag.arizona.edu/OALS/ALN/aln44/barkinfinal.html

Chapela, Gonzalo and David Barkin (1995) *Monarcas y Campesinos: Desarrollo Sustentable en Oriente de Michoacán*, Centro de Ecología y Desarrollo, Mexico

Chi Chase, Michelle (1998) 'Tour de force: Industry aims for higher return in Mexican tourism', *Business Mexico*, May 1998

Consejo Nacional Empresarial Turístico (1996) *Evaluación económica, estrategias y perspectivas del sector turismo en México*, Mexico

de Sicilia Muñoz, Rosa Alejandrina and Alvaro López López (1998) 'Distribución geográfica de los municipios turísticos de México', *Notas* (de INEGI), no 2, pp1–8

El Planeta Plática, an electronic periodical (http://www2.planeta.com/mader/planeta/planeta_index.html)

Kersten, Axel (1997) 'Community based ecotourism and community building: The case of the Lacandones (Chiapas)', *El Planeta Platica*, (May) (http://www2.planeta.com/mader/planeta/0597/0597lacandonia.html)

Locke, Mary (1997) 'Maya Echo – A cultural voyage', *El Planeta Platica*, August (http://www2.planeta.com/mader/planeta/0897/0897maya.html)

Mader, Ron (1998) *Mexico: Adventures in Nature*, John Muir Publications, Santa Fe, New Mexico

Morales, Teresa (1997) 'Community museums of Oaxaca', *El Planeta Plática*, February (http://www2.planeta.com/mader/planeta/0298/0298oaxaca.html)

Nigh, Ronald and Fernando Ochoa (1997) 'Conservación y desarrollo comunitario en Laguna Miramar: Una estrategia integral', *El Planeta Plática*, February (http://www2.planeta.com/mader/planeta/0297/0297miramar.html)

Robles Garcia, Nelly Margarita (1996) *El Manejo de los Recursos Arqueológicos en México: El caso de Oaxaca*, PhD dissertation, University of Georgia, Athens

Chapter 3

Regional and Domestic Mass Tourism in Brazil: An Overview

Antonio Carlos Diegues[1]

Introduction

Tourism is a very important sector of the Brazilian economy, and, as in many other developing countries, it was used by successive governments as a means for fast economic development and foreign currency exchange. In 1995, 55 per cent of all international tourists came from South America, especially from the Mercosur countries (Argentina, Brazil, Uruguay and Paraguay). The number of tourists from the North has declined in the last few years, due to increasing violence and the high costs of touring in Brazil. On the other hand, domestic tourism has been growing steadily since the early 1970s. Although it is not possible to estimate the exact number of nationals participating in tourism activities, today the sector demonstrates its weight in the Brazilian economy and its potential for developing backward areas. The present study aims to assess the social and economic importance of national and regional tourism in Brazil, as well as the environmental and socio-cultural impacts of tourism-related activities.

'Regional tourists' will be defined as those visitors whose country of origin is in South America. We will confer special attention to those visitors coming from the Mercosur countries, as they represent the majority in this category.

According to the WTO, which defines a 'domestic tourist', as 'any person residing in a country, who travels for a period not exceeding 12 months' (WTO, 1993), one could imply that most travellers using air travel are 'tourists', as the number of embarking and disembarking passengers is equivalent in the statistics for a given year. Domestic tourists frequently use cars when going on holiday, especially when travelling to neighbouring states. It is not possible to provide accurate figures on the number of tourists who travel by car. Another methodological difficulty emerging from this definition is that it is impossible to quantify the number of passengers travelling exclusively for leisure, recreation and holiday purposes, as the available data also include those who travelled to visit friends and relatives, for business and professional activities, for health treatment and religious purposes.

In the first part of the chapter we deal with domestic and regional tourism at the national level, trying to assess the importance of such a social phenomenon. The second part focuses on regional and domestic tourism to the north-east region of Brazil, a priority area of the government for tourism investment. The north-east is a fast growing tourist area and places such as Salvador (Bahia), Recife (Pernambuco) and Fortaleza (Ceará) are state capitals that receive a significant number of tourists. However, most domestic and regional tourism is still concentrated in the south-west and southern regions of Brazil where important tourist centres, such as Rio de Janeiro, São Paulo and Florianópolis (Santa Catarina), are located. The third part of the chapter looks at the case of the state of Ceará that presents a range of social and environmental concerns similar to those in other states of the north-east. Considering the large extension of the country and the environmental and social specificities of each region, the analysis of a case study will provide a more insightful approach to the issues presented in the chapter. In terms of socio-economic impacts, the state of Ceará deserves attention. Tourism is already one of the main economic activities of the area, the government has given it priority in its development plans, and an important on-going project for tourism development called PRODETUR (Projeto de Desenvolvimento do Turismo) is already taking place. Another interesting fact about Ceará is the emerging organization of local communities towards the structuring of 'community-based tourism'.

Apart from definitional difficulties, the research process faced another problem: the lack of information and data available on this particular aspect of the tourism industry, as most of the information refers to international tourism. Domestic tourism has no particular records and only estimates can be provided on the basis of Brazilian passengers using air travel as a means of transportation, as mentioned above. Information on regional tourism is more accurate, as it is considered a subcategory within international tourism. And even here, more accurate information is found only for regional tourists travelling by air, and few data can be collected on those visitors who come from neighbouring countries by car and bus.

Domestic and Regional Tourism at the National Level

The Importance of Tourism for the Brazilian Economy

In 1995, Brazil received 1,991,416 international tourists, compared to the 249,000 who visited the country in 1970, the growth in the industry being remarkable. In 1995, some 55 per cent were regional tourists. Although it is difficult to assess the actual magnitude of domestic tourism, it is estimated that it has increased consistently in the last ten years. It could be said that domestic tourism is far more important in number and income generation than international tourism.

In 1994, activities linked to tourism generated, directly and indirectly, an income of US$40.39 billion and US$7.80 billion in direct and indirect taxes, which is equivalent to 8 per cent of gross domestic product (GDP) (EMBRATUR/ABRESI/SEBRAE, 1996). It has been estimated that there was a total investment of US$7.3 billion, or 5.6 per cent of total economic investments. In 1994, the sector employed, directly and indirectly, from 8 to 10 million workers, resulting in US$16 billion paid as salaries. The tourist industry employs one out of eleven workers in the country.

Currently, the most important problem that the tourist sector faces is that of outbound tourism. There is an astonishing growth of Brazilian nationals travelling abroad. In the last 15 years, outbound tourism has grown by 495 per cent, compared to the 17 per cent growth in international tourists to Brazil for the same period. In 1995, around 3,100,000 Brazilian nationals travelled outside the country,[2] of which 67.1 per cent were tourists and 61 per cent came from the rich areas of the south (São Paulo, Rio de Janeiro and Minas Gerais). The average Brazilian tourist travelling abroad spends around US$1635 per vacation (EMBRATUR/ABRESI/SEBRAE, 1996).

As far as the balance of payment is concerned, Brazilians are spending more outside Brazil (US$341 billion) than international tourists are spending in Brazil (US$209 billion) (Cacex, 1995). This tendency can be explained by the existence of a growing middle class that prefers to visit other countries, particularly the United States, as the costs of air tickets and accommodation are comparatively lower than in Brazil. Another reason is that travelling abroad, especially to the United States and Europe, confers a higher status than travelling inside the country.

History of National Tourism in Brazil

Tourism as a social phenomenon started in Brazil in the 1940s and 1950s during the process of import-substitution through which the urban–industrial sector emerged as the leader in the Brazilian economy. There was an expansion of the urban–industrial working class and middle class, particularly in the south-eastern part of the country, mainly São Paulo and Rio de Janeiro. In these decades and in the subsequent ones, the working class consolidated their labour rights, including the right to annual vacations. During this period, there were strong migration movements from the north-eastern states to the growing urban areas of São Paulo, Rio de Janeiro and other state capitals of some southern states. Some of these migrants return regularly to their areas of origin to visit relatives and friends.

In the 1950s, Brazilians were already visiting Rio de Janeiro, then capital of Brazil and known for its natural beauties, as well as the surrounding hydro-mineral resorts in the mountains between São Paulo and Rio de Janeiro.

During the 1960s, the movement of national tourists increased due to the establishment of the first car industries that led to the rapid construction of roads which gradually replaced railways. The road network was also greatly enlarged with the construction of the new capital Brasília, situated in the geographical centre of the country, and thousands of kilometres away from the main economic centres, such as Rio de Janeiro and São Paulo. New roads were built to the north, such as the Belém–Brasília highway, linking Amazonia to the southern regions.

During this decade the first roads linking Rio de Janeiro, São Paulo and Belo Horizonte to the coastal areas were built, leading to the construction of secondary houses for tourists along the coast. In the process, local fishermen and peasants were expropriated from their houses and beaches, and used the newly built roads to migrate to larger cities, looking for better living conditions. In most cases, they ended up in the outskirts of these cities, living in slum areas. Concomitantly, the traditional way of life of the coastal communities was disrupted, and traditional cultural practices and festivals started gradually to be abandoned. This process was particularly acute along the coast of São Paulo and Rio and became more serious in the following decades. Many of the traditional inhabitants became housekeepers of summer-houses, receiving small salaries in exchange (Diegues, 1983). Together with the improvement of the roads, two categories of visitors appeared: the vacationers, who spent several weeks on holiday on the coast, mostly in their secondary houses, and the 'tourists' who spent only a weekend in the area. From the 1980s onwards, there was a boom in the construction of secondary houses, particularly in the coastal areas near large metropolitan centres, such as Rio de Janeiro, São Paulo, Florianópolis, Recife and Salvador.

Rodrigues (1996b) argues that the increase in mass tourism in the 1970s is due to: a) the growth of the urban middle class (professionals, traders, public officers and qualified workers in the industrialized sector); b) the higher participation of women in the labour market, increasing the family income; c) the increasing number of families owning a car; d) amelioration of highways; e) the means of communication, travel agencies and publicity; f) rapid urbanization and g) the growth of the construction sector, building summer-houses in the coastal and mountainous areas.

National Policies for Tourism

The first institutions and policies for tourism promotion were initiated in 1958 by President Kubitschek and the creation of the Brazilian Commission for Tourism (COMBRATUR), linked directly to the presidency. In 1962, a new division for Tourism and Sports was created, replacing COMBRATUR, and was linked to the Ministry of Industry and Commerce.

In 1966, during the military regime, the Brazilian Enterprise for Tourism (EMBRATUR) was set up, centralizing policy-making at the federal level. The potential for tourism development was emphasized with the formulation of the first national policy for the sector and the creation of the National Council for Tourism. In subsequent years, agencies for tourism promotion were created at the state level (Becker, 1995).

Tourism was then considered a 'national strategic industry' by the military regime and the federal government had the task of establishing appropriate policies for fostering the growth of this new sector. EMBRATUR had the right to establish subsidiaries with government and private capital. Special financial incentives were given for the construction of hotels and other tourist infra-structure in the country. In 1977, a federal decree allowed the government to create Special Areas of Tourist Interest (Áreas Especiais e Locais de Interesse Turístico). In the first 20 years of the decree (1967–1987), the number of hotel rooms in Brazil increased from 16,313 to 120,000. Around 70 per cent of the new hotels were built through these special fiscal incentives (Becker, 1995).

In the mid-1980s, the military regime was replaced by a democratic government and this transition gave place to a more liberalized tourist industry with more participation of the private sector. During this decade, the number of travel agencies increased significantly, as will be seen later. In 1981 the first National Policy for the Environment was formulated to assess the relationship between tourism and environmental preservation. From 1986 onwards, environ-mental impact analysis was required for any major environmental disturbance caused by road and infrastructure construction, particularly along the coastal areas. In 1987, EMBRATUR launched the first programme for ecotourism, following the experience of other countries.

In 1991, EMBRATUR changed its name to the Brazilian Institute for Tourism, linked directly to the presidency of the republic, with the task of formulating, coordinating and fostering the execution of the National Policy for Tourism (TNT). The fiscal incentives for tourism, however, were discon-tinued. The main objectives of this new policy were to foster domestic and international tourist flows and to improve tourist infrastructure, adapting it to regional characteristics.

PLANTUR (National Plan for Tourism), 1992–1994

The main instrument of the National Policy for Tourism is PLANTUR (National Plan for Tourism), presented by EMBRATUR for the period 1992–1994. This plan aims at the development of 'tourist poles' with adequate infrastructure (airports, hotels, etc), the creation of jobs and income, and the encouragement of private investments in the sector. The plan seeks to double the income from international tourism to an additional US$46 billion, to create 490,000 new jobs, and to place tourism among the first three items for export. PLANTUR has several subprogrammes, such as:

- **Programme for tourism growth centres** These centres scattered around the country would concentrate the main investment in the sector, serving not only international but also national tourists. National tourism should be stimulated through low-price hotels and special travel arrangements. The financing for the subprogrammes should come from existing funds such as FUNGETUR (General Fund for Tourism Development), FINAM (Investment Funds for Amazonia) and BNDES (Bank for Socio-Economic Development).
- **Programme for domestic tourism development** This subprogramme seeks to spur mass tourism, particularly at weekends. It will be implemented in coordination with workers' associations.
- **Programme for tourism development in Mercosur** Tourists from the neighbouring countries of Mercosur – a common market created in 1991 with Argentina, Uruguay and Paraguay – represent a significant percentage of all international tourists. As these visitors usually come by car, the programme foresees road infrastructure amelioration. Trade companies among Mercosur countries were set up in order to improve the access routes of tourists.
- **Programme for international tourism development** This programme aims at promoting international tourism (particularly from Europe, Japan and the United States) as it has been declining in past years due mainly to the high costs of travelling and hotels, increasing violence in urban centres, especially in Rio de Janeiro, because of the impoverishment of a considerable proportion of the urban population. It is mainly a marketing strategy devised to promote tourism among young people, and ecotourism, particularly in Pantanal and in the Amazonian region.
- **Programme for ecotourism development** The interest for ecotourism appears more visibly in Brazil in the mid-1980s. In 1987, a special Technical Commission was created by EMBRATUR to study the potential for ecotourism and to propose measures to stimulate this activity in Brazil. In 1989, IBAMA (the Brazilian Institute for Environment Protection) and EMBRATUR signed an agreement in order to foster ecotourism, particularly

in national parks, on islands and in estuarine areas. In 1994, EMBRATUR and the Ministry for the Environment launched the 'Guidelines for a policy to ecotourism'. This document has indicated the following large ecosystems as priority areas for ecotourism development: the Amazonian Forest, the Atlantic Forest, Cerrado (central savannah), Pantanal, Araucaria and pampas (flat areas) of the southern region, mangroves, coast and islands. Priority was given to ecotourism in protected areas, particularly in those under federal jurisdiction: 35 national parks, 23 biological reserves, 21 ecological stations, 16 environmental protected areas, 9 extractive reserves and 39 national forests. And particular attention was given to the 100 already existing private protected areas.

- **Programme for PRODETUR (Programme for the Development of Tourism)** PRODETUR is the most ambitious tourism development proposal for the north-east region of Brazil. It was initiated in 1991 by EMBRATUR and SUDENE (Superintendency for the Development of the Northeast). The programme's budget of US$16 billion is funded both by the Inter-American Development Bank and the federal government. It aims to provide an incentive to tourist activities (both international and national) in the region through state and private investments. Its objectives are: to increase tourist demand for the area, and to generate employment and income through several activities linked to the construction sector (the expansion of airport facilities, roads, sewage systems). Given the importance of this programme, a more detailed analysis will be made later.

Policy Guidelines for the Period 1996–1999

In 1996, EMBRATUR launched a new document 'Política Nacional de Turismo: Diretrizes e Programas 1996–1999' (National Policy for Tourism: Guidelines and Programmes, 1996–1999), setting the objectives for tourism development for the next four years (EMBRATUR, 1996c). In general terms, the document included again most of the objectives and strategies of previous plans, emphasizing the role of international tourism.

The municipalization of tourism was given a higher priority. Around 660 municipalities, from a total of 1570 with potential to participate in the programme, have joined in, and 29 workshops involving 1000 people were organized to train local tourist agents and other professionals to plan tourist activities in their municipalities. The organization of ecotourism also drew the attention of the government, and 11 workshops involving around 440 people took place. Efforts concentrated also on the establishment of charter flights inside Brazil, facilitating them also among sub-regions within Mercosur. This document considers domestic tourism as a means of transferring income from the rich southern regions to the poor north and north-east regions.

General Comments about the Existing Programmes

Most of the goals of the government proposals and programmes for tourism development in the Policy Guidelines document for the period 1996–1999 seem to be unrealistic, especially regarding the overoptimistic forecasts for the rapid increase in the demand for international and domestic tourism. After the stabilization of the currency in 1994 when the Brazilian currency (real) was over-evaluated in relation to the US dollar, the costs of air travel and accommodation became very high for tourists. The over-evaluation of the national currency has also induced a fast-growing movement of Brazilian tourists to the United States and Europe. Today the number of national tourists outside Brazil is higher than the international tourists coming into the country. As mentioned earlier, many potential domestic tourists prefer to travel abroad as it confers prestige and reflects a higher social status, is cheaper than domestic travel and they can purchase goods at lower prices than in Brazil. This situation may be reversed, but the process will take time. Recently, travel agencies, together with hotels and airline companies, started organizing tourist packages in order to diminish the cost of travel and accommodation. This strategy is giving positive results, particularly for those who visit the north-east.

There is a lack of coordination between government agencies and programmes. There is, for instance, a National Programme for Coastal Management which was set up to monitor the conservation of coastal ecosystems. Their proposals are often in conflict with those of the government tourist development agencies, many of which might imply the construction of new roads and large hotels in very fragile areas, threatening the environment and local human cultures.

More emphasis should be given to social development policies to alleviate rural and urban poverty, particularly in areas where tourist development projects are being implemented. Existing social marginality and urban violence are factors that withdraw tourists from those areas. Many tourist centres are inside or close to urban centres where violence and criminality are high (Rio de Janeiro, Salvador, Recife).

Although the programmes aim at creating new job opportunities, most of the local populations are not qualified and trained for these new jobs, and might reinforce the already existing social marginalization and boost the large informal sector. Substantial efforts should be made to incorporate this population in the planning and implementation of the tourist activities. More adequate links should be established between communities with rich cultural patterns and diversity and tourist projects, particularly in the north-east, where cultural tourism might become an important tourist attraction, but this potential is not yet fully utilized.

The recent decentralization policy in tourism in which more power is given to municipalities is a positive trend, but, in general, these municipalities are not properly equipped to plan and implement tourism development activities. A positive trend is that some municipalities are creating their own commissions for tourism development.

As subsidies for tourism have been discontinued, the government is proposing joint ventures between the government and the private sector. However, the behaviour of the private sector should be regulated as, very often, private investors buy the land or even expropriate it from the local communities in those areas where investments are planned, causing social tension. Furthermore, tourism is perceived in many municipalities as the predominant activity rather than a complementary activity to the existing ones (small-scale fisheries, agriculture, etc). Therefore, given the seasonal characteristic of tourism-related activities, this often leads to social and economic disruption of regional economies.

The Tourism Industry

Since the early 1970s, EMBRATUR has created a special fund for tourism development, using fiscal incentives. From 1969 to 1993 over 1403 projects were funded through this system, particularly the construction of hotels, representing an amount of over US$1 billion. Over 66,711 hotel rooms were built during this period, creating around 60,000 jobs. In the period 1976–1995, FUNGETUR financed 1099 projects (US$398,810 million dollars), in particular building 16,049 hotel rooms and creating 19,962 jobs (EMBRATUR, 1996a).

According to EMBRATUR/ABRESI/SEBRAE (1996), there are 18,026 hotels and hostels in Brazil, with 500,000 rooms. Around 49 per cent are located in the south-east region, 21 per cent in the north-east, 19 per cent in the southern region, and 11 per cent in the northern-central regions. There are few high-category hotels, totalling less than 1000 rooms. The total investments in hotel construction reached US$19 billion in 1995. These hotels employ 287,265 people who receive approximately US$1.3 billion per year (EMBRATUR/ABRESI/SEBRAE, 1996).

From 1990 onwards few hotels were built. In 1980, for instance, 5144 new hotel rooms were built. In 1992 there were only 34 new rooms, while there were 965 in 1995. This last increase represents less than one-fifth of the number of rooms built in 1980 (EMBRATUR, 1996a). There was a 30 per cent increase in the number of travel agencies between 1992 and 1995. The north-east presented the highest increase during these three years, revealing the tourist potential of the region. In 1993 these agencies employed 93,690 people on a regular basis and 24,474 freelancers, generating an income of US$9 billion. In 1994 there were 800 car-renting firms operating, using around 70,000 cars. Around 50 per cent of these firms were located in the south-east region, 17.4 per cent in the north-east, 12.l per cent in the south, 12.1 per cent in the centre and 8.5 per cent in the north. Around 900,000 tourists rented a car in 1994, spending US$240 million. In 1994 this subsector employed 16,000 people on a regular basis and 48,000 on a non-regular basis (EMBRATUR/ABRESI/SEBRAE, 1996).

The Ongoing Crisis of the Tourism Industry in Brazil

In spite of Brazil's high potential for regional and domestic tourism, the sector underwent a crisis throughout the 1990s as part of the overall economic recession the country had been facing since the end of the 1980s.

In the 1970s the Brazilian GDP grew at 7 per cent a year, decreasing to 1.3 per cent per year in the 1980s. From 1990 to 1992 the GDP grew at 1.5 per cent per year, and since 1994 there has been a slight recovery, reaching around 2 per cent per year. There is also growing unemployment, particularly in the industrialized centres like São Paulo where it reaches over 18 per cent of the population (Paiva, 1996). Some other economic trends affecting tourism have been observed since 1994 with the implementation of the stabilization plan. The middle class has been deeply affected by unemployment and a decrease in income has resulted in a reduction of the family budget, therefore making it more difficult to plan long holidays. On the other hand, the decreasing price of second-hand cars has been a positive effect, enabling many workers to buy and use these vehicles for short recreation trips.

The number of domestic tourists using air travel as a means of transportation decreased from 1988 to 1992, with a slow recovery in 1995. Tourism from neighbouring countries is the only sector that has been growing steadily. The high costs of air travel, hotels and meals in Brazil constitute the main discouraging factors influencing both domestic and international tourists when it comes to choosing their holiday destination. The hotel industry also claims that, due to the lasting financial recession of the country, not enough investment is being made in the construction of new hotels and in the recovery of existing ones. Another problem that hinders tourism development in Brazil is increasing urban violence – another product of the economic recession.

Regional Tourism

Regional tourists are those visitors who come from neighbouring countries in Latin America, as Brazil has borders with most of them (except Chile and Ecuador). Tourists from Argentina and Uruguay used to visit Brazil before the 1970s, since when the number of tourists from other neighbouring countries has increased significantly. Roads and communications have improved and tourists from neighbouring countries have started to visit the beaches of the southern states of Rio Grande do Sul and Santa Catarina. Many of them have bought second homes, particularly on beaches, such as Camboriú in Santa Catarina.

Table 3.1 *Number of international and regional tourists in Brazil*

Origin	1975	1980	1985	1990	1995
International tourists	512,000	1,625,422	1,735,982	1,091,000	1,991,000
Regional tourists	168,960	941,007	996,087	527,000	1,106,000
Regional/international	33.0%	57.9%	57.4%	46.0%	55.4%

Source: EMBRATUR, 1996a

The number of regional tourists is increasing steadily. In 1990, some 527,000 people visited Brazil and this figure doubled in 1995, reaching 1,106,062 – over 50 per cent of all international tourists. Table 3.1 shows a comparison between international and regional tourists from 1966 to 1995.

The number of international tourists increased around tenfold between 1966 and 1995, reaching its peak between 1975 and 1980 when the Brazilian economy was booming. In this period, regional tourism represented more than half of the amount of international tourists. During the 1980s, this percentage remained steady. It decreased in the early 1990s, due to political instability, economic recession and urban violence. In 1995, it started increasing again, reaching almost 2 million international tourists in 1995 (see Figure 3.1).

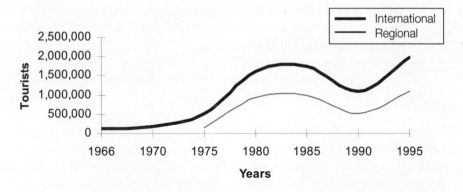

Figure 3.1 *The number of international and regional tourists*

In 1995, Argentines represented 32 per cent of all tourists, followed by 11 per cent of North Americans, 10 per cent of Uruguayans, 5 per cent of Paraguayans and 3 per cent of Chileans.

According to recent research undertaken by EMBRATUR (1996b), Argentines visited mainly Florianópolis (29.7 per cent), Foz de Iguaçu (25.6 per cent), Rio de Janeiro (12.0 per cent), and Camboriú (10.7 per cent). Most Argentines visited the country for touristic purposes (81.5 per cent), for business (12.6 per cent) and to attend conferences (2.2 per cent). Around 17 per cent of them were traders, and 22 per cent were professionals. They stayed around 12 days, spending US$45 a day (US$87 for those staying in hotels).

Domestic Tourism

Domestic tourism in Brazil has been motivated by the following purposes:

- Pilgrimage and religious functions: This movement of visitors to religious sanctuaries is old, but has become an important activity since the end of the last century. Visits to national Catholic sanctuaries, such as Aparecida Virgin and Bom Jesus de Iguape in São Paulo, Círio Procession in Belém and Bom Jesus do Bonfim in Salvador, became a source of massive tourism, particularly after the 1960s when the road system was improved.
- Leisure: This concentrates the bulk of domestic tourism. Tourists are mostly interested in visiting coastal areas and mountains. Beaches have remained the main attraction for massive domestic tourism, particularly after the 1960s. Tourism to mountainous areas is gaining in importance, particularly as beaches tend to become overcrowded around metropolitan areas, such as São Paulo and Rio de Janeiro. National parks are also receiving larger numbers of tourists, mostly to Parque Nacional Iguaçu, Parque Nacional de Itatiaia and Parque da Serra do Mar.
- Business, conferences and meetings: This very selective form of tourism is also increasing. Many cities situated between the large business and university centres of São Paulo, Belo Horizonte and Rio de Janeiro, particularly in hilly areas, are specializing in this kind of tourism (Caxambu, Serra Negra, Águas de São Pedro).
- Family visits: This is an important form of tourism as internal migration in Brazil is high, particularly between the poor north-east and the rich south-eastern regions.

Unfortunately, specific data on the different types of domestic tourism are scarce. EMBRATUR usually takes the number of national passengers embarking or disembarking at airports as the only indicator, making it impossible to assess the precise proportion of those who travel exclusively for leisure purposes.

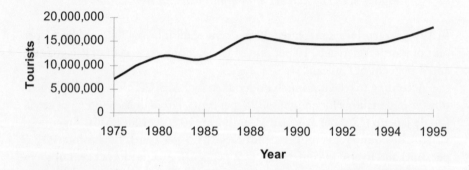

Figure 3.2 *The number of domestic tourists disembarking in airports*

The south-east region is the main touristic producer and receiving centre. It includes São Paulo, with 5,524,130 embarking passengers in 1995, and Rio de Janeiro, with 3,177,105. These principal cities, from where some 55 per cent of all domestic tourists depart, are also the main cities receiving tourists – around 45 per cent of all disembarking passengers. The second most important tourist receiving region is the north-east, which includes some of the most important tourist areas in the country like Bahia, Pernambuco and Ceará which received around 2,865,597 passengers in 1995.

Table 3.2 *National passengers disembarking at Brazilian airports*

Year	Passengers	Year	Passengers
1975	7,018,265	1990	15,911,397
1980	11,772,040	1992	14,447,586
1985	11,370,828	1994	15,082,626
1988	15,916,932	1995	18,077,747

Source: Embratur 1996a

As mentioned earlier, the main problem about using the number of passengers as an indicator is that because of the high price of air travel, the majority of Brazilians (around 96 per cent) use other means of transportation, such as cars and buses, for their touristic trips. Thus, most internal travellers are not accounted for in the national statistics.

EMBRATUR (1996a) estimates that around 128 million nationals travel as tourists per year. This figure, however, seems to be grossly exaggerated. Rodrigues (1997), based on the distribution of the population according to consuming patterns, has a much lower estimate for the number of potential domestic tourists: around 40 million people. This author also argues that in the last two years, due to the stabilization of the Brazilian currency, some 13 million additional people entered the market of potential tourists.

One more accurate estimate concerns the tourists (including weekend trips) going to the beaches close to São Paulo, such as Santos and Praia Grande. According to the Department of Roads of São Paulo, around 12 million people went from São Paulo to the nearby coast in 1995. In 1994, bus companies had approximately 28,455 buses, and the bus terminals in São Paulo alone catered for 38,752,096 passengers. The main cities to which domestic tourists went were São Paulo, Rio de Janeiro, Brasília, Salvador, Recife, Fortaleza, Curitiba and Pôrto Alegre.

Domestic and Regional Tourism in the North-East

The Potential and Constraints for Tourism in the North-East

The north-east of Brazil, where the federal government decided to invest heavily in tourism development, has 3300 kilometres of coast, with beautiful tropical beaches, estuaries, dunes, lagoons, a stable, high temperature, and sunshine almost all year round. This region encompasses nine provinces: Maranhão, Piauí, Ceará, Rio Grande do Norte, Paraíba, Pernambuco, Sergipe, Alagoas and Bahia.

The Social Situation in the North-East

The north-east is the most underdeveloped area of the country where modern cities, such as Fortaleza in Ceará, and industrialized centres, such as Salvador, Aratu and Camaçari in Bahia, coexist with large slum areas. The north-east is home to one-third of the Brazilian population (40 million inhabitants) and more than 50 per cent of the rural population of the country. The area is known as 'poverty reserves' where the interaction between low income, illiteracy and environmental degradation feeds new cycles of poverty and marginality (Martine, 1991). In 1991, a study showed that 35 per cent of all Brazilian families (or 43 million families) were living under the poverty line, but in the north-east the percentage is even higher: 53 per cent of the families are under the poverty line, earning around US$30 per capita per month (CNUMAD, 1991). Per capita income in the region varies from US$541 to US$1,563 in Bahia, compared to US$4140 in São Paulo (Moraes, 1995).

Land tenure is highly concentrated and most of the 2.8 million holdings belong to poor farmers. Chronic droughts affect part of the region, provoking a historical migration movement of part of the rural population to the rich southern regions of the country and, more recently, to the state capitals of the north-east. It is estimated that in the 1970s over 16 million people migrated inside Brazil, coming mainly from the north-east and going to the rich south. Most of the migrants came to São Paulo and Rio to work in the construction sector and they went back regularly to their place of origin to visit their relatives.

Urbanization was a rapid process in the north-east, particularly after the 1970s. The region today includes three large metropolitan areas: Recife (Pernambuco) with 2.5 million inhabitants, Salvador (Bahia) with 2.4 million inhabitants, and Fortaleza (Ceará) with 2.2 million inhabitants. The urbanization rate in most coastal municipalities has been prominently high: 26 per cent in Ceará, 34 per cent in Rio Grande do Norte and 31 per cent in Pernambuco, leading to a high concentration of the population in the state capitals. In some north-eastern states, a large proportion of the population lives in these coastal municipalities, such as Ceará (65 per cent) and Pernambuco (38 per cent). In general, besides the state capitals, the remaining coastal populations live in small towns, with few economic alternatives, except artisanal fisheries and seasonal tourism.

The combination of rapid industrialization in some state capitals of the north-east, accelerated urbanization in all of them, and insufficient employment opportunities, resulted in massive urban poverty in the region. Slum areas proliferated in most of them, resulting in severe health and sanitation problems. The indicators for the region are below the national average. In Brazil, only 40 per cent of the families have water and sanitation facilities, but in the north-east the proportion is only 15 per cent. In the urban areas of Brazil, 54 per cent of the families have water and sanitation, but in the urban north-east only 27 per cent have these services. The lack of sanitation causes (1986) high child mortality rates in the region (75 children out of 1000 died before the age of one year) compared to the southern areas (37 out of 1000 children). In the rural areas of the north-east child mortality rates are even higher (130–160 children out of 1,000 died before the age of one year).

The situation has been aggravated in the last few years as government investments in health and education have not increased, resulting in the extinction of important health services and epidemic control agencies, inviting diseases like cholera and dengue (breakbone) fever to become endemic in some areas.

The impoverishment of favela dwellers is more critical today due to the low economic growth rate of the country as a whole in the last ten years. Most tourists arrive in the modern state capitals, like Salvador and Bahia, which have developed in order to attract tourists. At the same time, a fast growing middle class has appeared in these capital cities, which are basically dependent on tourism and other services. The modernization of the coastal line of these capitals includes the opening of large avenues in areas previously inhabited by poor people, as has occurred in Fortaleza and Salvador. These poor inhabitants have been transferred to other areas far from the coastal line, affecting small-scale fishermen and other people living from a growing informal sector (small shop-owners, construction owners, etc).

The growing mass of unemployed people has resulted in increased urban violence, particularly in large cities and at important tourist centres such as Salvador and Recife. Thus, while efforts are made to attract tourists via the modernization of the urban centres by increasing the number of shopping centres and large avenues, growing urban poverty and violence have become a constraint to tourism development.

The Present Situation of the Tourism Industry in the North-East

Existing figures show a fluctuation in the number of regional and international tourists in the north-east for the period 1985–1995 (Figure 3.3). There was a

34 per cent increase in the number of international tourists in the period and a decrease of 18 per cent of domestic tourists to the region. There are no specific figures for South American tourists, but the number of Argentines, the majority of neighbouring tourists visiting Bahia and Pernambuco, has decreased to around 50 per cent from 1985 to 1995. It is important to note, however, that the number of regional tourists has doubled from 1990 to 1995, revealing that these visitors are staying mainly in the southern areas of Brazil that are closer to their countries of origin, particularly Argentina, Uruguay and Paraguay.

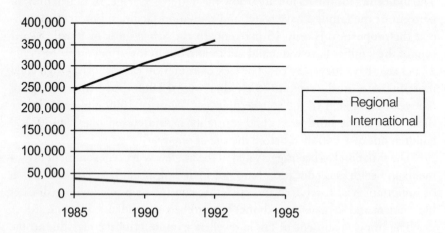

Figure 3.3 *The number of international and regional tourists in the north-east of Brazil*

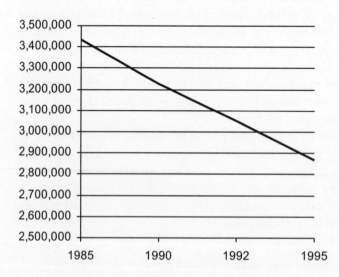

Figure 3.4 *The number of domestic tourists disembarking at airports in the north-east*

Tourist infrastructure increased significantly during the period 1985–1995. The number of hotel rooms in the region nearly doubled. The most significant growth occurred in the state of Ceará where the number of rooms grew threefold from 1985 to 1995. This significant increase can be explained mainly by the existence of fiscal incentives until 1991. Travel agencies in 1995 were almost ten times the amount of 1985, increasing from 153 to 1328.

The total private investment in the tourism industry represented US$364 million during the period 1982–1992, creating 12,575 direct employment opportunities. The PRODETUR document estimated the private investment by 2000 to be of US$223 billion, of which US$112 billion in foreign investments.

Table 3.3 *Number of tourists in the north-east of Brazil*

Origin of tourists	1985	1990	1992	1995
International tourists	243,944	307,099	361,063	na
Regional tourists	na	na	na	na
Argentines	36,339	27,321	26,343	16,641
National tourists	3,434,979	3,244,469	3,050,637	2,865,597

Note: na = not available
Source: PRODETUR, 1994

The PRODETUR project has estimated an unrealistic number of regional and national tourists visiting the region in the year 2000: more than ten times the current number of regional tourists and three times the number of national tourists.

Table 3.4 *National and Mercosur tourism demand for the year 2000*

Demand of tourists from Mercosur	453,000
Demand of domestic tourists	6,424,000

Source: PRODETUR, 1994

Profile of Regional Tourists

Research undertaken by PRODETUR (1994) reveals that regional tourists usually travel to the north-east with their families, spending individually around US$80 a day. They stay an average of seven days, and their preferred attractions are beaches, local excursions, shopping, festivals (carnival) and typical dishes. Other research undertaken by EMBRATUR (1996b) reveals that 85.7 per cent of regional tourists come to Fortaleza exclusively for recreational purposes. Some 30 per cent of them are entrepreneurs, university academics and students, staying an average of ten days in the state, spending US$120 per capita. The main complaints were lack of tourist information, public cleanliness and insufficient airport facilities.

The PRODETUR Project

PRODETUR aims at increasing tourist demand and the length of stay of tourists in the area, encouraging new investments in infrastructure and creating employment. The project's total budget is US$1,670 million, of which US$750,000 are from the Inter-American Development Bank (IDB) and US$920,000 from government funds. The main subprogrammes focus on growth poles and tourist corridors.

PRODETUR covers the most important coastal ecosystems in the region where thousands of small-scale fishermen and peasants live. Even before the PRODETUR project was approved in 1991, high investments had already been made along the coastal areas of many of the north-eastern states. In the beginning of the 1980s, the Parque das Dunas – Via Costeira (Dune Park and Coastal Avenue) – transformed 8.5 kilometres of the coast around Natal. Along this tourist road 23 high-standard hotels were planned (three of which have already been built), damaging some fragile dunes. In 1993, the construction of the Linha Verde (Green Line), 142 kilometres of asphalted road linking Salvador to the northern part of the state, gave way to the planning of many hotels and other infrastructure development. This area is also sparsely inhabited by small-scale fishermen. It is within this context that PRODETUR is being planned and implemented. The following locations have been chosen for investments:

- Maranhão: São Luís and Alcântara. Main investment: recovery of the historical monuments, airport.
- Ceará: Costa do Sol Poente (east coast of Ceará). Main investment: airport, sewage system, roads, environmental recovery (the establishment of protected areas).
- Rio Grande do Norte: Rota do Sol (southern coast). Main investment: airport, roads, sewerage system.
- Paraíba and Pernambuco: Costa Dourada. Main investment: sewerage system, roads.
- Sergipe: Aracaju and São Cristovão. Main investment: roads, sewerage system.
- Bahia: Costa do Descobrimento. Main investment: roads, sewerage system, airport.
- Alagoas: northern coast. Main investment: sewerage system, roads.

Impacts of PRODETUR

Although PRODETUR was designed to cover the nine states of the north-east, development has only started in Ceará and Bahia, as only in these two states was the government ready to provide national funds as a counterpart to the Inter-American Development Bank loan. However, tourism development projects started also in other north-eastern states like Paraíba and Rio Grande do Norte.

On the basis of existing experience, it is clear that these projects will have strong ecological, social and cultural impacts. As was seen earlier, the north-east is the least developed and poorest region of the country with the highest illiteracy levels, appalling health conditions and lack of urban infrastructure. The region is particularly vulnerable to environmental degradation for a number of factors. The general socio-economic conditions make the local population less prepared to tackle environmental problems than in other regions of Brazil. Ecological regulations are less enforced here than in the more developed southern part of the country. Hotels and roads are built without the appropriate environmental impact analysis. Dunes and mangrove areas are being destroyed, as is occurring in Rio Grande do Norte and Paraiba. Paradoxically, part of this environmental degradation is caused by the coastal poor who build their houses on state-owned mangroves and dunes when they lose their land due to infrastructure development.

At the same time, expectations about tourism as the best way to create employment and to develop the area are higher here than elsewhere. But the fact that there is a large portion of the local population who are illiterate and who do not have the necessary skills to work in high-standard hotels makes this optimism unrealistic. Most of them are independent producers, small-scale fishermen and peasants who are not ready to work long additional hours every day.

It can be foreseen that some of the main consequences of PRODETUR will be:

- A probably higher concentration of investments in coastal areas while little consideration will be given to the rural populations living in and around the project areas, causing a higher migration from rural areas to urban centres.
- The privatization of beaches and 'commons' will result in a higher level of expulsions of the coastal population from their land.
- The cost of living will increase, particularly for the poor population.
- The development will end in growing segregation between tourists and the coastal poor.
- Changes in the cultural pattern and in the traditional way of living are likely to take place. Customary activities such as artisanal fishing might be further disrupted.

In summary, the north-east of Brazil presents a high tourist potential represented by its natural beauties, particularly sunny and sandy beaches, and the rich cultural heritage of its population. In contrast, this is also the poorest region in Brazil, the most affected by the current economic situation, and where the income gap between the rich and the poor is the highest. The ecological and cultural impacts of PRODETUR will be numerous, especially as the tourist model chosen by the authorities is similar to the Cancún experience in Mexico (Chapter 2). New roads along the coast are being built in several states of the region where new high-standard hotels are being planned close to the beaches where traditional poor communities of fishermen live. The names selected for some sections of the coast (Golden Coast in Pernambuco, Sun Coast in Paraíba) resemble the highly crowded beaches in Spain and France.

Domestic and Regional Tourism in Ceará

The Potential and Constraints for Tourism in Ceará

The state of Ceará is known for its 183 kilometres of coast, tropical beaches, sunshine and stable hot climate (26° Celsius all year round). In the last decade, Ceará has considerably invested in the tourism sector, showing the highest increase in hotel room construction in the north-east. The capital city became one of the most modern Brazilian cities, and its international airport has a growing number of charter flights to the United States and Europe. The coastal area has been inhabited traditionally by small-scale fishermen, particularly raft-fishermen, who possess a rich and diversified culture, represented by festivals and dances, such as côco and maracatus. Until recently, the main economic activities were cotton growing, cashew nut production and lobster fishing. All these traditional practices have declined in the last decades and tourism has emerged as an important economic activity.

In 1992, around 15 per cent of domestic tourists using air travel chose Ceará as their vacation site and around 26 per cent of Argentine tourists travelling to the north-east have visited Ceará. In 1993, income from tourism represented 1.95 per cent of GDP equivalent to US$178.1 million, and it increased to US$519 million in 1996 (Almeida, 1997), employing around 61,000 people in 1994.

Table 3.5 *The number of domestic, regional and international tourists in Ceará*

Origin of tourists	1985	1990	1992	1995
Domestic			373,180	446,712
Regional (Argentine)	243	878	6865	
International	3018	9659	17,013	

Source: PRODETUR, Recife 1993.

The Social Environment in Ceará

A survey undertaken in 1993 by local authorities indicated that the social situation of coastal communities is alarming. Around 50 per cent of the local population is considered to be below the poverty line, earning salaries of around US$100 a month. The illiteracy rate is very high, reaching over 40 per cent, and the health situation is appalling, with diseases such as cholera and dengue fever threatening the population. Sanitary conditions are poor and on many beaches there is even an absence of tapped water or a sewerage system. Fishing, the main economic activity of the area which employs around 60,000 people, is going through a serious crisis as artisanal fishermen are being expelled rapidly from their beaches by land speculation. Lobster fishing is also decreasing, due to overfishing by the industrial fleet located in the capital.

PRODETUR in Ceará

Development plans include the amelioration of the highway linking the capital Fortaleza to the western beaches, the upgrading of the local airport, and the improvement of the sewerage system in tourist areas. This project, locally called PRODETUR, covers 117 kilometres of the western coast, encompassing six municipalities (Caucaia, São Gonçalo do Amarante, Paracuru, Paraipaba, Trairi and Itapipoca).

Table 3.6 *Investments by PRODETUR in Ceará (in US$1,000)*

Investment per item	US$
Airport	109,672.00
Sewerage	52,216.00
Energy	16,799.00
Services/equipment	14,601.00
Studies	10,000.00
Marketing/training	3248.00
Total	216,536.00

Source: PRODETUR, Recife, 1993.

There are 15 large private projects involving US$500 million planned for Ceará. The most outstanding one is the Sun and Fun Recreation Park, occupying an area of 500 hectares in the isolated estuary of the Cauípe River. Hotels and other tourist infrastructure have also been planned for the estuaries of Curu and Mundaú, areas of a very fragile ecosystem used by artisanal fishermen (Rodrigues, 1996a). There are also two hotels and a marina planned for Mundau estuary, and one hotel and a country club in Cauípe, in addition to the Sun and Fun Recreation Park.

Environmental and Social Impacts of PRODETUR in Ceará

Environmental impacts

The coastal line of Ceará extends for 573 kilometres of which 60 kilometres are already undergoing rapid erosion. Important dunes of the eastern shoreline have been occupied by hotels and tourist second homes, resulting in serious environmental disasters. Examples of this damage are Canoa Quebrada, Caponga, where the sea has already destroyed 120 metres of beach, Almofala which has lost 170 metres of beach, and Icaraí which has lost 350 metres (Rodrigues, 1996a). Another example is the town of Pecém in the PRODETUR area. In the last 15 years it has been growing in an uncontrolled way with the construction of tourist houses on mobile dunes. As a result, erosion has already taken 150 metres of the sandy beach, where small-scale fishermen used to live. Houses and streets were destroyed by waves. A large commercial harbour is being planned for this area. The consequences of this project are largely unknown, particularly in regard to the coastal landscape that now attracts tourists. Tourist attractions are disappearing, but small-scale fishermen are those who suffer the most.

Social and cultural impacts

In April 1995, a seminar organized by the Coastal Forum and the Bank of the North-east to analyse the impacts of PRODETUR, there were different views concerning the impacts of tourism on coastal zones and human communities. Government and financial institutions were optimistic about the consequences of PRODETUR, emphasizing the perspectives for income and employment growth. Most NGOs and universities were critical about the social and cultural impacts of tourism development, based on the already existing consequences of this activity. Local community members were eager to improve their income and employment situation, and felt encouraged by the perspective of ameliorating the infrastructure, but, at the same time, were afraid of losing their land as most of them were considered 'squatters'. Most non-governmental participants criticized the lack of information about PRODETUR and the lack of interest of the government in explaining the main points of the project to the local population. The main negative points of the project raised by NGOs, universities and local communities were as follows.

The privatization of beaches and loss of access to land and natural resources

They argue that even before the implementation of the project, beaches and coastal land are being privatized by large economic groups. In the last ten years a rapid process of land concentration has taken place and many coastal poor families have been displaced in order to build hotels and other infrastructure.

It has been mentioned that around 20 rich families control most of the land in the coastal area. As these families are in one way or another linked to the state administration, they already know where infrastructure, such as roads, will be built and, therefore, they buy as much land as possible within the project area. Artisanal fishermen, after selling their houses or after having been cheated by land speculators, had to move to areas far from the beach, losing their access to the sea. Many examples were given on how beaches are privatized, such as Paracuru beach, where the local community will be resettled outside the beach. Local groups and NGOs are trying to promote environmental protection of the existing dunes to stop the high level of erosion, but they feel that their efforts will be jeopardized as an important economic group linked to the state governor has bought the land. The construction of a PRODETUR-funded road on the environmentally fragile Mundaú-Guajiru beach is leading to the expropriation of 30 of the 100 coastal 'people's houses'. In Jericoacara, a distant beach on the western coast, the sea water is already polluted as around 4000 tourists arrive during the summer season and no appropriate infrastructure exists. Small-scale fishermen who used to own the beach in the past were expropriated from their land by land investment firms and are now living in a slum area (Nova Jeri) far from their working place (Coriolano, 1996). In Trairi municipality, on a beach called Fleicheiras, mangroves have been destroyed in order to build a hotel and a road. Most of the fishermen have been displaced to areas far from the beach and find it difficult to earn a living from fishing.

In the same seminar, participants denounced the existence of a large tourist project called Nova Atlântida in the beautiful coastal area of Almofala where a lagoon and dunes exist. This large area belongs to the remaining 17 communities of the indigenous tribe Tremembés, who live on 4674 hectares of land that has not yet been demarcated. Spanish, Italian and national tourist development groups have already bought the area, threatening the way of life of these indigenous communities and are planning to transfer the inhabitants into a 2-hectare plot, where the Indian Tremembés will not be able to live from fishing and forest harvesting.

On Cumbucu beach, 30 kilometres from Fortaleza, a Brazilian–French group has invested in a large tourist resort that has expelled several families of small-scale fishermen from the beach. Some of those fishermen today work as tour guides, taking tourists in their raft boats to trips around the hotel. This resort was planned to attract high-income tourists, but as the beach is close to the capital city, this area has become a 'popular area', as urban day-trippers come by bus to enjoy the 'hotel beach'.

Changes in the traditional way of living of coastal communities

Those who are opposed to large tourism development projects such as PRODETUR argue that large-scale tourism will disrupt the way in which coastal communities live. Since most of them make a living from artisanal fishing and the loss of coastal land causes them to abandon fishing activities, many of these fishermen become employed as housekeepers in second homes. As the development of small-scale fisheries is not a government priority, no assistance is provided to artisanal fishermen. They affirm, correctly, that artisanal fishermen could benefit from tourism if they were supported in their efforts to sell their fish and lobsters directly to the restaurants and hotels. In order to ensure the continuity of those communities, the access to their land should be guaranteed as they are being threatened by the expropriation of their land along the beaches and estuaries.

NGOs and universities claim that local inhabitants will not be employed by the high-standard hotels to be built, as over 37 per cent of them are illiterate. At the same time, experience has proved that autonomous fishermen can hardly be transferred to other activities that require full-time dedication and special training.

Cultural changes

Local groups and NGOs are already worried about the cultural impacts of PRODETUR over traditional communities. They criticize the fact that government and private groups organize carnivals outside the traditional season to attract tourists, using non-local music and traditions. At the same time, no assistance is given to local groups that make efforts to maintain live local dances and music, such as the forró, maracatús and papangus. They claim that PRODETUR funds are only allocated to restore the architectonic patrimony of some cities, but nothing is done to promote the 'living culture' of coastal communities. They also claim that more assistance should be given to promote the traditional economies of the coastal communities, particularly artisanal fishing.

Increase in 'sexual tourism', prostitution and use of drugs

A recent parliamentarian commission in Ceará organized the assessment of the impact of tourism, concluding that the prostitution of children has increased dramatically, due to increased poverty and tourism development. However, it is not possible to assess to what extent domestic tourists participate in sex tourism or find it a motivation to visit the north-east, for most eyes usually turn to foreign visitors when evaluating this problem. An increase has also been observed in the use of drugs by young people in coastal communities, as middle-class tourists tend to use drugs during their vacation.

Lack of participation of local communities in the planning of PRODETUR

Local communities and NGOs argue that PRODETUR was designed without the participation of local groups and will benefit mainly private investors. NGOs and local groups, particularly the Forum do Litoral, have requested a copy of the PRODETUR project, but the government has not been willing to provide it. They call for more transparency in government actions.

Positive Trends on Community-based Tourism and Reactions of Villagers to Tourism Development

In the 1980s and early 1990s, coastal communities, with the support of the Catholic Church and NGOs, started their organizations in order to react against threats to their lands and growing impoverishment. Some communities were threatened by land speculators and, on some beaches, the houses of fishermen were burned by armed jagunços. Industrial fishing of lobsters led to the overexploitation of resources and conflicts with artisanal fishermen.

Ceará fishermen and coastal communities have a strong tradition of resistance. A local NGO called Terramar, created in 1991 to support the artisanal fishermen's claims, was able to mobilize some coastal communities to defend their rights to the land and to call the attention of the government to the poor living conditions of small-scale fishermen. In 1994 a Coastal Forum was created to ensure the participation of local communities in the development of the coastal area. The first actions took place in the eastern part of the coast, in the municipality of Icapui, where a leftist party – PT (Partido dos Trabalhadores) – won the elections. Priority was given to implement community-based tourism and to assist artisanal fishermen. In Icapui, the first cooperative of artisanal fishermen was organized in 1993, and local mobilization has resulted in the functioning of 27 different local organizations, dealing mainly with small-scale fisheries development and community-based tourism.

Currently, at Redonda beach, a municipality of Icapui where 486 families of nativos (local people) live, a project organized by Terramar encourages traditional activities such as lobster fishing. In 1994, the community organization forbade the selling of a plot on the beach without the agreement of all villagers. The nativos have built five lodges and local restaurants to receive tourists. In order to control lobster fishing, the Redonda community has bought a boat to survey illegal lobster fishing. This is a pioneer project, involving IBAMA, and officially responsible for the surveillance of fisheries. They have introduced an innovation – 'the people's tribunal' – to bring to trial those who disobey the agreement they reached on responsible fishing. They have also produced, in cooperation with the government, a management plan for lobster fisheries. In this respect they became a model for other regions of Brazil where the responsibility for fishing surveillance relied only upon IBAMA.

In 1994, at Balbino beach in the neighbouring municipality of Cascavel, 52 families denounced the destruction of mangroves on their beach and their local association obtained the support of the Catholic Church and other NGOs.

Instead of accepting the construction of big hotels, the association has built local lodges (pousadas) and restaurants to host tourists. In 1997, as a result of their fight, the government has ensured the property of the land, providing the local association of the nativos with a land title. They have organized several conferences and meetings in association with the NGO Terramar to discuss the impact of tourism on coastal communities (Tupinambá and Limba, 1997). The last meeting, organized by Terramar and the International Collective in Support of Fishworkers (headquarters in India), was held in August 1997. Over 160 community leaders met to discuss measures to ensure responsible fishing and press the government to assist artisanal fishermen. This meeting was attended not only by the authorities of Icapui, but also by three other municipalities that decided to join efforts in order to promote responsible fishing and tourism. The mobilization of NGOs, local communities and universities is attracting the attention of federal institutions that are responsible for fisheries management and tourism development.

Areas Requiring Further Research

It should be noticed that official data concerning domestic tourism are scarce, as statistics concentrate mainly on international tourism. However, this aspect of the tourism sector has become an area of academic research in some universities and research centres, particularly in São Paulo.

There are two phases in research on tourism in Brazil that are closely related to different periods of the development of the activity. The first phase encompasses the period from 1970 to 1985 when tourism started to gain momentum and economic importance. This period was also marked by economic incentives from EMBRATUR to construct hotels and infrastructure. It also coincided with the increase in the number of international and domestic tourists. During this period the first courses, and even colleges, on tourism were created in the southern region, particularly São Paulo and Rio de Janeiro. Most of the publications were diagnosis and technical reports, taken as a basis for feasibility studies of infrastructure development and done by economists and technical advisers linked to government institutions.

Since the early 1990s there has been a growing number of university dissertations based on a more critical analysis of the impacts of tourism on the different ecosystems and local populations. In this second phase, researchers started to study these impacts, particularly along the south-western and southern coasts, from Rio de Janeiro to Santa Catarina, the north-east and Pantanal. The main subjects of these academic papers were ecotourism, the impact of large tourist infrastructure on the environment and local populations, and community-based tourism.

It is clear that tourism is an emerging subject for academic research, and it will receive more importance in the near future, given the growing environmental and social impacts of large projects such as PRODETUR. Areas that require further research are the following:

- Statistics and studies on domestic tourism at the national level, as this sector has become more important than international tourism.
- Community-based tourism is definitely an area that requires more research and reflection, as in some regions local communities are trying to take advantage of tourism. Communities on the western coast of Ceará, along the southern coast of São Paulo, are examples of this new tendency.
- Socio-cultural impacts of large tourist projects are also a research field in need of more attention from researchers, especially in the south of Bahia, in the PRODETUR region and along the area between São Paulo and Rio de Janeiro. Very little thought has been given to the potential of domestic tourism to valorize local cultural diversity and livelihoods. How can traditional communities take advantage of regional and domestic tourism, and how can they accommodate this new economic season within their calendar of traditional activities, such as farming, fishing and forest harvesting?
- Nature tourism and ecotourism also need more research as they are emerging strategies for tourism development, particularly in the Amazon and in the world's largest wetland, Pantanal. A growing number of small travel agencies specialize in nature tourism, taking visitors to national parks and isolated rainforest areas. What are the impacts of this growing interest in the natural environment and traditional communities? How can local people be incorporated into this activity, as guides, owners of community lodges, etc?

Conclusions

Domestic and regional mass tourism is a recent phenomenon that started in the 1970s with the rapidly growing middle classes, the establishment of paid holidays for some sectors of industrial workers, the expansion and amelioration of transportation – mainly roads and aeroplanes – and the development of hotels, hostels and campgrounds.

It is difficult to estimate the number of domestic tourists, but it could be said that around 40 million, or one-third of the population, are taking holidays that may vary between a weekend to three weeks (according to the law, workers should have three weeks vacation annually). Approximately 18 million of these tourists use air travel, but most of them use buses and cars as a means of transportation. Domestic tourists are more numerous in the richer south-western states, such as São Paulo, Rio de Janeiro, Brasília, Paraná, Minas Gerais, Santa

Catarina and Rio Grande do Sul. Most domestic tourists take their vacation in the summertime during the school holidays – from December to February – the destination usually being the coastal areas. Tourism in the mountains is popular also in Serra do Mar-Mantiqueira, between São Paulo and Rio, catering for those interested in national parks (Itatiaia National Park, Serra do Mar State Park, etc). Tourism in the Amazon is also growing, even though this distant area is preferred mainly by international tourists. There is growing domestic tourism to the large wetlands – Pantanal – particularly for sport fishing and ecotourism. More recently, Brazilians have been taking their holidays in Europe and the United States in particular, and the number is growing rapidly, reaching 3 million in 1996. This number is higher than international tourists, involving around 2 million people. This is caused mainly by the high costs of domestic flights, particularly to the north-east, and the status associated with travelling abroad. Domestic tourism is currently more important, by far, than international tourism, in terms of numbers and income generation.

Regional tourism also started in the 1970s. Argentines, followed by Uruguayans and Chileans, are the majority among regional visitors, who in total represent today more than half of the international tourists. There is a governmental effort to foster tourism from Mercosur countries. There are today some 1,100,000 tourists from neighbouring countries that use mostly air travel as a means of transportation, but it can be said that an equal number of them use cars and buses when their destination is Brazilian states in the south, particularly Santa Catarina, Paraná and Rio Grande do Sul. It is estimated that their number will grow in coming years, pending on the possibility of the lowering costs of air fares and hotel rates that are high in Brazil, as a consequence of the over-evaluation of the national currency.

It is hard to evaluate the economic impact of domestic and regional tourism with precision. It is clear, however, that this form of tourism is the highest source of income and employment in many coastal areas, such as those between Rio de Janeiro and Santos, Santa Catarina and Rio Grande do Sul in the south and some north-eastern states, such as Ceará, Pernambuco and Bahia.

Today the north-east is one of the rapidly growing tourism areas of Brazil, particularly for international tourism, and it has been chosen as the priority region for tourism development to be implemented through PRODETUR. The role of tourism seems to be ambiguous for the poorest region of Brazil, where the gap between rich and poor is also the largest. On the one hand, it is seen by some state governments as the only alternative for raising income and employment, particularly in coastal areas. NGOs rightly argue that, given the seasonal characteristic of tourism, it cannot be considered the only economic activity in an area, but a complementary one among the already existing practices. The challenge is how to integrate tourism with the regional economy and society without disintegrating traditional economic networks, especially those related to small-scale fisheries and agriculture. The disorganization of the traditional economic network was occurring even before the arrival of mass tourism, and it was caused by the intensification of market relations and the higher dependence of small-scale producers vis-à-vis urban economies. Tourism offers income and employment opportunities during the summer season, but after the four-month period, the economic and social situation of coastal communities remains as bad as it was previously. Furthermore the long-standing economic recession continues to deeply affect the tourism sector. Most of the small producers who decide to abandon activities, such as small-scale fisheries and agriculture, find temporary employment in the construction sector, which is also affected by the economic recession.

The state of Ceará was selected as a case study because it summons both the potential and difficulties related to tourism development. In this state, tourism associated with the construction sector was given the highest priority by the state government. The negative aspects of tourism are clearer in this state than elsewhere in the region. But, at the same time, Ceará is today the state where open discussions are taking place concerning the positive and negative aspects of tourism. More than that, coastal communities have started to organize and propose their own alternatives to integrate tourism into their traditional economies. In some communities, this integration has already started, as these communities, although reinforcing artisanal fishing, are building their own lodges and restaurants to receive tourists. Fish products are sold not only in their own lodges and restaurants, but also to other hotels. In some municipalities such as Icapuí, a cooperative for tourism services has been established and it is run in cooperation with locally organized fishing cooperatives. Locally managed tourism is related to locally managed fisheries and coastal zone management. This integrated coastal management is too recent to serve as a model but it is being recognized as one of the leading experiences in Brazil in this area.

Notes

1 Research assistant: Fabio Eduardo De Giusti Sanson.
2 Of these 3,100,000 tourists, 750,000 went to the United States, 600,000 to Argentina, 550,000 to other neighbouring countries, 550,000 to Europe, 250,000 to Mexico and the Caribbean, 200,000 to Asia and the Middle East, and 200,000 to other destinations.

References

Almeida, M (1997) 'Turistificação: Os novos atores e imagens do litoral cearense', in *Turismo e Meio Ambiente*, João Pessoa, Associação dos Geógrafos Brasileiros

Becker, B (1995) *Levantamento e Avaliação da Política Federal de Turismo e seu Impacto na Região Costeira*, Ministério do Meio Ambiente/Programa Nacional do Meio Ambiente, Brasília

Cacex (1995) *Boletin Informativo*, Ministério de Indústria e Comércio, Brasilia

CNUMAD (1991) *Subsídios Técnicos para a Elaboração do Relatório Nacional do Brasil para a CNUMAD*, Comissão interministerial, Brasília

Coriolano, L (1996) 'Turismo e degradação ambiental no litoral do Ceará', in A Lemos (ed), *Turismo: Impactos Socioambientais*, São Paulo, Hucitec

Diegues A C (1983) *Pescadores, Camponeses e Trabalhadores do Mar*, São Paulo, Ática

EMBRATUR (1996a) *Anuário Estatístico*, Brasília

EMBRATUR (1996b) *Estudo da Demanda Turística Internacional*, EMBRATUR, Brasília

EMBRATUR (1996c) *Política Nacional do Turismo: Diretrizes e Programas, 1996–1999*, EMBRATUR, Brasília

EMBRATUR/ABRESI/SEBRAE (1996) *A Indústria do Turismo no Brasil: Perfil e Tendências*, São Paulo

Martine, G (1991) *A Questão Populacional no Brasil: Elementos para a Agenda da Fundação MacArthur*, Instituto SPN, Brasília

Moraes, A C R (1995) *Os Impactos da Política Urbana sobre a Zona Costeira*, Ministério do Meio Ambiente, Brasília

Paiva, M (1996) 'Globalização e segmentação: Reflexões sobre o mercado de trabalho em turismo do Nordeste', in A Lemos (ed), *Turismo: Impactos Socioambientais*, São Paulo, Hucitec

PRODETUR (1993) *Programa de ação para o Desenvolvimento de Turismo no Nordeste* – PRODETUR, Recife

PRODETUR/NE (1994) *Programa de Ação para o Desenvolvimento do Turismo no Nordeste: Estudo de Mercado Turístico do Nordeste*, Fortaleza

Rodrigues, A (1996a) 'Percalços do planejamento turístico: O PRODETUR-NE', in A. Rodrigues (ed), *Turismo e Geografia: Reflexões Teóricas e Enfoques Regionais*, São Paulo, Hucitec

Rodrigues, A (1996b) 'Desafios para os estudiosos do turismo', in A. Rodrigues (ed), *Turismo e Geografia: Reflexões Teóricas e Enfoques Regionais*, São Paulo, Hucitec

Rodrigues, A (1997) *Turismo e Espaço: Rumo a um Conhecimento Transdisciplinar*, São Paulo, Hucitec

Tupinambá, S and M Limba (1997) 'O papel da organização comunitária na gestão ambiental', in A Filho (ed), *Proceedings of the International Workshop on Artisanal Fisheries*, Labomar/UFC/CIDA/Memorial University of Newfoundland

WTO (1993) *Recommendations on Tourism Statistics*, Madrid

Chapter 4

The Economic Role of
National Tourism in China

Krishna B Ghimire and Zhou Li

The economic significance of international tourism in China is widely recognized. What is less known is the role and extent of domestic tourism, which is substantial and rapidly growing. The present chapter focuses on this aspect. It is based mainly on the available secondary sources, together with the experience of authors who have visited a few tourist destinations. The chapter is divided into six parts. Part one presents an overview of the development of domestic tourism since the reforms; some insights relating to the social backgrounds and interests of domestic tourists are provided in part two, followed by an evaluation of the government's domestic tourism policy in part three. Parts four and five deal, respectively, with the economic impact of domestic tourism at the regional and local levels and a number of problems arising from the rapid growth of domestic tourism. Further reflection and research in this field are required, as discussed in the concluding remarks in part six.

A Brief Overview of the Development of Domestic Tourism over the Past Two Decades

Although China is a country blessed with numerous tourist resources, the capacity of the tourist industry to generate income had long been underestimated and its resources were underexploited or improperly used without contributing to the development of the local economies or the improvement of the people's standard of living. No efforts were made to attract international tourists or to increase the rather low demand for domestic tourism. However, since 1978, when a liberal economic policy was introduced, important changes have taken place in the understanding of the economic role of tourism. Prior to this date, the activities related to tourism were largely seen by the Chinese authorities as 'non-productive', as they involved no concrete material production or the generation of added value (Xu Dixin, 1980). The potential role of the tourism sector in the national plan of social and economic development was first mentioned in the Seventh Five-year Plan (1986–1990). In 1991, in the Ten-year Programme for National Economy and Social Development and the outline of the Eighth Five-year Plan, tourism was defined as an industry and highlighted as a key sector of the service industry whose development should be accelerated. In 1992 the Central Committee of the Communist Party of China (CPC) and the State Council stressed these aspects in a resolution and reinforced the importance of tourism. The main result of defining tourism as an industry was that state-owned travel services engaged in international tourism were converted into enterprises that had to assume responsibility for their profits or losses[1] (Sun Gang, 1997).

With the gradual acceptance of the industrial nature of tourism, views of the relevant state authorities on incoming tourism shifted from political assignments to economic activities, which greatly accelerated tourism develop-ment. In recent years, tourism revenue from incoming tourists has sharply increased and even exceeded the targets set. For example, the aim was to earn US$10 billion from tourism by the year 2000, but, as indicated in Table 4.1, tourism earned over US$14 billion in 1999. This is in sharp contrast to the previous situation, in which planned long-term targets had never been set.

Table 4.1 *Foreign exchange earnings from incoming tourism since the economic reforms*

Year	Tourism receipts (million US$)	Total foreign exchange (million US$)	Total (%)	Year	Tourism receipts (million US$)	Total foreign exchange (million US$)	Total (%)
1978	262.90	10,012.90	2.63	1989	1860.48	54,400.48	3.42
1979	449.27	14,109.27	3.18	1990	2217.58	64,307.58	3.45
1980	616.65	18,736.65	3.29	1991	2844.97	74,684.97	3.81
1981	784.91	22,794.91	3.44	1992	3946.87	88,886.87	4.44
1982	843.17	23,163.17	3.64	1993	4683.17	96,423.17	4.86
1983	941.20	23,171.20	4.06	1994	7323.00	128,363.00	5.70
1984	1131.34	27,271.34	4.15	1995	8733.00	157,513.00	5.54
1985	1250.00	28,600.00	4.37	1996	10,200.00	161,260.00	6.33
1986	1530.85	32,470.85	4.71	1997	12,074.00	194,770.00	6.20
1987	1861.51	41,301.51	4.51	1998	12,602.00	196,362.00	6.42
1988	2246.83	49,766.83	4.51	1999	14,099.00	209,000.00	6.75

Source: National Tourism Administration, China Statistical Yearbooks (1978–1999), the State Statistics Bureau, China Statistics Publishing House, Beijing; Xinhua News Agency, The New Progress of the China Tourism of 2001, 13 February 2001, Beijing

While a rapid increase took place in international tourism after the end of the 1970s, the sector that experienced even faster growth was domestic tourism.[2] Before the 1970s wages were on the whole low in both urban and rural areas, and there was generally little relationship between a worker's income and his/ her efforts. But this has changed since the reforms. During the last two decades, the correlation between a labourer's income and his/her endeavours became linked, thus encouraging people to work harder for improved wages and providing different compensations for workers with different qualifications.

The increase in staff and workers' income strongly heightened domestic demand for travel, and the enlargement of income differences led to a diversity of demands for domestic travel. In addition, business-related domestic tourism also expanded during the transformation process from a planned economic system to a market one. The introduction of a five-day working system on 1 May 1995 has had a favourable impact on the increase in travel demand. The number of residents in cities and towns travelling for leisure purposes increased and the domestic tourism revenue rose by 34.4 per cent and 20 per cent respectively (Qian Jianping, 1996).

When domestic tourism was in its infancy in the early 1980s, tourist expenses were at a comparatively low level because of the prevalence of generally low earnings. A survey of domestic tourists made in Hangzhou municipality (the capital of Zhejiang province) at the time showed that 68.7 per cent of tourists wished to spend less than RMB3 a day[3] for a bed (Cheng Wendong, 1992). A survey (ibid) made in Xi'an, the capital of Shaanxi province, indicated that the per capita expenses of domestic tourists were RMB18.4 a day. Since then, the level of tourist consumption has risen continually, in step with the increase in the income level. Per capita expenses in 1996 were RMB165.6 a day. In recent years, some organized tourist parties made up mainly of businessmen and their family members in relatively developed areas of Guangdong, Beijing and Shanghai have asked travel services to arrange return air tickets and hotel accommodation of three-star and above level. The consumption standard in these instances was similar to that of overseas tourists.

Until 1984 domestic tourism statistics were not included in the agenda of governmental authorities (the State Tourism Administration and the State Statistics Bureau). It can be seen in Table 4.2 that the number of domestic tourists has been increasing steeply, with the proportion of domestic tourists to tourists as a whole at around 90 per cent. The proportion of domestic tourism revenue to total tourism revenue has been rising steadily, topping 70.8 per cent in 1999. Over the past ten years the increase in domestic tourism has exceeded the annual growth rate of the national economy. The importance of domestic tourism to the national economy is now quite evident.

According to the available information, in 1985 domestic tourism revenue and its share in GDP were RMB8 billion and 0.93 per cent respectively. In 1997, they rose respectively to RMB185 billion and 2.26 per cent. In some tourist areas their role was even greater. The share of tourism revenue in GDP of such provinces as Yunnan, Shaanxi, Zhejiang, etc attained more than 5 per cent. Beijing achieved a proportion of over 10 per cent (He Guangwei, 1997). The tax revenues earned from tourism in Hainan province made up around 20 per cent of its total tax revenues, and thus became a key industry of the province. Tourism was initially developed in 1992 in Lijiang prefecture of Yunnan province, where profits and taxes amounted to RMB30 million in 1995, ie 25 per cent of the area's revenue of RMB120 million (Sun Gang, 1996).

A significant level of public investment has been made in tourism in recent years. For example, during the 15 years between the Sixth Five-year Plan and the Eighth Five-year Plan (ie 1981–1996), total investment in tourism brought into line with the State Plan of Capital Construction was only RMB4794 billion, including a fiscal allocation of RMB573 million, loans (to be paid back yearly by travel services after their business began) amounting to RMB4045 billion and funds raised by organizations independently (from retained profits of state-owned travel services) of RMB131 million. All the funds invested during this period were unfavourably matched to state investment in medium and large projects. Furthermore, the investment was used for tourist facilities receiving overseas visitors. However, although the government invested little or nothing in domestic tourism directly, foreign tourist-oriented facilities developed by the government, such as hotels, also received domestic tourists. In this sense, there was therefore an indirect investment in domestic tourism from the government (Sun Gang, 1997).

By the end of 1996 there were 3257 class C travel services fully engaged in domestic travel business in China and 965 A and B class travel services also had domestic travel business. In 1994 the organized tourists among national residents in towns and cities totalled 2.75 per cent of all tourists. In 1995 and 1996 this rose to 5.55 per cent and 7.58 per cent respectively, indicating that the share of tourist groups organized by travel services, as compared to total tourists, tended to increase rapidly (The State Tourism Administration, 1997, p49).

Similarly, in the early 1980s there were only about 160 civil aeroplanes in China and airport facilities were undeveloped. By the end of 1995 civil aeroplanes amounted to 852 and civil air lines to 694; both had quadrupled. The situation was similar for highways, railroads and water transport. Although it would be wrong to suggest that this expansion was solely due to the tourism sector, the latter probably played a significant role.[4]

By the end of 1996 there were 811 national forest parks with an area of 7.2 million hectares, 36 scenic spots of protected nature regions were being developed, and 24 additional forest tourist sites, such as hunting farms and wildlife zoos, were also opened. The total area involved was 9 million hectares, with 3403 tourist vehicles and craft, 76,257 beds for guests in forest parks (on tourist sites), and reasonable service facilities (Xu Jing, 1997).

Table 4.2 *Number of domestic tourists and tourism revenue in China since 1984*

Year	Number of domestic tourists (million persons)	Share of total tourists (%) (billion yuan)	Revenue of domestic tourism	Share of total tourism revenue (%)
1984	200	93.04		
1985	240	93.08	8.0	52.98
1986	270	92.20	10.6	54.86
1987	290	91.51	14.0	56.90
1988	300	90.44	18.7	59.36
1989	240	90.74	15.0	58.59
1990	280	91.07	17.0	58.72
1991	300	89.69	20.0	55.22
1992	330	89.65	25.0	52.61
1993	423	90.80	86.4	76.40
1994	524	92.30	102.4	61.84
1995	629	93.13	137.6	65.58
1996	639	92.59	163.8	68.30
1997	644	92.77	211.3	67.49
1998	694	91.62	239.1	69.5
1999	719	90.81	283.2	70.8

Sources: National Tourism Administration, China Statistical Yearbooks compiled by the State Statistics Bureau, China Statistics Publishing House

It was expected that if the number of sightseeing spots was increased, entry conditions improved, and more options made available for tourists, crowding in some famous tourist spots would be somewhat eased. Statistical results in Sichuan show that in 1996, while visitors tended to increase in some conventional scenic areas, such as Giant Leshan Buddha, Baoguang Temple, Dazu Stone Inscription, Mount Ermei, etc, there was a great decrease of domestic visitors in comparison with the previous year (Chen Yanbai, 1997). This demonstrates that the growth in the number of recently developed areas and spots leads tourists to explore new scenic locations.

Social Backgrounds and Expectations of Domestic Tourists

Generally speaking, no language barriers are involved in domestic travel,[5] and consequently this type of travel is generally individualized and seldom organized. In China, however, the ratio of organized domestic tourists to overall domestic tourists has been increasing on a year-by-year basis by almost 4 per cent to date, whereas the overseas rate is around 2 per cent. This is probably due to the greater number of travelling activities organized with public funds in China.

In fact, many labour unions in enterprises, women and youth organizations and schools in China organize travel activities themselves instead of resorting to travel services. For example, every ministry, large to medium enterprise, company, university, etc. has one or more sanatoriums located at famous scenic sites. These only cater to internal officials, managers, employees and their family members. If the number of tourists who do not deal with business hotels and restaurants is taken into account, the number of organized domestic tourists can be considered as double. Though the existence of such a situation is due to the organized sources formed during the last 50 years, the more important reasons are the intensified competition among enterprises during the transition from a planned economy to a market one, the increase in the desire of workers to travel, and the utility of organized tourism as one of the methods of strengthening an enterprise's internal cohesive force, as is the case in companies, universities, and even ministries.

People from rural areas have also begun to get involved in tourism activities. Inferences based on relevant materials show that 250 million tours were made by farmers in 1993, 319 million in 1994, and 383 million in 1995 and 1996 respectively, thus exceeding half of the total number of domestic tours nation-wide (see Table 4.3).[6] In particular, the expenses of some farmer touring parties from coastal areas in the east exceeded the average expenses of parties composed of urban residents because their income per capita was generally higher than that of average urban workers or city residents. Tourism among farmers has also undergone a rapid expansion in the middle and western regions. An event that caused great sensation throughout the country was 'a great touring party of 100 people', formed actually by 99 farmers from Xinjiang Uygur autonomous region, who travelled around 14 cities across the country at their own expense. In recent years, some farmers from the remote mountainous areas who are becoming wealthier have begun to travel for leisure purposes (Qian Jianping, 1995).

As noted earlier, while statistics concerning China's international tourism are exhaustive and quite systematic, domestic tourism statistics only became available as late as 1993. This situation is consistent with the development process of domestic tourism in China. The statistical data indicate that tours taken by rural residents exceed those of urban residents in terms of number, but the tourist expenditures of rural residents are less than those of urban residents. This indicates that domestic tourism revenue is chiefly contributed by urban residents (see Table 4.3).

Table 4.4 suggests that officials, technical personnel and businessmen make up a large proportion of domestic tour participants. Businessmen and private entrepreneurs constituted one-quarter of the total number of tourists, and the former group's share has increased spectacularly. Workers are another important category of tourists, although their proportion is stable or has even declined slightly, probably because of reduced public subsidies for workers' travel and visitor facilities in tourist locations.

Table 4.3 *Profile of domestic tourism in China*

	Total		Urban residents		Rural residents	
	Travellers (million)	Expenditure (billion)	Travellers (million)	Expenditure (billion)	Travellers (million)	Expenditure (billion)
1993	410	86.40	160	71.40	250	15.00
1994	524	102.35	205	84.82	319	17.53
1995	629	137.57	246	114.01	383	23.56
1996	639	165.64	256	138.64	383	27.00
1997	644	211.27	259	155.18	385	56.09
1998	694	239.12	250	151.51	444	87.61
1999	719	283.19	284	174.82	435	108.37

Note: Tours of rural residents is the product of the tours of urban residents and the ratio of tours of rural residents to the tours of urban residents; the latter is inferred from typical survey sources of passenger traffic volume on railways and highways. Per capita travelling expenses are the product of the per capita travelling expenses of urban residents and the ratio of the per capita expenses of rural tourists to the per capita expenses of urban tourists; the latter is inferred from the sampling survey of urban and rural resident households by the State Statistic Bureau.
Sources: As per the above.

Table 4.5 shows the daily expenses of different groups of domestic tourists. Private entrepreneurs and businessmen are the groups spending the most. This is understandable, as these are wealthier classes in China. Moreover, their work is usually connected with specific tasks, with a fair amount of the expenses being reimbursed. This is also the case with government officials and technical personnel, which is the next important group of domestic tourists.

Table 4.4 *Composition of urban residential tourists in China (%)*

	1993	1994	1995	1996	1997	1998	1999
Administrative staff	21.5	26.9	10.2	9.8	7.9	8.0	6.2
Technical staff	19	22	22.1	14.6	15.3	13.9	–
Teachers	5.2	4.9	5.2	4.5	4.8	4.8	16.1
Businessmen	5.9	7.8	6.4	19.5	18.9	17.8	17.8
Service staff	2.2	1.6	1.9	3.6	3.4	3.2	5.7
Students	12.8	6.1	12.8	12.3	13.2	13.1	13.8
Retired personnel	8.3	12.1	12.5	13.2	12.4	16.1	15.3
Workers	17.1	13.8	19.3	16.7	17.6	15.7	16.8
Private entrepreneurs	8	4.8	9.6	5.8	6.5*	7.4*	8.3*
Total	100.0	100.0	100.0	100.0	100.0	100.0	100.0

Note: Categorized by profession; * equals 'others'
Source: The State Tourism Administration of the People's Republic of China, Investigation Team of Urban Social and Economic Conditions of the State Statistics Bureau, 1993, 1994, 1995 and 1996

Table 4.5 *Consumption per capita by urban residents in tourism (RMB/day)*

Year	1993	1994	1995	1996	1997	1998
Administrative staff	81.47	93.88	152.96	191.7	186.6	205.5
Technical staff	72.26	97.50	120.40	160.6	154.9	184.3
Teachers	55.53	74.20	102.33	137.7	137.2	140.2
Businessmen	120.79	123.95	161.37	173.9	187.2	193.4
Service staff	86.73	98.47	126.24	145.7	162.9	151.2
Students	36.95	55.45	59.16	77.5	84.3	89.2
Retired personnel	39.84	51.80	59.57	90.7	104.1	118.6
Workers	52.98	66.30	93.49	111.2	131.8	123.8
Private entrepreneurs	136.01	141.19	221.08	–	–	–
Others	37.79	56.07	101.63	200.0	133.5	158.8
Total	65.46	85.09	103.33	139.1	141.8	150.1

Note: Categorized by profession
Source: The State Tourism Administration of the People's Republic of China, Investigation Team of Urban Social and Economic Conditions of the State Statistics Bureau, 1993, 1994, 1995 and 1996

Table 4.6 demonstrates a clear correlation between the level of education and the demand for travelling among urban dwellers. The majority of urban tourists are educated above junior middle school. The tourists who have primary school education or less are few. This may also mean that there is some correlation between the level of education and income in urban China. No information is available on rural tourists and their level of education, which may be somewhat different, given a generally lower level of education in rural areas.

Table 4.6 *Composition of urban residential tourists in China (%)*

Level of education	Total	1993	1994	1995	1996	1997	1998	1999
Above college	29.6	25.8	31.3	29.2	31.9	32.0	31.7	33.0
Senior middle school	37.4	38.4	39.2	35.9	35.9	35.3	35.1	35.7
Junior middle school	21.6	20.1	20.7	23.4	22.2	22.4	22.9	21.5
Primary school	8.7	10.6	7.4	9.8	7.1	7.4	7.9	7.5
Other	2.7	5.1	1.4	1.7	2.9	2.9	2.4	2.3
Total	100.0	100.0	100.0	100.0	100.0	100.0	100.0	100.0

Note: Categorized by education
Source: As per the above

Table 4.7 shows that the main interest of urban domestic tourists is natural scenery and leisure. This is not surprising, as many come from mega-cities characterized by noise, pollution and generally hectic lifestyles. It seems that the younger the tourists, the greater the interest in natural scenery, especially mountains (cf Youngblood, 1997). There is a considerable interest for sports among domestic tourists and there are no distinguishable differences among different age groups. Table 4.8 shows that there is a notable correlation between income level and travel demand. Table 4.9 demonstrates that most domestic tourists take tours lasting one week, probably because Chinese workers do not have long vacations. However, the number of tourists who take vacations for more than a week is not negligible.

As for the quality of travel services, very few domestic tourists were either very satisfied or dissatisfied. Most expressed a moderate view of a mediocre service. However, roads, transport facilities, hotels, restaurants and tourist information systems are greatly lacking in many areas visited by Chinese tourists, especially in remote and mountainous areas. There is little control over the quality of tourist services and facilities, even though prices are generally fixed by the authority. This was, for example, the case of Jiuzhaigou (Sichuan province), a well-known destination for Chinese tourists. In 1992 the area received 270,000 Chinese and 400 foreign tourists. The alpine landscape, pine forests, clear lakes and waterfalls are the main attractions. During a visit of the first author in 1993, it was found that tourists were charged higher accommodation prices than the official rates and there was little control over the quality of food served or the organized cultural and sightseeing programmes. At the same time, in several locations, tourist accommodation centres had completely absorbed the original villages. A few people from these villages had opened shops and sold handicraft goods, but there was little benefit to the rest of the community (personal observation; see also Ghimire, 1994). This is of course a common occurrence in many parts of the developing world where tourists are received.

Table 4.7 *Major interests in domestic tourist activities of urban residents in China (1993–1996) (%)*

	>51	31–50	17–30	<16
Natural scenery	44.66	48.74	50.45	52.61
Cultural heritage and legacy	9.68	10.89	10.50	6.26
Local conditions and customs	6.31	5.13	5.48	2.19
Leisure and vacation	11.18	13.32	13.44	19.11
Sports	21.20	12.29	12.39	13.98
Festival activities	2.11	5.14	4.81	2.00
No answer	4.87	4.48	2.92	3.84
Total	100.00	100.00	100.00	100.00

Note: Categorized by age
Source: As per the above

Table 4.8 *Relation between monthly income of domestic tourists and their tours*

Year	< RMB100	RMB100–200	RMB200–500	RMB500–1000	> RMB1000
1993	2.6	31.6	56.7	7.9	1.1
1994	5.6	6.0	55.8	27.7	5.0
1995		15.2	31.5	43.8	9.5
1996		–	5.5*	24.4	70.1
1997	–	–	5.4*	20.0	74.6
1998	–	–	5.5*	18.6	75.9
1999	–	–	5.6*	17.9	76.5

Note: * Tourists with a monthly income below RMB500
Source: As per the above

Table 4.9 *Distribution of the length of stay of domestic tourists on tour (%)*

	1 day	2–3 days	4–7 Days	8–14 Days	>15 Days	Average
1993	29.1	17.8	24.6	16.3	9.8	
1994	23.3	24.9	25.8	16.5	7.6	6.63
1995	29.5	26.1	21.3	14.3	8.8	5.73
1996	28.3	34.8	20.5	10.3	6.1	6.20
1997	25.1	34.7	22.3	10.8	7.1	4.7
1998	33.2	35.9	16.9	8.0	6.0	6.2
1999	27.9	36.3	20.4	9.7	5.7	5.8

Source: As per the above.

Recent Government Policies and Measures for the Promotion of Domestic Tourism

In the early years of the economic reforms, the concerned state authorities focused their attention on the importance of international tourism in earning foreign exchange and raising revenue. Not only were specific targets set, but detailed promotional programmes were also initiated. This is a common phenomenon in other developing countries. However, domestic tourism was not expected to grow fast. For instance, in the Eighth Five-year Plan, the number of incoming tourists to the country was projected at 33–35 million and foreign exchange earnings from tourism at US$3.6–4 billion by 1995. By the year 2000, the number of incoming tourists was expected to be 4.5–5 million and foreign exchange earnings from tourism US$6–7 billion (Chronicle of Tourism Events in China, 1995). But the promotion of domestic tourism was not even mentioned. Domestic tourism began and evolved spontaneously because of the stimulus of the market. Few economic or policy incentives were provided by the government, which has responded only as a means of coping with the changing domestic tourism situation and demand.

In 1991, after hearing a report given by the director of the State Tourism Administration during a National Tourism Working Conference, Prime Minister Li Peng spoke about the considerable development potential of domestic tourism during the Eighth Five-year Plan period (Chronicle of Tourism Events in China, 1995). He urged that the State Tourism Administration at various levels should focus on better planning, organization and management of domestic tourism; guide and encourage self-sponsored travel; and propel domestic tourism towards healthy and balanced growth.

In 1993, the general office of the State Council put forward five specific targets for domestic tourism development (ibid):

1   domestic tourism should be integrated into the national economic plan and social development;
2   fair competition practices should be developed in the domestic tourist market sector;
3   efforts should be made to develop tourist products for ordinary people;
4   work should be directed towards improving quality and safeguarding tourists' interests; and
5   tourist administrative authorities should take charge of the management and coordination of domestic tourism-related affairs.

In 1994 about half of the provinces nationwide held working conferences on domestic tourism and sought to make domestic tourism a burgeoning provincial sector for economic growth.

While domestic tourism had started to flourish, large state-owned travel services continued to concentrate their efforts on international tourism as the benefits were higher and they did not expect enormous revenue to accrue from domestic tourism. In any event, the prices for board and lodging charged by large state-owned travel services were too high for average domestic tourists. The expansion of the demand for domestic tourism provided favourable opportunities for the growth of smaller agencies under different systems of ownership, especially for collective and private hotels. It is interesting that the political incidents of June 1989 in Beijing, followed by a marked drop in international tourism, impelled large state-owned travel services to engage actively in domestic tourism. From then on they extended their interest to exploring the domestic tourism market.

The existing data and analyses concerning domestic tourism do not cover a long period because they were not available until domestic tourism was taken into the management context by the government. On the basis of the available figures (see Table 4.2), it can be said that although domestic tourism is characterized by short-term trips, lower per capita expenses and so on, it represents more than half the share of the national tourism revenue because of its large volume, ie domestic tourism has now become the mainstay of tourism revenue. This shift in the development of tourism made the relevant state authorities recognize that it was imperative to clarify the general status of domestic tourism. Consequently, beginning in 1993, the State Tourism Administration entrusted the State Statistics Bureau with the responsibility of conducting research and developing appropriate policies.

Governmental support played a very important role in developing China's international tourism. As stated above, domestic tourism in China was virtually induced by the market demand. The government established a number of macro-controls mainly to conform with its expansion. The following are some of the concrete institutional measures aimed at better regulation and management of domestic tourism (China Tourism Yearbook, 1995, 1996, 1997)

- **Requirement of a deposit by travel services.** This is a concrete measure to resolve claims, as in some travel services contracts have been broken, or else the agencies have collected higher charges and reduced the services. It is specified that the travel services shall deposit a guaranty of RMB600,000 (for class A travel services), RMB200,000 (for class B travel services) and RMB100,000 (for class C travel services) with the supervisory and administrative offices. When claims from tourists arise and are accepted, the supervisory and administrative offices in charge of tourism service quality shall instruct the corresponding travel services to compensate. In case compensation is refused by a travel service, the supervisory and administrative authorities will offset the amount against the previously deposited guaranty and will reimburse the tourists so as to safeguard their interests. From July 1995 to September 1996, altogether 1765 claims from tourists were accepted, of which 1605 were from domestic tourists, making up 91 per cent and totalling over RMB1.7 million of reimbursement.
- **Upgrade order and public security on tourist sites.** So as to improve the quality of tourism, the relevant authorities have revoked more than 1000 small class C travel agencies and curbed various activities unfavourable to a touristic environment.
- **Restructure the system for the establishment of tourism prices.** In the past tourist prices were established 'from above to below'. After the reforms this was eliminated. On 24 April 1993, the State Tourism Administration and the State Price Administration dispatched a circular on the problems concerning the administrative pattern of reform of international tourism prices, in which it was explicitly proposed to change the government-dominated pricing system 'from above to below' into one 'from below to above', in which travel enterprises set the prices and charged their own rates on the basis of their operational costs and supply and demand. These prices were then submitted to the State Tourism Administration for publication.

- **Upgrade toilet facilities for tourists.** In view of the fact that on some tourist sites toilets were substandard, plans were made to build a number of standardized tourist toilets within three years. By the end of 1996 this objective had been achieved; 1896 high-standard toilets had been built, thus eliminating or alleviating the 'dirt, mess and inferior conditions' that had existed in scenic spots. Complaints by tourists on this subject have decreased accordingly (Tieling, 1997).
- **Environmental protection.** Establish laws, policies and economic measures that will encourage tourist enterprises to practise sustainable utilization of tourism resources. On the whole, tourist enterprises tended to utilize readily available natural resources without much care for their long-term protection and sustainable use.

The Capacity of Domestic Tourism to Strengthen Regional Economies and to Alleviate Local Poverty: A Few Cases from Different Provinces

The following cases reflect the economic impact of tourism in locations where the development of potential attractions seems to have led to a significant increase in GDP and per capita income of the population. The Chinese government has defined an above poverty level as a situation where the average annual net income and grain consumption per capita exceeds RMB800 and 400kg (criterion set by 1996) (Fu Min, 1996). Unfortunately, it is not possible to assess in this study who has benefited most from touristic activities or the extent to which the revenues from tourism have been reinvested to stimulate other economic sectors so as to create solid economies independent of just one main activity.

In the cases below, reliable data and previous in-depth analysis are very scarce; they should merely be seen as an attempt to gather the relevant existing observations, experiences and information. The intention is to show the potential of tourism development in terms of income generation if profits are reinvested with a view to solving the more acute social and economic problems of the community. The government – which is nearly the only source of information in the field – has focused mainly on the positive impacts of tourism. Increase in per capita income and growth in GDP are the only two factors that have been examined and the only two indicators available when evaluating economic impacts. It is thus very difficult to assess the quality of the economic growth that has taken place in any of the locations rapidly developed for tourism, or simply to corroborate the data provided by the source. Nevertheless, tourism development appeared to have offered the government a viable option for poverty alleviation in some poor areas with tourist resources.

The cases described below come from a variety of regions, including the north-east (Jilin and Liaoning), north China (Beijing Tianjin, Hebei), south-central China (Hubei, Hunan), south-western China (Yunnan, Guizhou) and north-western China (Ningxia). They have been chosen for their availability rather than their particular geographical locations.

Hongqi village in Antu county (Jilin province, north-eastern China) took advantage of its location at the site of the famous scenic Changbaishan Mountains to build a folklore village with government support. A traditional hotel, song and dance hall, and an outdoor illuminated entertainment centre were rebuilt and decorated, and quality indoor toilets were constructed at the initiative of 20 farming families. The folklore village was opened to tourists after a year's efforts. The performances of the folk song and dance team were well greeted by visitors. Between August 1995 and October 1996, 18,000 visitors were received, tourism revenue was RMB760,000 and the average household income in the area reached RMB13,000 (Wang Yuejin, 1997).

The three towns of Xian Ren Dong, San Jia Shan and Lian Hua in Bing Yu Gou (Zhuang He county, Liaoning province), also in the north-east of the country, were impoverished and remote sites, located in an attractive mountain region; per capita income was less than RMB200. After a ten-year effort they became well-known popular tourist destinations. The development of tourism enabled these towns to increase their annual economic revenue by RMB150 million (Sun Gang, 1996).

Shapotou (Zhongwei county, Ningxia province) in north-central China is located at the southern fringe of the Tenggeli Desert; its climate is arid. Before tourism was developed, most residents cultivated a small area of land at the edge of the desert and seldom dealt with the outside world. The yearly per capita income of more than 10,000 families (a population of more than 40,000 inhabitants) was just RMB200. This was 60 per cent less than the average yearly per capita income of peasants throughout the county (RMB500). However, the natural scenery in Shapotou is quite unique: there is boundless desert, and an orchard of over 30 mu on the Mingshashan Mountains at a perpendicular height above 100 metres; the Yellow River is to the south of the orchard, and on the opposite bank rise the Xiang Shan Mountains, the site of the Great Wall. In 1985 Shapotou began to develop its tourist reserves, and in 1996 its yearly per capita income was RMB1770, which not only exceeded the average of peasants in the county, but was also 70 per cent higher than the per capita income in Ningxia. More than 10,000 people became engaged in tourism. Foreign funds of more than RMB20 million were poured into the county and over 1000 people were provided with employment opportunities. It is the county with the greatest number of foreign-funded enterprises among the counties in Ningxia (Sun Gang, 1996).

Kundian Manzu autonomous county is located at the edge of the Yalujiang River, on the border with Korea. It has abundant tourist resources, but these have not been utilized because of their inaccessibility. In recent years the national tourist demand has jumped abruptly, creating favourable conditions for touristic development. By the end of 1996, 12 scenic tourist locations had been developed, revenues earned directly from tourism reached RMB26 million and social and economic benefits generated indirectly from tourism amounted to RMB220 million (Meng Jialu, 1997).

Xia Ying Shui village in the Fangshan district of Beijing is located in a remote, poor mountain area, with per capita land of less than 1 mu. In July 1992 a great karst cave containing valuables and underground caves was found while a small colliery was being dug. The Party branch of the village decided to collect its own funds for development of the cave. Before the development of tourism, the per capita income had been less than RMB500. In 1995 the per capita income exceeded RMB2000. About 80 per cent of the labour force in the village are engaged in tourism. More than 30 villagers above the age of 60 receive pensions; RMB100,000 were invested in establishing and maintaining an elementary school; a ground satellite station was built and cable television systems were installed in every household (Sun Gang, 1996).

In north-central China (Hebei province), Gou Ge Zhuang village at Ye San Po (Lai Shui county) had been an isolated area since the late Ming and early Qing dynasties, with little influence from the outside world. It has a population over 2000 people, representing more than 300 households; the per capita income was below RMB60 in the early 1980s. Visitors began to come to the village in the mid-1980s, and catering and accommodation facilities were rapidly developed. In 1988 per capita income had reached RMB650, thus exceeding the comparatively rich villages in the area. Farmers organized tourism cooperatives and competition was regulated and shifted from individuals to more organized groups of farmers. Lincheng county in the same province was a relatively poor location which possessed scenic caves, mountains and forests, as well as cultural relics. In 1990 the county government decided to invest in tourism development as a means of alleviating poverty and increasing local wealth. Over the last 6 years, 11 villages and more than 3600 households have benefited directly from tourism and half appear to have improved living standards (Liu Zhenli and Wang Bing, 1996).

Ji county in north-central China is the only mountain county in Tianjin municipality that formerly had some impoverished villages. Huang Ya Guan village, located beside the Great Wall, was one of these villages, with a per capita income of RMB165 in 1984. After the development of tourism, Huang Ya Guan headed the list of the top ten major tourist sites in Tianjin. The precipitous mountainous topography shifted from being the cause of poverty and backwardness to the source of wealth. Seven towns, 52 villages and 120,000 people, representing 16 per cent of the county's population, benefited directly from tourism. In 1995, per capita income in Huang Ya Guan village reached RMB1852, which was more than ten times the income of a decade ago (Sun Gang, 1996).

Set in the mountains, Yichang county (south-central province of Hubei) hosts the Xiling Gorge, one of the three famous gorges of the Yangtze River. In 1990, in 45 per cent of the villages in the county (ie 248 villages), the per capita net income of the peasants was below RMB350. Tourism revenue in 1995 topped RMB13.78 million and the net per capita income of the peasants rose to RMB1208. The improvement in living conditions is particularly evident in Yangjiachong village, where the Golden Lion Cave is located. Each of the 40 families who lived in the village had members doing business at the cave. One of the results of the increase in income was the proliferation of colour televisions and tape recorders in about 80 per cent of the households (Sun Gang, 1996).

Further south, Nanyue at the foot of the Hengshan Mountain (Hunan province) is a town created mainly as a result of tourist development. The three other 'towns' of the four under its jurisdiction have also benefited from tourism. In the 1980s, per capita income of the farmers in the area was below RMB180. Some one-third of the area's total population lacked adequate food and clothing. In 1995, 2.06 million visits were made by domestic and overseas tourists to Nanyue, and the total income generated by tourism reached RMB310 million, accounting for 65 per cent of the local GDP. Farmers in the mountain areas have thus been provided with the possibility for income and improvement in their living conditions. In 1995 farmers in the area had an average per capita income of RMB2048 (Sun Gang, 1996).

In Guizhou province in the south-west, the Tianhe scenic spot in Guiyang city includes four villages, more than 800 families and over 5000 people, with a per capita cultivated area of 0.82 mu. Between 60 and 70 per cent of the peasant families used to take out loans to buy grain. In 1992, this scenic location having been opened up to the outside, 96 per cent of the families had enough to eat and wear, and the yearly per capita income rose from RMB200 to RMB1200 yuan. Similarly, in 1984, Shanglangde Miao village in Leishan county had 148 families (680 inhabitants), with a per capita net income of about RMB200. In 1997 the income earned from tourism exceeded RMB300. By developing the Fanjingshan Mountains, Yinshan county raised its GDP from RMB90 million in 1990 to RMB285 million in 1995; its total tourism revenue of RMB47.5 million accounted for 16.7 per cent of its GDP. It was estimated that 648 villages, 95,457 families and 330,000 people had benefited from tourism. In recent years Longsheng county has devoted major efforts to exploiting tourist resources such as Aiking Hot Springs, Longji Terrace, and Zhuang. Consequently this has helped to attract a significant number of visitors. Direct revenues and indirect benefits earned from tourism were close to RMB100 million. The annual per capita income of people along the tourist route increased from RMB200 to RMB1200. Gui Yang city, in the Hua Xi district in the same province, developed its tourist resources by opening popular tourist routes. The area is mountainous and rich in tourism attractions, although it lacks water.

In Li Cun, one of the villages in the area, per capita cultivated land is only 0.04 mu. About 30 per cent of the farming families were recipients of government relief programmes. In 1995 the village raised RMB120,000 and voluntarily contributed 18,000 man-days to building a road connecting the village and the arterial highway, together with routes for sightseeing and exploring scenic spots such as Gleam of Sky, Dragon King Well and Lotus Pond. By providing tourist facilities and cultural performances, it encouraged citizens of Gui Yang city to visit the area. By 1996, tourism revenue had exceeded RMB200,000, with an apparent drop in poverty levels (Sun Gang, 1996).

Yunnan province, bordering Burma, Laos and Vietnam, has attempted to take advantage of its abundant natural and historical resources to promote tourism. In 1995 about a million tourists were received, including 100,000 from overseas. Tourism revenue reached RMB200 million in the area, representing 13 per cent of the local GDP, and taxes and profits amounted to RMB300 million (25 per cent of local fiscal revenue) (Yu Jianming, 1997).

The per capita income in Zhangshiyan in Zanhuang county increased from RMB270 in 1988 to RMB3000 in 1995. Tourism development started in 1988, when the number of visitors amounted to 30,000. By 1995 this number had risen to 420,000. As a result of the relevant policy implementation, the local infrastructure improved in terms of transport facilities, communication systems, and water and sewage drainage. The income of nearby villages also increased significantly (the data were collected by the second author in field investigation in Zhanhuang county, 1997).

The above examples show a significant growth in GDP and per capita income. But apart from these encouraging statistics, we must look at the negative consequences of rapid tourism development. The lack of research on these particular aspects makes it very difficult to assess the extent to which tourism has contributed to the welfare of the communities involved and to estimate the actual redistribution of tourism benefits among the local populations, the role of tourism in helping developing local and traditional industries and other sectors of the regional economies, and to judge improvements in health standards and literacy levels.

In some cases it has been mentioned that television sets, stereos or satellite dishes have proliferated after tourism development took place. A greater access to such luxury items might imply an increase in the villagers' incomes, but it does not necessarily mean better living conditions. Matters such as a reliable source of electricity, access to clean drinking water, proper sewerage facilities, improvement in healthcare and educational premises should be looked upon when government officials and independent researchers evaluate the newly developed sites.

Careful project planning and implementation are not only necessary to take maximum advantage of tourism benefits, but also to minimize the negative impacts of tourism.

Problems Related to the Rapid Growth of Domestic Tourism

Up to now, the tourist sector in China has been seen exclusively from the positive angle. Possible negative impacts have been largely neglected in official and unofficial studies and evaluations. As such, the information cited above should be considered with caution. Domestic tourism is a relatively new phenomenon. More precise knowledge is currently needed on the nature, extent, social backgrounds and expectations of domestic tourists. Information on their possible negative impact on the local economy, culture and environment is nearly absent. There are few site-specific tourism plans and rational arrangements for tourism development targeted specifically at national tourists.

The environmental sector is one area where limited information exists on the negative impact of domestic tourism, although very little distinction is made between the relative influence of national and foreign tourists. Nevertheless, as domestic tourism is already extensive, various impacts are clearly probable. A number of surveys point to the destruction of the natural environment in tourist reserves (cutting into mountains, opening up land, building roads, dredging river courses, etc) in order to develop tourist facilities. The other serious problems are waste disposal, and air and water pollution.

In this respect it should be remembered that although domestic tourism has grown at a rapid pace, the expenditure capacity of the average tourist is generally low. Most Chinese tourists are far more willing to accept inferior touristic conditions, while preferring to spend less money rather than to spend more and enjoy better conditions. This may also be a consequence of the lack of awareness campaigns.

Currently, the use of tourist resources is uncontrolled and chaotic. Under the former system of planned economy in which the government was the sole investor, the problem of low investment efficiency did exist, but the use of tourist resources was controlled. After the reforms, tourist resources could be exploited by all the central and local government authorities at different levels, as well as by communities, enterprises and individuals. Many regulations exist only on paper. The present situation is thus inevitable, even though investment efficiency was improved.

The impact of urban culture and consumerism is visible at many tourist sites frequented by domestic tourists, even in relatively remote areas. Ethnic culture and costumes are commonly being utilized for the promotion of tourism but the community receives little in return. Integration into the market system is generally taking place very rapidly, in accordance with the government's current economic and political policies, and the tourism sector in particular has helped to promote this process. People are selling more and more in the market to satisfy their consumer needs. They are frequently losing in the exchange process. Although the law does not allow the sale and purchase of land in the open market, mortgaging is increasingly common at certain tourist sites. Currently, social differentiation is based principally on the difference between those who can invest in tourism and other business activities, and those who cannot.

Conclusion

The primary conclusion is that domestic tourism in China is clearly sizeable, involving several million people and bringing in substantial revenue. Domestic tourism is more important than international tourism in terms of both the number of tourists involved and the amount of revenue earned. It is now a well-recognized and stable economic sector. Recent government tourism policy has focused more on domestic tourism, although there is still an apparent bias in favour of international tourism. Detailed site-specific domestic tourism planning is scarce and the domestic tourism policy is yet to be integrated with such sectors as agriculture, industry, manufacturing, services and transport.

Indeed, the development of domestic tourism seems to be more a response to market demand than to the government's promotion measures. Ironically, it was the decrease in the number of foreign tourists following the Tiananmen events in the late 1980s that caused the national tourism market to turn to Chinese tourists, by offering competitive prices and diversified activities that were more suited to the interests of national tourists. The rising income in both urban and rural areas, and the rapid expansion of the middle class, have more or less assured the demand for leisure travel. This is assisted further by the influence of the Western consumer lifestyle and leisure ethic that promotes mass tourism. In China, as in much of Asia, the growing middle class aspires to 'catch up' with its counterparts in the West, at times simply imitating in order to appear affluent and sophisticated.

In 1996, the State Tourism Administration suggested that in the period between 1996 and 2000, the accumulated number of domestic tourists would amount to 4.06–4.28 billion and domestic tourism revenue would add up to RMB1000–1050 billion. Some 35.7–36.8 million overseas tourists and US$58 billion foreign exchange revenue would be received. It is expected that from 2001 to 2010 the number of domestic tourists would increase yearly by 8 per cent, and tourism revenue by 15 per cent every year. It is calculated accordingly that the visits paid by Chinese domestic travellers would reach 2–2.5 billion, with domestic tourism revenue attaining RMB1000–1050 billion by 2010. During the same period, it is estimated incoming tourists (including compatriots in Hong Kong and Macao) to the country and foreign exchange revenue would account for only US$64–71 million and US$38–43 billion respectively (The State Tourism Administration of the People's Republic of China, 1996). This clearly indicates the relative importance of domestic tourism in the coming years.

The overall economic role of domestic tourism at the national level is incontestable, although how different figures are derived and linkages with the other sectors of the economy are conceived is an aspect that requires further clarification. The area where the information is especially lacking is the nature and extent of the impact of domestic tourism at the local level. This study has referred to a number of cases involving a certain level of impact of domestic tourism on the local economy and society, but this information is extremely sketchy and obtained mainly from the tourist authorities who are obviously more keen to emphasize the positive aspects of domestic tourism.

More in-depth information and investigation is required on the extent to which different investments and the transfer of wealth to rural, less privileged areas are taking place. Is the development in domestic tourism helping to valorize and develop local products, instead of imports from urban areas or abroad? Does it support cottage industries and local business? How is domestic tourism fulfilling investment demand for and the improvement of local infrastructure and utilities such as water, electricity, telephone, communication systems, and healthcare facilities? More importantly, what has been its role in generating employment and income in local areas?

Finally, any extensive investigation and analysis of the local-level impact of domestic tourism must involve a critical look at the consequent social stratification process. The key question is: who is gaining and who is losing? And what are the prospects for local groups to come together to formulate institutional arrangements so that the potential economic gains are fully enjoyed locally, while seeking to control the negative impacts?

Notes

1   Before 1992, the state-owned travel services engaged in international tourism were under the Foreign Ministry. Its main function was to execute government foreign policy. The generation of profit was not its principal objective and it did not bear any responsibility for the loss incurred in management as well.

2   The definition (The State Tourism Administration of the People's Republic of China, 1994) of domestic tourists in China includes: residents in mainland China, outside their usual residences, beyond 10km for more than six hours, engaged in such activities as touring, vacationing, visiting and calling on friends, etc (medical appointments, recuperation, conventions, and economic, technological, cultural, educational, sports and religious activities are also included). The following are excluded from this definition: personnel remaining outside for more than half a year; personnel travelling on business; leaders above the rank of minister on inspection tours in various places; resident staff in offices elsewhere. This definition is basically the same as that accepted by the WTO.

3   The personal experience of the second author also confirms this attitude. In the decade between the end of the 1960s to 1970s, when working in agriculture in a border area more than 4000km away from his area, he went home to visit his family five times. Each time he seized the opportunity for sightseeing in cities during the daytime and travelling by train at night to save accommodation expenses.

4   According to Tisdell and Wen (1991, p177–184), cumulative investment in transportation (which only included tourist vehicles, roads and cruises), shopping facilities, tourist attractions and domestic tourism facilities to the end of 1986 was 4.1, 1.2, 1.6 and 3.2 billion respectively. The total cumulative investment in tourism (29.6 billion for hotels and 18 billion for other tourism facilities) did not include investment in tourist restaurants, travel agencies and tourist education. There were 1300 travel agencies, 24 universities or departments and 200 vocational schools providing tourism education with financial help from government or other sources. Of the total foreign investment in China in 1984, for example, 69 per cent was allocated to the tourism sector and within the sector to hotel construction. During the 1980s, Beijing was the main focus for foreign investment in the tourism industry, accounting for 74.6 per cent of the total.

5   It should be noted that in the 1990s there has also been an increase in the number of Chinese people (mainly from urban areas) travelling abroad following the relaxation on foreign travel. Some citizens went to neighbouring countries such as Russia, DPR Korea, Mongolia, Burma, Laos, Nepal, Singapore, Thailand, Malaysia, etc, for sightseeing. There were also self-sponsored travellers to other regions of the world. According to the public security department, outgoing tourists among Chinese citizens totalled 4,530,500 in 1995, 21.1 per cent higher over 1994, 2,053,900 of them for private purposes, accounting for 45.4 per cent, 25.1 per cent higher over 1994; 1,259,900 were organized, making up 61.3 per cent. Their main purpose of travel outside the country involves seeing social conditions and customs in other regions and countries, and purchasing cheaper industrial products. Most of these people probably combine their travel with official business and visiting overseas relatives, but some apparently travel purely for leisure (cf *Financial Times*, 26 May 1997).

6   So far farmer samples have been unavailable in specified travel sampling surveys. Figures concerning farmer tourists are based on the results of per capita travelling expenses in typical survey data of passenger traffic volume on railway and highway, as well as sampling surveys of urban and rural resident households by the State Statistics Bureau.

References

Chen Yanbai (1997) 'Local tourism of Sichuan Province', in Editorial Board of China Tourism Yearbook, *China Tourism Yearbook 1997*, China Tourism Publishing House, Beijing

Cheng Wendong (1992) 'Speech on the conference of national tourist market', *Tourism News*, no 6

China Tourism Yearbook (1992) (also for the years 1993, 1994, 1995, 1996 and 1997), Editorial Board, China Tourism Publishing House, Beijing

Chronicle of Tourism Events in China (1995) Editorial Division, China Tourism Publishing House, Beijing

Financial Times (1997) 'China's fledgling tourists spread their wings', 26 May

Fu Min (1996) *Action of Extinguishing Poverty by China Government*, Hubei Science and Technology Press

Ghimire, Krishna (1994) *Conservation and Social Development: A Study Based on an Assessment of Wolong and Other Panda Reserves in China*, Discussion Paper No 56, UNRISD, Geneva, December

He Guangwei (1997) 'Seizing the Opportunity, Fulfilling the tasks of '97 travel year', in Editorial Board of China Tourism Yearbook, *China Tourism Yearbook 1997*, China Tourism Publishing House, Beijing

Liu Zhenli and Wang Bing (1996) *Newly Edited Chinese Tourist Geography*, Nankai University Press

Meng Jialu (1997) 'Local tourism of Liaoning in 1996', in Editorial Board of China Tourism Yearbook, *China Tourism Yearbook 1997*, China Tourism Publishing House

National Tourism Administration, *China Statistical Yearbooks* (1978–1999), the State Statistics Bureau, China Statistics Publishing House, Beijing

Qian Jianping (1995) 'Domestic tourism in 1995', in Editorial Board of China Tourism Yearbook, *China Tourism Yearbook 1995*, China Tourism Publishing House

Qian Jianping (1996) 'Domestic tourism in 1996', in Editorial Board of China Tourism Yearbook, *China Tourism Yearbook 1996*, China Tourism Publishing House

The State Tourism Administration of the People's Republic of China (1996) *The Ninth Five Year Plan and Long Range Objective Programme in 2010 for Tourism Development in China*, China Tourism Publishing House, Beijing

The State Tourism Administration of the People's Republic of China, Investigation Team of Urban Social and Economic Conditions, the State Statistics Bureau of the People's Republic of China (1993) *Sampling Survey Data of China's Domestic Tourism 1993* (also for the years 1994, 1995 and 1996), China Tourism Publishing House, Beijing

The State Tourism Administration (1997) 'The class evaluation of travel services', in Editorial Board of China Tourism Yearbook, *China Tourism Yearbook 1997*, 49, China Tourism Publishing House, Beijing

Sun Gang (1996) 'Alleviation poverty from tourism', *Tourism News*, no 12

Sun Gang (1997) *New theory of Tourist Economics*, China Tourism Publishing House

Tieling (1997) 'Development and protection of tourist resources', *China Tourism Yearbook 1997*, China Tourism Publishing House

Tisdell, C and Jie Wen (1991) 'Investment in China's tourism industry: Its scale, nature and policy issues', *China Economic Review*, vol 2

Wang Yuejin (1997) 'Alleviation poverty draw support from tourism in Hongqi village, Antu County', in Editorial Board of China Tourism Yearbook, *China Tourism Yearbook 1997*, China Tourism Publishing House, Beijing

Xinhua News Agency (2001) *The New Progress of the China Tourism of 2001*, 13 February 2001, Beijing

Xu Dixin (1980) *Dictionary of Political Economics*, People Press, Beijing

Xu Jing (1997) 'Management of National Forest Parks', in Editorial Board of China Tourism Yearbook, *China Tourism Yearbook 1997*, China Tourism Publishing House

Youngblood, Robert (1997) 'The long trek up a Chinese mountain', *International Herald Tribune*, 28 February

Yu Jianming (1997) 'Local tourism of Yunnan Province in 1996', in Editorial Board of China Tourism Yearbook, *China Tourism Yearbook 1997*, China Tourism Publishing House, Beijing

Chapter 5

Domestic Tourism in Thailand: Supply and Demand

Mingsarn Kaosa-ard, David Bezic and Suzanne White[1]

Introduction

The kingdom of Thailand possesses a physical and ethnic richness that has led to its establishment among the world's major tourist destinations. A variety of historical, cultural and natural endowments serve to propel Thailand's illustrated tourist appeal. Its location at the crossroads between East and West has produced a unique heritage that combines elements of ancient Indian, Chinese and Cambodian cultures with features of the Khmer kingdoms. Thailand also includes diverse natural attractions that provide international and domestic tourists with scuba-diving areas, sun and sand recreation and mountain excursions. Thailand's 70 national parks provide outdoor enthusiasts with an opportunity to experience the country's flora and fauna in a natural environment. The parks also serve as a popular get-away destination for Thai urban-dwellers looking to escape temporarily the crowds and pollution of the city.

In 1996, an estimated 7.44 million international tourists visited Thailand and their collective expenditures of 201,389 million baht proved to be the country's primary source of foreign exchange that year (TDRI, 1997a). The year earlier, Thailand ranked tenth worldwide in tourism receipts and was the 19th most visited global destination in terms of foreign tourist arrivals.

Supplementing this substantial degree of international visitation is an increase in the number of trips made by Thai tourists within their own country. The rapid growth experienced by the Thai economy over the past decade has been accompanied by an expansion of the country's middle class and a rise in domestic tourism. More and more Thais are finding the time and financial resources to travel and are expected soon to account for a greater share of tourism-related expenditures within the kingdom than their foreign counterparts. The number of in-country trips made by Thai tourists in 1996 totalled approximately 42.5 million and projections suggest that this figure will more than double to 97 million by the year 2003 (TDRI, 1997a).

In addition to the foreign exchange it supplies thanks to international tourism, other less recognized, indirect economic contributions of the tourism sector include its role as an income redistributor and the tourism-related production it induces. The economic importance of domestic tourism has usually been regarded as a means to prevent the foreign currency outflow provoked by outbound tourism. There is a general lack of information and systematic studies on the potential of domestic tourism as an agent for economic development and income redistribution.

While the benefits are relatively obvious, the costs of domestic tourism – stemming largely from mismanagement – are less apparent. Currently, most studies refer to international tourism, even though domestic tourists outnumber international ones and may cause equal or greater damage to a site. Both groups differ in terms of motivations, preferences and destinations for their travels and, as a result, might provoke different types of impacts. The absence of effective measures to address the cultural, social and environmental impacts of domestic tourism makes evident the need for in-depth studies that are capable of clearly assessing the many consequences of this expanding phenomenon. The ramifications of improper tourism management are far-reaching and the failure to recognize this is akin to inviting unsustainable development of the sector.

Overview of Some Issues Related to Tourism

As many other developing nations, Thailand has viewed tourism as a means to quick and easy foreign exchange earnings. This approach has resulted in the formulation of policies that seek to encourage and promote visitation while largely neglecting carrying capacity issues. The government's perception of the need to increase demand has often been the main obstacle to a tourism strategy that best serves the long-term interests of Thai society. Policies have tended to concentrate upon marketing at a time when investments are needed for environmental maintenance and protection. This approach is further reflected in recent budget cuts which have served to alter restoration plans.

As the number of Thai and international tourists continues to climb, increasing pressure will be placed on infrastructure such as roads, water and electricity supply, and telecommunications and environmental resources required to support visitors' demands. The development of resorts and facilities in locales deemed attractive by visitors – typically in pristine, natural areas where management capacities are at an embryonic stage – has often caused irreversible damage to the ecologically sensitive surroundings and detracted from its future tourist appeal. These pressures are made more acute by what appears to be an increasing demand among tourists for nature-oriented sites and activities – for example, visits to pristine beaches and national parks, camping, trekking, rock climbing and kayaking. This increasing demand comes at a time when such areas are declining in availability. Rapid economic development, the expansion of the manufacturing sector and government-sponsored mega-projects, such as the eastern and southern seaboard, have all led to consistent encroachment of areas formerly considered to be prime tourism locations. As the competition for land and space intensifies, consideration of environmental constraints will become necessary in future tourism strategy formulation.

In addressing this shortcoming, competition for Thai society's limited economic resources will intensify as infrastructure improvement and the expansion of tourist facilities require the diversion of funds away from alternative uses and sectors. This diversion imposes an implicit 'cost' on those segments of society that do not benefit directly from the tourism industry.

The above trends suggest that without careful planning and policy revision, the long-run sustainability of Thailand's tourism industry is precarious. The demand-oriented policies of the past, which focused on increasing (mainly foreign) tourist numbers, must be altered in favour of a more supply-conscious approach. Policies that fail to remain mindful of carrying capacity, infrastructure and domestic traveller issues will surely result in unsustainable development of the industry. Rendering these negative repercussions more pressing is the fact that these policies also invite environmental degradation and a potential decline in the standard of living among some segments of Thailand's population. Economic turmoil, however, has increased the need for foreign exchange and makes it difficult to divert government attention to domestic tourism.

The issues of demand-focused national policies and environmental constraints are topics that will be referred to frequently throughout this chapter. Analysis of various tourist groups in Thailand will be considered, with emphasis on the role played by domestic tourists. For the purposes of this discussion, a domestic tourist will be defined as 'any person residing in a country, who travels to a place within the country outside his/her usual environment, for a period not exceeding 12 months and whose main purpose of visit is other than the exercise of an activity remunerated from within the place visited' (WTO, 1993). It should be noted that the WTO applies this definition to domestic tourists making trips for a variety of reasons, including leisure, visiting friends/relatives, business, health treatment and religious pilgrimages, among others. In this chapter, the definition will be applied primarily to those who travel in pursuit of leisure, recreation and holidays.

The broad concept of regional tourist is more difficult to define. However, in view of the geographic proximity and economic similarity of the ASEAN nations to Thailand, tourists from within this group will be considered as regional tourists. Visitors from China, Japan and Korea will also be classified as regional tourists although their home countries are not in ASEAN. Finally, outbound tourists will be defined as Thai nationals who travel abroad and stay at least overnight, but no longer than 90 days for voluntary leisure or business purposes. Other definitions will be clarified as required.

The chapter begins with a short discussion on the evolution of the tourism industry in Thailand. Domestic tourists' preferences, motivations and economic importance are outlined in part two. Part three focuses on the supply side of tourism development in Thailand by considering the country's physical and environmental carrying capacities. The cultural and social implications of promoting the tourism sector are discussed in part four and the final part outlines the national government's past and present approach to tourism policies. The chapter ends with recommendations regarding future policies in support of the sustainable development of the domestic tourism industry in Thailand.[2]

Antecedents of Domestic Tourism

Historically, travel in Thailand consisted mainly of religious pilgrimages to Buddhist temples and holy places and was limited in scope. Following the Second World War international tourism started to gain importance and the Tourism Organization of Thailand (TOT) was established (Meyer, 1988, p63; Tahiar, 1972). The necessary physical infrastructure for tourism was constructed and translated into success when the number of international arrivals, predominantly wealthy Americans, increased consistently throughout the 1950s and 1960s. The onset of the Vietnam war in the 1960s provided the biggest boost to tourism in Thailand as the country became a popular rest and recreation (R&R) destination for US military personnel. The servicemen's tourist pursuits often revolved around the procuring of sex services and this led to the rise of tourist-oriented prostitution.

Prior to the GIs' arrival, the country was home to only one high-class beach resort. This resort, located at Hua Hin, was established by the Thai royalty and catered primarily to the country's elite (Kanywerayotin, 1987). However, following the GIs 'discovery' of Pattaya in 1959, the number of resorts in Thailand increased drastically. The town's consequent success and rapid economic growth served as a catalyst to copycat vacation site development throughout the country's coastal regions.

The end of the Vietnam War led to a departure en masse of the GIs and a fundamental shift in the type of tourist typically found in Thailand. Mainly filling the gap left by Americans were Japanese, Middle Eastern and European visitors, and available tourist services began to change in response to their particular demands (Cohen, 1996, p9). Diversification also occurred in the quality of tourist services found in Thailand as the number of business travellers increased and world incomes rose. More and more high-end amenities, such as hotels, travel services, exclusive clubs and golf courses, became available and were increasingly used by Thais. At the same time, relatively inexpensive restaurants and accommodations were still available for 'backpackers' travelling on shoestring budgets.

Until the end of the 1980s, the tourism industry in Thailand catered mainly to foreign visitors. Domestic tourists travelled mainly by coach or trains and were accommodated at relatives' or friends' homes. Merit-making activities such as Thod Kathin (robe) and bathing cloth (Thod Pha Pa) ceremonies for monks have become important events or activities for domestic travel. Domestic tourism changed drastically after 1987 when Thailand's economic growth accelerated throughout the decade. Economic growth enhanced local income and hence domestic tourism. Towards the 1990s certain sections of the industry, including hotels and restaurants, began to cater more to the tastes of domestic tourists.

At the present time, the industry is grappling with questions regarding its sustainability and overall health. Recent trends that must be addressed in the search for a new, more appropriate management strategy include the rise of the domestic tourist, intensified regional competition, environmental degradation, the sector's ability to serve as a net source of foreign exchange and increasing pressures on the country's finite resources.

Domestic and Outbound Tourism in Thailand

Domestic tourism continues to grow and so does the number of outbound Thai tourists. This section examines some of the economic contributions and implications of Thai tourism by examining domestic and outbound tourists' expenditures. The geographical and societal distribution of economic benefits stemming from the tourism sector is also considered.

Domestic Tourists

The relative importance of Thai domestic tourists continues to grow as the country's development makes travel accessible to an increasing number of people and the recent economic slowdown induces more Thais to spend their holidays in the country. Much of this travel among the urban middle and upper classes has been encouraged by the development of transportation systems, the diffusion of motorization, and the recent rise in popularity of purchasing second 'weekend' homes in rural settings, away from the crowds and pollution of the cities. A prominent example of one such park is Khao Yai, located two hours north of Bangkok via car. The clean air and picturesque scenery of the area has also made it a popular choice for rich Bangkokians building 'orchard homes' for weekend retreats. Second homes such as these, which have risen in number along with the expansion of the Thai middle class, are a new and important source of internal trips and domestic tourism. In 1992, domestic tourists made an estimated 35.9 million trips within their country. Since that time, the numbers have continued to swell and some 97 million trips are expected by the year 2003, far exceeding estimates of 11.2 million international arrivals to Thailand for the same year.

Coinciding with the growth in the number of domestic tourists has been a growth in the size of their expenditures as a group. In 1990, they spent a total of 76,601 million baht (41 per cent of all tourism expenditures in Thailand that year). By 1996, domestic tourists' expenditures increased to a 45 per cent share of all tourism-related expenditures in Thailand that year. As Thailand has developed economically, more and more of its citizens have discovered that they can afford to partake in tourism-related activities and, as such, expenditures for leisure travel have increased accordingly. Influencing factors on the level of the household tourism expenditures include income, age of household head, education, sex, location of the household (ie urban vs rural), marital status and the nature of employment. For instance, a 1992 TDRI study indicated that single people and women living in Bangkok spent a higher proportion of their income on tourism expenditures compared to men. The study also indicated that expenditures were likely to increase with the age and level of education of the household head.

As this trend continues into the future, domestic tourists will become an increasingly important source of revenue for the country's tourism sector. In fact, TDRI estimates suggested that domestic tourist expenditures in Thailand would actually begin to outstrip those made by foreign visitors beginning in 1998. According to the estimates, domestic tourists would contribute 247,080 million baht (51 per cent) to the tourism sector in that year, while international tourists would be the source of an additional 233,852 million baht (49 per cent). The estimates also implied that the share of tourism revenues in Thailand attributable to domestic tourists would climb even further, eventually reaching 54 per cent by 1999 and 57 per cent in 2000.

By comparing the number of tourist nights spent in Thailand by each tourist group, it is possible to gain an idea of the relative importance of domestic tourists. In 1992, Thais spent an estimated 97 million tourist nights while travelling within their own country. International visitors, on the other hand, spent a total of 31 million tourist nights in that same year. The implied share attributable to domestic tourists (approximately 75 per cent) was maintained again in 1996 when they accounted for 139 million tourist nights, compared to the 45 million nights spent by international tourists. This trend has been further reinforced in recent years as many Thais are now choosing to take holidays inside the country due to financial instabilities and devaluation of the national currency.

Domestic tourists' preferences

In 1997, approximately 9.95 million trips (21 per cent) of the nation's 47.29 million total domestic trips were made to Bangkok alone, with the rest being distributed in various provinces around the country. The second largest single domestic tourist destination will be Chiang Mai (1.89 million visits) followed by Nakhon Ratchasima (1.73 million visits). Estimates suggest that Bangkok's popularity as a destination among domestic tourists will be maintained into the future. In the year 2003, 15.07 million of the country's estimated 97.02 million domestic visits will be to Bangkok. These numbers translate as a 15 per cent share of total domestic trips in that year and a 5 per cent decline from the city's share in 1997.

It is interesting to note that Bangkok is the most favoured destination within Thailand for both domestic and international travellers. However, when it comes to the relative importance of other destinations among the two groups, much variation can be found. This is important in the context of the study as such diverging preferences are indicative of a need to distinguish between the two types of travellers when analysing Thailand's tourism sector.

Comparing preferred destinations between international and domestic tourists at the anticipated ten most popular destinations for 2003 reveals some of the differences between the two groups. Table 5.1 indicates that Bangkok is expected to maintain its current position as the most popular destination among the two classifications of travellers. However, looking beyond this, the similarities become much less apparent. For example, the predicted second most popular destination among domestic tourists, Nakhon Ratchasima, is nowhere to be found on the international group's top ten list. A reason for this divergence is that Nakhon Ratchasima is generally lacking in 'typical' tourist attractions – hence, it tends to be overlooked by international visitors. On the other hand, the area is home to a large number of Thai citizens who have migrated to Bangkok in search of employment opportunities. When these migrants return home to visit family and friends, their trips are classified as domestic tourism and serve to boost the region's apparent tourist popularity. Foreign tourists, in particular European ones, prefer seaside excursions compared to Thais. Further examples of diverging preferences can be found in the differing popularity among the two groups of Phuket (ie third for international tourists vs tenth for domestic) and Kho Samui (sixth for international while not even among the top ten for domestic tourists). For further insight into domestic tourists' most favoured destinations and a comparison of these to international tourists' preferred sites, see Table 5.1.

Domestic tourists' motivations

By understanding the demands of tourists, domestic and international alike, the Thai government can formulate tourism policies that most effectively

Table 5.1 *The ten most popular provincial tourist destinations*
(projections for 2003)

Domestic tourists		*International tourists*	
Province	No of Thai tourists ('000s)	Province	No of international tourists ('000s)
Bangkok	15,070	Bangkok	9160
Nakhon Ratchasima	4133	Pattaya	2819
Chiang Mai	4006	Phuket	2582
Phetchaburi	3812	Chiang Mai	1431
Pattaya	3547	Hat Yai	1058
Chon Buri	3512	Kho Samui	815
Rayong	3009	Sungai Kolok	574
Kanchanaburi	2834	Krabi	496
Had Yai	2554	Kanchanaburi	384
Phuket	2467	Rayong	362

Source: TDRI estimates, 1997b

promote policy objectives. In order to arrive at effective policies, it is important to know what tourists' purpose of travel is, what locations and specific attractions are preferred in their eyes, what information sources are utilized in shaping their demands and what types of activities are undertaken in their role as tourists. Authorities can then proceed to manage the country's tourism resources in such a way that encourages the attainment of various goals, possibly including some that lie beyond the tourism sector. For example, income distribution across various localities in Thailand can be achieved by encouraging the country's urban rich to travel to, and spend money in, the poorer rural areas. In order to do this, however, a prior understanding of domestic tourists' tastes, demands and motivations is required.

Domestic tourists in Thailand are likely to travel within the country for the purpose of visiting relatives and friends. Of the 626 domestic tourists surveyed by TDRI, 29 per cent of domestic visitors to the north-east and 27 per cent to Bangkok named this as their purpose of travel.

Bangkok's prominence as the country's capital city and centre of business makes it an obvious destination point and has also led many people from the north-east to migrate there in search of employment. As many of these migrants make periodic trips to visit the people they have left behind, voyages from Bangkok to the north-east are commonly motivated by such personal visitation purposes. In fact, the TDRI survey revealed that 67 per cent of the domestic respondents whose destination was the north-east had begun their journeys in Bangkok.

Domestic tourists are also likely to travel within the kingdom for business purposes. It was found that 24 per cent of domestic tourists travelling to the north-east and 19 per cent of those heading to Bangkok, cited this as their purpose. The fact that none of the Thai respondents travelling to the country's west or east were doing so for business purposes reflects the diversity of attractions and development within Thailand. Table 5.2 provides further details on the travel objectives of domestic tourists.

Table 5.2 *Objectives of domestic tourists travelling to various regions (%)*

Purpose	North	North-east	Destination Bangkok	South	West	East
Recreation	54.62	15.79	12.80	86.08	73.75	80.56
Business	5.88	23.68	18.90	1.27	0.00	0.00
Conference	7.56	0.00	3.05	0.00	0.00	1.85
Visit relatives/friends	12.61	28.95	26.83	2.53	7.50	0.00
Official trip	6.72	2.63	11.59	2.53	0.00	0.93
More than 1 reason	8.40	28.95	23.78	6.33	17.50	15.74
More than 2 reasons	4.20	0.00	3.05	1.27	1.25	0.93

Source: TDRI, 1993 p75

Tourists' proclivity towards specific attractions has been found to differ according to age, gender, income and occupation. In order for the sector to be managed effectively, the preferences of specific target groups must be identified. A 1993 survey[3] revealed that most travellers to the north, south, west and east do so for strictly holiday-related purposes (as opposed to business or family/ friend visitation purposes). The south, west and east regions were found to attract tourists largely as a result of their natural beauty, while the north had a more diverse array of perceived attractions. For example, 30 per cent of respondents travelling to or in the north cited natural attractions as the focus of their visit, while 13 and 8 per cent named religious and historical sites, and cultural activities respectively as their focus. Finally, the north, Bangkok and the east had the greatest prevalence of tourists who were attracted to the region by seminar and conference facilities and events.

It was found that young tourists prefer natural attractions as approximately 53 per cent of employed females in the 25-year age group identified 'nature' as their first choice. In comparison, only 36 per cent of employed females in the 50–60-year age group made the same choice. Older tourists, particularly females, expressed a greater relative penchant for historical and religious attractions as well as for cultural activities. Male tourists showed a degree of favour towards entertainment attractions and this preference tended to diminish with age. Among the higher income group, preference for the entertainment industry was found to be statistically insignificant while 'nature' and 'shopping centres' were popular for those aged below 30 years. For the 50–60-year age group, preferences differed in that 'historical or religious places' were a most favoured attraction rather than 'shopping centres'. However, 'nature' was also a favourite among this age group as well.

The information gained in the above estimation was subsequently utilized in constructing a ranking of domestic tourists' most preferred attractions, the results of which are outlined as follows:

- Sea and beaches.
- Mountains and waterfalls.
- Religious and historical places.
- Cultural activities.
- Entertainment.
- Shopping.

An important determining factor of tourists' preferences for different attractions is the information that they receive in this regard. Travel information not only can play a significant role in shaping people's travel choices, but can also influence the degree of success realized by government tourism policies in meeting their objectives. As a result, it is essential that the authorities have some knowledge on what informational resources are being used by tourists planning their trips. A 1992 TDRI survey queried 625 domestic tourists on their sources of travel information and found that their main source of information was personal acquaintances (31 per cent), followed by 'others' (28 per cent) and tourist agencies (15 per cent).

Outbound Tourism

The rapid economic growth and rising income levels over the past decade have made it possible for a greater number of Thais to travel, not only within Thailand but outside it as well. Outbound tourism represents an outflow of currency induced by Thai nationals travelling abroad. The number of outbound tourists has doubled since 1990, implying an annual growth rate of 15 per cent over this period. This trend also comes at a time when neighbouring ASEAN countries such as Malaysia and Indonesia have launched aggressive marketing campaigns in an attempt to attract international and regional visitors. These campaigns have been successful at drawing tourists, including Thai nationals, to their respective countries, and have further encouraged growth in the number of outbound Thai tourists. Thai outbound tourists tend to confine most of their international travel to countries within the region. For example, in 1996, approximately 78 per cent of Thais travelling abroad chose countries in East Asia as their destination (TAT, 1996, p50). The ASEAN subgroup accounted for 40 per cent of all outbound destinations, while the single largest country was Malaysia with a 21 per cent share. Following Malaysia were Singapore and Hong Kong, both with approximately 15 per cent shares.

Coinciding with their increasing numbers has been the rise in the amount of currency outflows prompted by outbound tourists. In 1992, approximately 40,556 million baht (US$1590 million; US$1 = baht 25.50) flowed out of Thailand as a result of trips taken abroad by Thai residents (Cacnio, 1995, p13). By 1995, this amount totalled 83,948 million baht (US$3372 million; US$1 = baht 24.89) and in 1996 it increased further to 105,621 million baht (US$4171 million; US$1 = baht 25.32). As a result of these increases, Thailand's net balance of foreign exchange earnings from tourism declined from what they would have otherwise been in the absence of outbound travel.

An intent to revert this unfavourable trend was to promote domestic tourism, as well as to motivate Thais to do their shopping in the country. In 1994, the Tourism Authority of Thailand (TAT), together with the Association of Thai Tour Operators (ATTO), designed the 'Thais Tour Thailand' campaign. It consisted of the organization of 'Sales Fairs' addressed to all ages jointly, with a special programme targeted to young people during the summer school vacation or off-school periods. It is usually at this time when well-off parents send their children to learn languages abroad. The aim of the campaign was to induce parents to consider other special activities for their children, especially nature and sports-related activities. By awakening young Thais' interest in environmentally friendly activities, the TAT hoped to be able to reach their families and friends as well (Cacnio, 1996). The TAT allocated a bigger marketing budget for local promotion of Thai destinations while allowing its provincial offices their own budgets to handle local promotional drives (Jansen, 1996). TAT spent 87 million baht advertising local tours in 1995 (Muqbil, 1996). Other promotional mechanisms for making the domestic market more attractive were tour packages and hotel rooms to be sold at special rates with operators earning only nominal profits, and special discounted air fares from Thai Airways International and Bangkok Airways.

However, outbound tourism has experienced a slow-down in recent years. For example, the number of outbound tourists in 1992 had increased by 26.42 per cent over the previous year's total, while this same measure of growth equalled only 1.37 per cent in 1996. International unrest, domestic political problems and devaluations in the Thai baht are among the main reasons for this decline. But some travel agents and tourism organizations have also attributed the decrease to the effective promotional campaigns carried out by the TAT (Muqbil, 1996).

Outbound tourism and its consequent currency outflow has prompted the Thai government to tackle the problem by promoting domestic tourism. Once again its campaigns have focused on marketing and allocating generous sums to advertising. Even though environmentally friendly activities are at the centre of its campaigns, environmental impacts by the growing numbers of Thais travelling in the country still remain unobserved. As we will see in following sections, in spite of some policy attempts – often put aside because of insufficient funds – little has been done to assess properly the impacts of the heavily pro-moted domestic tourism.

The Distribution of Economic Benefits from Tourism

Although the tourism sector has provided Thailand with large amounts of foreign exchange and has served as an impetus for domestic expenditures, not all of the country's citizens have benefited equally from these flows. One reason lies in the obvious fact that different regions of the country have varying degrees of tourist appeal and, as a result, they receive diverging amounts of tourists in any given year. Even in those areas that do receive many tourists, the distribution of benefits may not be all that favourable due to the structure and nature of tourism expenditures, and the 'leakage' problem that results from multinational companies repatriating their incomes to their parent companies.

It is important to remain aware of the fact that a relatively low tourist presence in a particular area does not necessarily imply that this same area receives a low degree of *net* tourism benefits. Popular tourist destinations might realize greater benefits in the form of expenditure injections to the local economy, but they are also more likely to face higher costs in the process. These costs might come in the form of higher housing and food prices, environmental degradation, cultural change and/or increased pressure on local infrastructure. By avoiding these costs, areas with low tourist presence implicitly receive benefits that are not directly measurable.

Based on the earlier illustration of Bangkok's dominance in attracting tourists, it is not surprising to find that it is also Thailand's premier earner of tourism revenues. In 1995, a total of 105,220 million baht was spent on tourism within the metropolis. Of this total, 59,576 million baht came from domestic tourists. Second to Bangkok in 1995 was Phuket, which was home to approxim-ately 14 per cent of all tourism expenditures within Thailand's ten most popular destinations that year. This share resulted from the 31,001 million baht that tourists spent in the province in 1995. Of this total, domestic tourists contributed 3744 million baht. As far as future trends are concerned, Bangkok is expected to maintain its position atop all provinces in terms of tourism earnings, as noted earlier. TDRI predictions suggest that in the year 2003, domestic and international tourists will spend a total of 364,535 million baht within Bangkok. Of this amount, 80 per cent is anticipated to be the result of domestic tourists' expenditures while the remainder will come from foreigners. Phuket is also expected to retain its current position as the second most prominent earner of tourism income, with projected earnings in 2003 reaching 57,725 million baht (25 per cent of which will come from domestic tourists).

By influencing tourists' spending and travel patterns, the Thai government is afforded the opportunity to address some distributional issues within the country. Advertising and promoting relatively poorer regions to tourists can lead to increased economic activity in the area and, if managed correctly, can provide the local populations with improved standards of living. The broad scope and non-transparent character of tourism expenditure flows through different segments of society render it a difficult issue to examine with any degree of precision. National data and information on these matters are not readily available and the distribution of tourism's benefits is hard to quantify as a result.

The Chiang Mai Flower Festival

Although estimating the costs and benefits distributed at the national level is difficult and the information on domestic tourism is rather limited, the Chiang Mai Flower Festival provides an illustration of the impact of subsidizing specific promotional activities for tourism purposes. A study of the Flower Festival (TDRI, 1993, p175) posed the following two questions: to what extent does the festival create additional income over and above the normal peak season; and what are the costs and benefits to the parties involved?

The Flower Festival was initially used to promote horticultural production, and its promotion as a tourist attraction was introduced at a later stage. It has three main features: a procession of flower-decorated vehicles, a flower and garden competition and a beauty contest. The last activity is generally a by-product of the procession. The Provincial Office, with the help of the Provincial Agriculture Office, organizes the parade and local business, while government offices and educational institutes provide the flower vehicles. The Chiang Mai municipality is responsible for decorating the public park where the horticultural contests are held. Lately, it has been felt that the private business sector, in particular the large hotels that receive the greatest economic benefits, were inadequately supporting the festival. The private sector argued that because the event is held during the peak season it does not create a great deal of additional income. Furthermore, they argue that the festival attracts mainly domestic tourists who do not stay in large hotels, preferring to camp in national parks or stay with friends or family.

In 1992, the festival reaped an estimated total income of 105 million baht, approximately 45 million baht of which (ie 75 per cent) was above normal peak period income. Costs to the government (all agencies combined) and the private sector were roughly equal and in the amount of 1 million baht for each party. While the hotel sector provided an unimpressive vehicle valued at 120,000 baht, this sector gained an additional income of 9.05 million baht. The return on each baht of investment was 75 baht, more than three times the average return. Although the Flower Festival appeared to be slightly more attractive to domestic versus international tourists, 85 per cent of the income accrued in the hotel sector went to the large hotels (where domestic tourists traditionally do not stay).

The empirical results also confirmed the general speculation that tourism income from this festival does benefit small producers. This being said, the large operators accrue the greatest share by far. Wages for the people of Chiang Mai, and the students who join the procession without pay, were computed and the local community's contribution was valued at approximately 155,500 baht. Therefore, for every baht invested, the event (excluding imputed wages) generated an extra income of 20 baht.

The Supply and Carrying Capacity of Tourism Resources

The primary focus of Thailand's tourism development has so far been on facilitating demand and increasing the number of domestic and, in particular, international tourists within the country. As these efforts prove 'successful' and tourist numbers continue to grow, the existing capacity of infrastructure and the environment may become inadequate to satisfy tourists' needs without heavy damages or costs being imposed on local communities and environmental assets and functions.

Physical carrying capacity involves man-made facilities, the supply of water and electricity, communications services, transport, etc. Environmental carrying capacity refers to the maximum extent to which an area can be used before the surrounding environmental and ecological systems become degraded to the point where restoration is difficult or irreversible. These concepts are difficult to define as they are location specific and vary with geographical conditions, and the frequency and intensity with which tourists use a site.

The carrying capacity of the environment and infrastructure is a crucial issue since this chapter proposes that the actual constraint to tourism development in Thailand is an inadequate supply of natural and man-made resources rather than insufficient demand. Based on this premise, the government's current approach to tourism development (ie marketing and promotion) is highly inappropriate for Thailand and will impose social and economic costs on its citizens, eventually resulting in a state of maldevelopment as opposed to the true goal of development.

Physical Carrying Capacity: Domestic Tourist Evaluation of Tourism Resources

The TDRI conducted a survey in 1993 that questioned 695 domestic tourists in different regions on their opinion of the country's tourism resources and facilities. The respondents perceived the main physical problems as being traffic (especially for Bangkok) and an inadequate supply of water, telecommunications service and public toilets. They also considered hotel accommodation to be satisfactory in all regions, with the north-east ranking the lowest. Roads were also deemed satisfactory, with the east receiving the largest number of recommendations for repair and improvements. Public transport received positive responses for regions other than Bangkok.

A more recent poll conducted by the Assumption Business and Administration College over the period 1 August to 9 October 1997, queried 1072 Thai tourists who had been abroad within the previous year on their opinions of the Thai tourism sector. With regard to areas in which they saw the need for improvement, 'safety' topped the list (cited by 83.5 per cent), followed by 'cleanliness' (77.1 per cent) and 'honesty of retailers and service sector employees' (eg taxi drivers) (63.3 per cent). Two items that reflect tourism resource supply capabilities followed in fourth and fifth places; 63.3 per cent named 'maintenance of tourist sites' while 62.5 per cent referred to the need to improve the 'availability of amenities'. It is interesting to note that the survey respondents saw 'public relations and advertising' as being only the seventh most important aspect in need of improvement. It thus appears that the primary level of importance attributed to this item by the government runs contrary to the actual perceptions of domestic tourists. Table 5.3 summarizes the results of this survey.

Environmental Carrying Capacity

Tourism mismanagement often results in environmental damage. As tourist numbers have increased, overcrowding has become a reality in many localities, and pressure on local infrastructure and the surrounding environment has grown. Problems such as water shortages, pollution from improperly treated sewage, the accumulation of rubbish and land scarcity have begun to plague popular tourist destinations, while particularly ecologically sensitive resources (eg coral reefs and forest ecosystems) have been threatened by a large tourist

Table 5.3 *Domestic tourists' regional evaluation of supplied tourism resources (ABAC survey, 1997)*

Item	% of respondents
1 Safety	83.5
2 Cleanliness	77.1
3 Honesty of retailers and service employees	73.4
4 Maintenance of tourism sites	63.3
5 Availability of amenities	62.5
6 Conservation practices of Thai citizens	60.3
7 Public relations and advertising	45.1
8 Prices of goods near tourist sites	39.5
9 Improved performance of tourist police	39.0
10 Other (eg maps, information, etc.)	6.0

Source: Bangkok Business, 11 October 1997, p5

presence. For example, studies conducted at Phi Phi, Samui, Phu Kra Dueng National Park and the top-class coral sites in the Similans have indicated the need to limit the number of tourists visiting these particular locations. Further systematic studies of popular attractions in Chiang Mai, Chiang Rai and Phetchburi (eg Phu Chee Fa, Doi Inthanon National Park and Cha-am Beach) indicate that carrying capacities must be expanded and that this expansion can occur through improved management and the regulation of tourist behaviour (TDRI, 1995).

Over two decades, Pattaya developed from a small fishing village to an internationally acclaimed tourist resort. Its status as one of Thailand's major tourist attractions peaked in the middle of the 1980s and it is estimated that by the late 1980s some 2 million tourists and 1 million travellers (ie visitors who stay less than 24 hours) visited Pattaya. The size of Pattaya's tourism, measured in numbers of tourists, is second only to Bangkok and double that of Chiang Mai. In 1990, total tourism revenues from the area represented 16 per cent of the country's total revenue for that year. By 1988 the number of visitors to Pattaya began to drop. This decline was first observed with negative growth for domestic tourists and was soon followed by dwindling numbers of international visitors to Pattaya. As the drop in visitors occurred prior to the Gulf War, the decline must have been the result of environmental degradation (eg unsuitable water quality for swimming, degraded coral reefs and unchecked development along the coastline). In the Pattaya case, tourism cannot deny the overexploitation and injustice it has worked on nature.

In other cities, such as Bangkok and Chiang Mai, tourism is not the sole culprit of environmental degradation. Poorly managed urbanization and explosive industrialization have extracted heavy tolls on the country's environment. In 1992, 72 per cent of the visitors to northern Thailand (Chiang Mai, Chiang Rai, Sukhothai, etc) were Thais. Although the number of domestic tourists to the north was increasing, the number of Thais visiting Chiang Mai in 1992 decreased by 29 per cent. Apart from a more diversified and expanded market for domestic visitors, another reason for this decline was the perception that Chiang Mai was 'changing and expanding too quickly, and failing to conserve its cultural identity' (Donavanik, 1993). Simultaneously with this decrease was an increase in the number of international tourists, probably allowing the authorities and tourism entities to overlook the problems that brought the decline in the number of domestic tourists.

Doi Inthanon National Park in Chiang Mai is Thailand's only subtemperate wetland and moss bog. In order to service tourists during the dry season, water was pumped out of it. Moreover, road construction through the upper watershed has diverted natural water-flows from the wetland. Consequently, the wetland is drying up and suffers from successions of weeds and grass.

Kho Samui is a destination mostly favoured by international tourists, but in the last few years the number of nationals visiting the island increased, reaching 25.42 per cent of the total number of visitors in 1995. The most serious problems that threaten Samui's environment at present are related to waste collection and disposal, the lack of a communal waste-water treatment system, and the lack of proper knowledge about sewage treatment and the environment in general. If the number of domestic visitors continues to grow as the tendency shows, the pressure on the island's environmental carrying capacity will be enormous. The TAT Action Plan for Samui, set up in 1995, stressed that to maintain a good balance in tourism development and to assess the different problems of the island, it was necessary to promote more grass-roots participation, inviting local people and enterprises to cooperate with government agencies (*Bangkok Post*, 5 December 1996).

In the past, little concrete action was taken to counteract the negative effects of tourism development. The government was not keen on stemming tourism growth as such action could jeopardize the foreign currency inflow that the industry provided. Meanwhile, the private sector lacked the requisite knowledge to address the large-scale environmental problems that were arising. In addition, they were unwilling to sacrifice future revenues by scaling back development or by incurring costs for infrastructural projects that did not provide adequate private returns. Rather than attempt to repair the environmental damage for which they were partially responsible, the private tourism sector often found it easier simply to seek out untouched, environmentally pristine locations for new development undertakings.

As the environmental problems at popular destinations continued to grow in number and severity, they began to pose a perceived threat to tourist satisfaction and, in turn, tourist demand. Seeing the sustenance of tourism revenues jeopardized, the government finally took some action in the form of the Environmental Quality Act of 1992. This act attempted to address national and economy-wide environmental problems and not simply those related to the tourism industry. Portions of it, however, were directly aimed at the sector's particular problems and circumstances (eg more stringent development restrictions on the islands). Unfortunately, bureaucratic inefficiencies and resource short-comings have prevented the act's measures from being effectively implemented. Indeed, the tourism industry in Thailand has reached a point where restoration and conservation are required for the sustainable development of the industry.

Ecotourism

Ecotourism has been defined as a visit to any particular tourism area with the purpose to study, enjoy, and appreciate the scenery – natural and social – as well as the lifestyle of the local people, based on knowledge about, and responsibility for, the ecological system of the area. Its implicit stress on the balance between nature and tourist activities, along with its emphasis on minimizing humans' impact on the environment, renders it an attractive

alternative to more traditional forms of tourism. By encouraging the maintenance of natural areas upon which its very existence depends, ecotourism can
also address some of the current conflict between tourism development and
the environment. Coincidentally, it has been playing a role of increasing
importance in Thailand's environmental and tourism management.

When using ecotourism as a policy tool, management techniques can be
employed to prevent it from extending beyond the carrying capacity of the
areas in which it flourishes. These techniques might include park wildlife
management, the imposition of a limit on the number of visitors to the area or
park and the use of economic instruments (eg user charges, taxes, tradable
permits) to influence ecotourists' numbers and behaviour.

The policies of the TAT specify eight broad issues that they believe should
be encouraged within the tourism sector, three of which are directly or indirectly
related to ecotourism:

1   The expansion of tourism to remote areas to facilitate a more equitable
    income distribution across the regions.
2   The conservation and renovation of cultural sites, natural resources and
    the environment so as to maintain and preserve Thai identity.
3   To nourish public participation in activities related to the development of
    tourism.

Beyond its own objectives, the TAT also views ecotourism as a means to
influence and change the behaviour of tourists and tour operators in such a
way that is more in harmony with nature and the environment.

A resource that has an obvious link to ecotourism is that of Thailand's
national park system. The parks are the venues in which large numbers of
domestic and, to a much lesser degree, international tourists engage in
ecotourism-related activities. Their growing popularity as ecotourism destinations is reflected in the fact that the annual number of visitors to the parks has
practically tripled over the past decade. In 1985, there were 4,050,313 mainly
domestic visitors to the parks, while by 1995 this number had increased to
12,047,542. This growth is perhaps reflective of an emerging preference for
nature-oriented activities and a fundamental shift in the type of destinations
preferred by tourists. The findings of several park studies conducted by the
TDRI (TDRI, 1997) indicate that these tourism activities are most intense
during the cool and dry season, especially on long weekends. During such times,
the number of park visitors often exceeds their recreation areas' carrying
capacities, resulting in overcrowding and pressure on the parks' resources. This
is especially common in parks that are located relatively close to large urban
centres (eg Doi Suthep and Doi Inthanon National Parks near Chiang Mai).

Further findings of Khao Yai, Doi Inthanon and Doi Suthep National Parks
indicate that differences exist among domestic and international tourists' use

of the parks. In addition to the fact that domestic tourists constitute a much larger proportion of the parks' visitors, it was also found that, as a group, they tend to stay for shorter periods of time and spend less per visit than their foreign counterparts. More specifically, it was found that domestic tourists stay for approximately 1–1.6 days and spend an average of 204–447 baht/person/day during the course of their park visits, while international tourists stay for 2–3 days and spend approximately 346–1023 baht per person per visit. The two groups were also found to differ in their activities once in the parks. Domestic tourists expressed a preference for leisurely, relaxed activities (eg walking, bathing and picnicking – an activity that results in a large accumulation of refuse due to the Thai tendency to transport food in several plastic bags and Styrofoam containers). Alternatively, foreign tourists were interested in more physically demanding activities such as trekking, hiking and rock-climbing.

The studies also indicated that the parks lack the facilities and management necessary for their long-run sustainability. The growing number of visitors has led to levels of rubbish accumulation that are beyond the parks' existing capabilities to handle. For example, in Doi Suthep, about three tonnes of rubbish has to be shipped out by truck per day. It was found that informational resources, environmental education and participation of the local people were also lacking, thereby mitigating the parks' ability to provide some of ecotourism's most essential elements. The TAT has pointed out that one of the main factors for ecotourism's 'failure' was the insufficient participation of the local communities due to poor management skills and weak bargaining power against the tourism industry. Although the TAT is promoting ecotourism in the domestic market, it is aware of the general lack of environmental concern that Thai tourists have for the places they visit, and exhorted the need for environmental awareness campaigns among tour operators and tourists alike (*Bangkok Post*, 10 May 1997).

In order to address some of these deficiencies, the TDRI has suggested that entrance fees should be raised to limit the number of visitors as well to provide additional revenue for preservation efforts. In order to control the number of people camping, it was suggested that visitors should be required to purchase overnight permits should they desire to remain on the parks' premises after dark. The number of issued permits could be modified according to each park's facilities and carrying capacity at the time of the year in question. With regard to visitors' behaviour, a system of deposit for bottles and containers was suggested to help in the monitoring and controlling of litter, as were restrictions on certain types of non-environmentally friendly materials (eg Styrofoam). Finally, it was suggested that visitors should be encouraged to use a larger area of the park so as to minimize the impact upon specific areas, particularly those near the parks' entry points.

The negative impacts of tourism are not limited to environmental and physical infrastructure – there are cultural and social implications as well. In some cases, tourism can serve to reinforce positive cultural activities, while on the other hand it may not. The next section examines the influence that tourism can have on the lifestyles of the local population.

The Cultural and Social Implications of Tourism

In a very broad and general sense, 'culture' can be viewed as a set of relationships that govern society. The abstract nature of these relationships often leads to the convenient adoption of more concrete items such as religion, rites and rituals, the arts and language to represent culture. Tourism has been cited as a potentially positive as well as a negative influencing force upon culture. Those who cast it with a non-negative role (Picard, 1993) tend to view culture as a set of relationships that are constantly evolving according to shifts in the prevailing economic, social, political and technological environments. In this light, tourism can serve a positive role by encouraging visited communities to preserve their unique traditions and culture, and in the process to enhance their tourist appeal. They might also be encouraged to undertake such preservation measures as a defence against the intrusion of external culture.

On the other hand, those who view tourism as a negative influence upon culture (Wood, 1980) tend to cite its ability to affect indigenous society by way of distortions (often introduced for the tourists' benefit) to traditional lifestyles, values and rituals. One of the most prevalent criticisms of tourism is that it exposes local residents to the values and consumption patterns of the tourists, who tend to have much greater purchasing power than themselves. It is surmised that this may influence the local way of life and the local populations' consumption demands as the visited communities attempt to emulate the apparently attractive lifestyles of the tourists. Often overlooked by the proponents of this view is the role played by the diffusion of mass media, especially television, in exposing communities to alternate lifestyles.

Another criticism lies in the local communities' professed deprivation of 'true culture' that results when a cultural event or lifestyle is promoted for tourism-related purposes. It is argued that the transformation of such traditional traits into a spectacle for tourists' pleasure serves to undermine the spiritual significance of the event or lifestyle.

It is difficult to frame domestic tourism within any of these particular currents. The cultural impacts inflicted by the nationals of a country upon others in a different region or socio-economic situation are far less evident than those induced by foreign visitors. Maybe because of the more subtle influence that domestic tourists have on the communities they visit, this aspect has been largely underestimated and neglected by the government and academics alike.

Some Impacts of Trekking in Northern Thailand

Trekking is a popular tourist activity in Thailand, and is becoming more attractive to a greater number of domestic tourists every year. Trekking tours take place mostly in the northern region and usually involve a visit to a hill-tribe community. As any other tourist activity, it has incurred socio-economic and cultural changes in those communities produced by the increased contact of villagers with lowlanders through travel agencies and guides and, obviously, with trekkers. However, commercial penetration, missionaries, resource extraction, military and government missions, video halls, development projects and other factors have also prompted them to change aspects of their traditional way of life (Dearden, 1996).

From the standpoint of domestic tourism, negative impacts related to Thai tourists are related to scattered waste disposal, making a great deal of noise, loud singing and graffiti on walls and trees. Environmental degradation was found to be the most evident effect of trekking domestic tourists.

Other cultural and social problems such as AIDS, procuring prostitutes and drugs are problems associated most frequently with foreign tourists. This being said, an eight-year-long study in an Akha village in the north of Thailand (Toyota, 1996) explains how heroin was introduced to the village by jungle guides, partly as a result of bringing heroin-addict tourists (including Thais) to it as a 'safe place to consume the drug'. At present, visitors to that village are mainly Thais (or individual foreigners) who go there to smoke opium or to take heroin, and who show no real interest for Akha culture. The same study also pointed out that opium addicts existed before tourism started due to depressing prospects for the future, poverty and a disadvantaged position in Thai society. When tourism started, villagers saw in the sale of opium an easy way of earning cash, and, helped by opium-smoking demonstrations for tourists, addicts proliferated. Drug addiction has led to economic differentiation among the villagers depending on their degree of ability and commitment to work. It has also produced changes in the division of labour within the family unit and the role of women in the community. Change in consumption patterns was also observed in villages visited by trekkers. As new products, such as chocolate, beer and Western-style clothes, were brought from the lowlands for tourists' consumption, many villagers became fond of them. Begging also spread and the initial open hospitality that trekkers enjoyed in the first stages of tourism shifted to 'charged' hospitality (Dearden, 1996; Cohen, 1996).

A major concern about tourism development in the villages in the initial period was the impact that additional cash flow from trekking was going to have on the communities (Dearden, 1996). After years of tourist excursions to the hill tribes, it was noticed that the social structure in the communities started to be more differentiated, whereas before it was relatively egalitarian. Changes in the villagers' occupations also took place, as the new scenario induced people to seek alternative means to earn their livelihoods, relegating their traditional occupations. For instance, massage was usually given by the young women of the family to their older relatives. When trekkers started to visit the village, women found that to offer massage to trekkers was a more profitable and easier activity than the work in the fields. In many cases the trekking tours have substantially increased the income of the rural communities, thus helping to lift the poverty line, while at the same time widening the income distribution within the villages.

Even though domestic tourists constitute the largest group of visitors to the north – for example, 95 per cent of visitors to protected areas in the 1980s were Thais (Brockelman and Dearden, 1990) – studies on the region and trekking in Thailand concentrate mostly on the impacts of foreign trekkers. Furthermore, trekking and other nature-related activities are being heavily promoted among young Thais. As numbers are multiplying fast, it is necessary to study more conscientiously domestic tourist behaviour and to tackle the diverse problems that they cause, while they enjoy the fragile natural and social environments, regardless of the type of activities they pursue. Another aspect that should not be neglected is that of the important role held by guides. When leading their tours, they constitute the link between two cultures and expose the image of the hill-tribe people to the trekkers. Jungle guides usually lack formal training and are misinformed as well as little interested in the local culture, leading to misinterpretation of the villagers' costumes and traditions (Toyota, 1996). Training courses have been organized by the government jointly with educational institutions, but they proved to be inaccessible for the hill-tribe people in terms of costs and requirements to enrol (ie knowledge of English).

Thailand's Tourism Policy

In the past, tourism management was largely developed in a 'top-down' fashion with directives coming from the monarchy or government, but the last 25 years have seen it become increasingly directed from below by private enterprise (Cohen, 1996, p4). The government and its agencies (ie the TAT and the Board of Investment (BOI)) now tend to concentrate on support, promotion and regulation within the sector (Eoseewong and Rabibhadana, 1992, pp3–6).

The history of tourism promotion dates back to 1924 when the Royal Railway of Siam established a Public Relations Section with the purpose of advertising Thailand and assisting foreign tourists travelling in Thailand. The section was later transferred to the Ministry of Commerce and Communications and assigned the additional function of training local guides. In 1936, the Cabinet approved a tourism project aimed at advertising and facilitating, as well as maintaining, tourism sites and accommodation. In 1949, the government advertised Thailand on an international basis for the first time with an international exhibition at the Museum of the Far East. In the same year, the railways' Public Relations Section was transferred to the Prime Minister's office and its name was changed to the Office of Tourism. The first independent national tourism office was established in 1959, along with the Board of Economic Development and the Board of Investment, and today this office is known as the Tourism Authority of Thailand (TAT). To date, tourism policy can be described as foreign-market oriented, focusing mainly on extracting income from foreign tourists. This argument is vividly supported by the fact that approximately two-thirds of TAT's annual budget (approximately 2500 billion baht or US$100 million in 1996) is aimed at marketing operations in the form of maintaining international marketing offices (see Table 5.4). The budget resources going to development and planning have actually declined.

From its inception, TAT has been required to service not only foreign but also Thai tourists. In recent years, increasing attempts have been made to promote domestic demand, but these efforts have mainly focused on reducing the outflow of foreign exchange resulting from Thai citizens travelling abroad. In one of his various speeches on tourism, Prime Minister Sarit encouraged Thai citizens and school children to travel to other Thai provinces to increase knowledge, understanding and love for their country. In the first stage of the revamped 'Thais Tour Thailand' campaign, started in 1994, a TAT official stated that the entity would try to build a new awareness through activities organized in conjunction with educational institutions, and promotion campaigns featuring film stars to attract the interest of teenagers. Better trip planning and booking services were also to be implemented. The TAT's markets promotion director added that 'It is a must to organize activities to educate all students to understand the tourism industry', but remarked that a low budget limited what the TAT could accomplish (Jariyasombat, 1997). The TAT is also seeking ways of encouraging domestic tourists to visit new destinations to preserve overvisited sites. For instance, in eastern Thailand, Thais who live in the region tend to 'flood' only a few famous destinations, such as Ubon Ratchathani, Si Saket and Yasothan, during their long holiday periods, exceeding the sites' carrying capacity and causing major environmental problems due to littering (Jariyasombat, 1997).

The misconception of tourism development in Thailand as being a demand as opposed to a supply issue occurs predominantly at the higher levels of government rather than at the sectoral management level. The TAT has recognized the need to rehabilitate and restore tourism sites, and published a report in 1997 identifying 172 sites that have been seriously degraded and require restoration efforts. The authority commissioned the TDRI to design the monitoring system mentioned in the previous section, but lacks the budget to implement it.

In an effort to maintain the appeal of the country's tourism product, the TAT has recently undertaken a new campaign entitled 'Amazing Thailand,

Table 5.4 *National tourism budget*

Item	Year		
	1994 (%)	1995 (%)	1996 (%)
1 General Administration Department	3.8	3.7	3.9
2 Planning and Development Department	24.1	16.1	13.2
3 Marketing Department	60.6	68.9	71.3
4 Hotel and Tourism Training Institute	0.4	0.5	0.5
5 Tourist Business and Guide Registration Office	0.7	0.8	0.8
6 Tourist police	10.3	10.0	9.9
Total budget	100	100	100
	(2162.65)	(2305.02)	(2545.24)

Source: Tourism Authority of Thailand

1998–1999'. The government hoped that this initiative would help attract a target of 17.18 million foreign tourists over the campaign's two-year period and that these visitors would spend a total of 772 billion baht. Domestic tourism will be encouraged via the campaign and if government projections prove to be correct, approximately 122 million internal trips would be made during the two-year period.

One of the objectives of the Amazing Thailand campaign was to promote the country as a regional centre for shopping. This goal was motivated by disappointing sales over the past few years, as well as by a general slump in the national economy. Other facets of the campaign included the promotion of Thai food, cultural events and ceremonies, package tours, ecotourism, and the promotion of Thailand as a location for international conferences and exhibitions. Marketing strategies ranged from targeting internal and foreign groups through the media to the coordination of relevant agencies (eg travel and airlines) in the distribution of Amazing Thailand publications.

The following section examines the development of the tourism sector from the context of national planning. Discussion will then focus on Thailand's traditional approach to tourism development: sectoral planning.

National Plans

The first and the second National Economic Development Plans (1961–1971) focused primarily on investments in basic infrastructure; emphasis was assigned to hydropower projects, road construction and irrigation works. The third plan (1972–1976) introduced the need for social development, but it was not until the fourth plan (1977–1981) that tourism was mentioned explicitly. During this period, tourism was first and foremost considered as a major means of earning foreign exchange income. The fourth plan targeted an increase in the number of international tourists from 1.4 million (1977) to 2.2 million by 1981. Although increasing the number of domestic tourists was stated in one of the tourism strategies, the need to target domestic tourists was not specified. To achieve their goal, the fourth plan called for the need to prioritize tourism sites, human resource development for the industries and the participation of local communities. In addition to a government budget of 375 million baht, foreign loans (250 million baht) and grants (20 million baht) were to be secured to assist with the preparation of physical planning and the implementation of tourism projects.

The fifth plan (1982–1986) further stressed the need to utilize tourism as a foreign exchange earner. This plan considered the importance of outbound tourists to the national economy and called for measures to reduce the number of Thais touring abroad. It also recognized tourism's impact on the environment for the first time, and emphasized land use and building control as necessary measures to prevent further negative impacts.

The sixth plan, spanning 1987 to 1991, was a period of high and sustained growth in Thailand. The 1987 'Visit Thailand Year' international marketing campaign was launched and highly successful. During this period, the Thai government secured a loan from the Overseas Economic Cooperation Fund of Japan (OECF) of approximately 1375 million baht for the development and promotion of the tourism industry. A total of 69 projects were carried out by eight governmental departments under Phase 1 (1994–1998) with the objective of developing and maintaining tourism sites. The loan marked the first time that the Japanese government provided funds for tourism projects in a developing country.

The seventh plan (1992–1996) was formulated and implemented at the height of Thailand's economic boom. The strategies contained within it reflected the country's economic confidence, as well as public concern for the environment resulting from rising incomes. Two major strategies were proposed: the promotion of Thailand as a regional centre for tourism in Indo-China, and the restoration and conservation of tourism resources. During this period, the government began to study the implementation of phase II of the OECF 1.4 billion baht work plan and the TAT began to publicize its concern regarding the degradation of tourism resources.

In the latest eighth plan, a more integrated and bottom-up approach was adopted for the planning and design process. The plan stressed three major strategies: increased international competitiveness, human resource development and environmental conservation. Measures for each subsector are no longer identified and, as a result, several government agencies have resorted to a sectoral master plan as a guiding policy document. This is important as once a sectoral master plan is approved by the Cabinet, it can be used as a budget reference instead of the national plan.

The ten years spanning Thailand's sixth and seventh National Economic and Social and Development Plans (1986–1996) can be referred to as the 'Golden Age of Thai Tourism'. National earnings from tourism reached almost

50 billion baht in 1990 and increased to almost 200 billion baht by its final year. The rapid growth of tourism income during this period is certainly not the sole result of government policies and its 1987 'Visit Thailand Year' campaign. Granted, the 1987 marketing strategy enhanced the labour-intensive component of the tourism sector, but the overall increase in tourism income can be attributed to a number of factors. First, the world economy was expanding at a high rate and this contributed to greater purchasing power. Second, Thailand had become known worldwide as approaching NIC (newly industrialized country) status, and enormous amounts of foreign investment capital flowed into the country. Expanded trade and foreign investment also brought more visitors to the country, which in turn diffused information about Thailand among travellers with higher purchasing power. Finally, during the sixth plan period, and in particular following the mid-1980s, Thailand's production structure underwent a dramatic transition from being based on an abundance of natural resources to one based on abundant labour supply.

Sectoral Planning

As stated before, tourism development planning was initially undertaken on a sectoral basis, ie conducted by the TAT and aimed mainly at developing tourism resources. The first National Plan on Tourism Development was prepared in 1976 by an international consultant. The various Provincial Tourism Plans that followed can be most accurately described as physical plans. The national plan emphasized developing provinces with high potential for tourism by improving infrastructure and amenities, especially access to tourist sites (the plan reflected the fact that at the time most of Thailand's tourism areas remained in 'virgin' states, and restoration and degradation were not yet a concern). There were no attempts to co-ordinate the physical and marketing components of the national plan, which recommended upgrading the TAT into a ministry with affiliated semi-public enterprises looking after the major tourism development projects.

The 1976 National Plan on Tourism Development emphasized the tourism sector as a major source of foreign exchange earnings. Since then Thailand has been confronting a balance of payments (BOP) deficit for several consecutive years. The problem with applying this approach for addressing BOP deficits is the tourism market's sensitivity to international and local political disturbances. For example, the 1992 political instability caused an economic depression in several major tourist provinces including Songkla (Hat Yai), Chon Buri (Pattaya) and Phuket, which are highly dependent on international tourists.

The majority of provincial tourism plans stressed data compilation as opposed to product development and only a few recommendations have been implemented. A number of reasons can be cited to explain why many of the recommendations have not been put into practice (TDRI, 1993). First, most of the provincial plans were not well publicized. Second, financial support has never been made available according to the plan. Third, the recommendations lack imaginative promotion schemes, concrete incentives and product development methods. Fourth, provincial plans have rarely been updated. Fifth, environmental degradation has diminished the potential of some selected sites (eg forests, waterfalls and lakes). Sixth, provinces may have created their own projects and plans independent of the provincial plans. Finally, local residents have objected to some of the plan's recommendations which intervene in their daily lives or occupations.

Concerning training, since 1961, the TAT has operated training courses for tourist guides in cooperation with universities. By 1995, more than 18,000 guides had been trained and 2272 university students from 21 institutions had received tourist guide certificates. Also, beginning in 1966, the TAT organized courses for restaurants and hotel employees with the purpose of achieving and maintaining a high standard of service. The Hotel and Tourism Institute was established in Chonburi province in 1979 with the assistance of the United Nations Development Programme (UNDP) and the International Labour Organization (ILO). The institute offers one- and two-year advanced training courses for accommodation, catering and travel management (2704 graduates received one-year certificates as of 1995). The institute also provides short-term training courses to international students from Asia and Africa.

Finally, beginning in 1990, the TAT has placed more importance on increasing public awareness about the significance of tourism resources. In this regard, the TAT has undertaken training courses for junior volunteers with the objective of promoting understanding and pride regarding the country's arts and culture, as well as provide training courses for youth leaders on the subject of the conservation and protection of tourism resources.

Future Policy Recommendations

Sustainable tourism requires balanced development in various sectors. The management for the enhancement of positive tourism effects and the mitigation of the negative impacts of tourism must be undertaken by various government agencies, with participation from the private sector. Sharing a common vision and coordination among various government agencies are considered the keys to future success. Greater marketing and physical coordination are also necessary within the TAT. Most importantly, effective tourism development requires strategies that recognize that demand expansion without commensurate investment in the augmentation and conservation of tourism resources is unsustainable. The country must realize that there is no cheap way to earn tourism income and that part of the income must be reinvested in the maintenance of resources. In this regard, funds and technical support for local governments for tourism development are necessary.

When formulating policies and designing action plans, government officials and related agencies should keep in mind that tourism is, above all, a means of improving the welfare of Thai citizens and returning benefits to taxpayers by increasing foreign exchange earnings, local incomes and employment perspectives of the residents in tourist areas. Tourism should be used to provide historical, social and cultural education, and to stimulate the Thai people's interest in nature conservation, while protecting the environment and retaining the country's cultural identity.

Some recommended measures with regard to the restoration and conservation of tourism resources are, for example, the demarcation of ecologically fragile areas in major tourist towns and their proclamation as environmentally protected areas according to the 1992 Environment Act (Articles 44 and 45); the establishment of a 'Nature Fund' to restore physical, historical and cultural tourism resources, supported by the central government and local tourism income; and campaigns to raise public awareness regarding the need to protect tourism resources.

Considering that one of the most common impacts of domestic tourists is littering, ecologically sound waste-disposal procedures – such as waste separation in major tourist towns, the recycling of beverage and food containers encouraged by fiscal incentives, and tax surcharges added on non-recyclable containers – should be undertaken. The management of conservation areas for tourism could be improved by establishing interagency guidelines with relevant agencies for promoting the use of pilot projects to minimize negative environmental impacts, design training programmes for tour guides, implement safety measures, control the number of tourists visiting a site, etc. Furthermore, the guidelines should ensure that new tourism sites are not publicized until the supporting infrastructure and the local authorities are ready to receive tourists. To enable continuous evaluation of environmental impacts and the efficiency of financial resources for tourism projects, tourism resource monitoring and information systems[4] could be set up.

The information made available to Thai tourists is not always accurate or useful. Efforts should be directed to provide information to their interest, such as destinations suitable for families and ways of combining tourism with merit-making activities, sports and health centres. With regard to the improvement of facilities (public or picnic parks, rest rooms and car parks) for domestic tourists, especial attention should be given to border towns (eg Mae Sod, Mae Sai, Nong Khai, Mukdahan, etc), which are the major tourism sites for domestic visitors. Alternatively, the TAT could provide planning or financial support to local municipalities for improving existing public parks and establishing new ones along major rivers (such as in Tak province) and important beaches.

In order to promote cultural and national identities, the national government should give its support to the Department of Fine Arts to establish additional Cultural Museums which provide historical information, and make their displays more interesting and accessible to everyone. Children and high-school students could be encouraged to appreciate and learn about the cultural diversity of Thailand and its different ethnic groups through educational programmes at their schools. Likewise, the curricula of tourism-related degrees at university level should include subjects that will form professionals who are aware of the implications that 'cultural' tourism may have on local communities. Government agencies should also be encouraged to arrange the designs of their provincial offices according to regional cultural features. The most important methods to improve the country's image are to control the growing sex industry by eliminating tours and publications on sex services in Thailand and to provide information about the AIDS problem in the country.

Conclusion

The Thai government's misconception that tourism development should be addressed through the implementation of strategies that increase demand, as opposed to maintaining the supply and integrity of tourism locations and attractions, was mentioned several times. One result of this approach is that a limited number of studies have been undertaken with respect to the interests, characteristics and expenditures of Thai outbound and domestic tourists. The Asian economic crisis will serve to apply further pressure on the tourism industry to fulfil its role as a valuable foreign exchange earner. Clearly, the long-term sustainability of the industry is dependent on the ability of tourist sites to absorb large numbers of international and domestic visitors. The strain on these sites and infrastructure is already being experienced in several areas such as the Similans and Phi Phi. It is imperative that the Thai tourism authorities recall that the success of tourism campaigns like Thais Tour Thailand and Amazing Thailand must be discounted to reflect the extra burden that increased demand can place on the service sector, physical infrastructure and the environment. Otherwise, the long-term sustainability of tourism as an income earner will be threatened and Thai citizens will be left with crumbling buildings, a degraded environment and inadequate infrastructure, not to mention irreplaceable cultural attractions.

The natural environment essentially serves the tourism sector as it does other sectors of the economy; it acts as both an input for tourism's development as well as a sink into which its output must be absorbed. Its continued development requires a pristine and healthy environment, while at the same time its very development potentially can undermine this survival by encouraging the degradation of the environment. In the case of Thailand, mismanagement and short-sightedness have rendered this potential a reality and many tourist sites have now been jeopardized as a result.

The two most common motivations for domestic tourists for travel are nature-related activities and visits to historical sites. Thais constitute the largest group of visitors to national parks and their lack of awareness concerning environmental problems results in serious damage to the local ecosystems. Although the Tourism Authority of Thailand has recognized the imperative need for campaigns to educate Thai people in ecologically-sound behaviour, the feasibility to implement effective programmes has been affected usually by the reduced budget allocated for those purposes. In regard to heritage sites, the problem is very similar. The TAT has acknowledged the necessity to restore a great number of sites, but good intentions have been overshadowed by insufficient capital to carry out the projects. In the meantime, in 1996 the Marketing Department received over two-thirds of the national tourism budget.

The cultural implications of domestic tourism have been largely underestimated or unobserved. The influence that they might have when remote communities are visited, their perception and attitude, and the strain they put on the cultural life of ethnic minorities, are all questions that should be raised in the promotion of ecotourism among Thais.

In reviewing its tourism policies, the Thai government must also remain mindful of the growing importance of the domestic tourism sector. An alteration to past tourism management strategies, which tended to focus almost exclusively on international visitors, may be in order. The spending habits, tastes, reliability and cultural traits of domestic tourists tend to differ from those of foreign visitors. Policies that recognize the variance in needs and demands are required. Failure to take these changing characteristics into account will result in ineffective and outdated strategies that are incapable of providing Thai society with the greatest possible benefits from the industry.

The Thai government has faced a dilemma. On the one hand, the devaluation of the baht may enhance Thailand's international tourist appeal and encourage more tourists to visit the country, thereby assisting the nation to recover from its present difficulties. On the other hand, the economic downturn obviously has had an impact on middle-class Thais who had previously been engaging in tourist activities. If the government decides to continue its past approach to tourism development (ie to increase demand through marketing and promotion strategies), the increase in tourists, combined with the existing carrying capacities of the environment, service sector and infrastructure will be likely to lead to irreparable environmental damage and socio-economic costs. Alternatively, the current economic climate may assist in persuading the government that the long-term viability (and economic returns) of the tourism industry demands that the existing constraints should be recognized and respected. The latter scenario is beneficial to both international and domestic visitors as well as to local populations, and may eventually contribute to the longer term sustainability of the tourism industry in Thailand.

Notes

1 The authors are staff of the Natural Resources and Environment Programme, Thailand Development Research Institute. They wish to thank Mariana Mozdzer of UNRISD for her crucial editorial and conceptual input into this paper.

2 TDRI reports and surveys, as well as TAT annual statistics, are the source of the majority of figures, data and statistics quoted in this chapter. Two of the often consulted reports (TDRI, 1993 and TDRI, 1997b) contain information that is related to this study and may be of interest to those seeking further insight into Thailand's tourism sector.

3 In attempting to make such identifications, a TDRI 1993 study applied multinomial LOGIT estimation techniques to survey data in modelling tourist preferences.

4 The large degree of environmental degradation induced by tourism prompted the TDRI to design a monitoring system (based on the needs identified by the TAT) to guide the sector's management. This system comprises two main parts, the first of which is computer-based interactive software called TOURINFO from which tourism information could be readily obtained at the provincial and site-specific levels. The second part is a non-computer-based information and monitoring system. The details contained in the databases would be used to construct a computer-based ranking of each site's relative importance, level of degradation and coinciding need for restoration. Based on this ranking, the government could then prioritize its restoration efforts and resource allocations according to the degree of urgency perceived for each particular site. In addition to this information system, the TDRI also recommended that the TAT establish a tourism resource and environmental management committee, as well as a tourism resource monitoring network that links the government with local conservation groups. Other recommended measures included encouraging the local media to delegate more coverage to the monitoring of tourism resources and the establishment of a telephone hotline that would provide a convenient link between conservation groups in the TAT network and the TAT itself.

References

Bangkok Business (1997) 'Tourism', 11 October
Bangkok Post – Horizons (1996) 'Samui prepares for green future', 5 December
Bangkok Post (1997) 10 May

Brockelman, W and P Dearden (1990) 'The role of nature trekking in conservation: A case study in Thailand', *Environmental Conservation*, vol 17, no 2, summer, Switzerland

Cacnio, P (1995) 'Trends in tourism to Thailand and ASEAN', *Bangkok Bank Monthly Review*, vol 36, no 2, 9 February

Cacnio, P (1996) 'Travel and tourism: In the road to a vigorous expansion', *Bangkok Bank Monthly Review*, vol 37, no 8, 19 August

Cohen, Erik (1996) *Thai Tourism*, White Lotus Press, Bangkok

Dearden, P (1996) 'Trekking in northern Thailand: Impact distribution and evolution over time' in M Parnwell (ed), *Uneven Development in Thailand*, Avebury, Hants, pp204–224

Donavanik, P (1993) 'Tourism in the north', *Bangkok Bank Monthly Review*, vol 34, 16 December

Eoseewong, N and M R Akin Rabibhadana (1992) 'Social and cultural impact from tourism: Case of Bun Bang-Fai', in *A Review Report on Tourism for the Master Plan*, TDRI, Bangkok

Jansen, P (1996) 'Thailand – Shopping till they drop', *Asia One*, Far East Trade Press Ltd, Singapore, 1 May

Jariyasombat, P (1997) 'TAT wants to expand domestic horizons', *Bangkok Post*, 19 July

Kanywerayotin, S (1987) 'King Rama VII paved way for tourism in Hua Hin, Petchaburi', *Bangkok Post*, 2 April, p32

Meyer, M W (1988) *Beyond the Mask*, Breitenbach, Saarbrucken

Muqbil, I (1996) 'Economic worries cause more Thais to stay at home', *Bangkok Post*, 20 August

Picard, Michael (1993) 'Cultural tourism in Bali: National integration and regional differentation' in Michael Hitchcock, Victor T King and Michael J G Parnwell (eds), *Tourism in South-East Asia*, Routledge

Tahiar, C (1972) 'The history of TOT', *Bangkok Post Industrial Review*, 27

TAT (Tourism Authority of Thailand) (1996) *Statistical Report 1996*, TAT, Bangkok

TDRI (Thailand Development Research Institute) (1993) *Tourism Master Plan: A Review* (in Thai), prepared for the Tourism Authority of Thailand (TAT), TDRI, Bangkok

TDRI (1995) *Tourism Monitoring System for Thailand*, prepared for the Tourism Authority of Thailand

TDRI (1997a) *Tourism Master Plan* (in Thai), prepared for the Tourism Authority of Thailand, Bangkok

TDRI (1997b) *Thailand Tourism: Vision 2012*, prepared for the Tourism Authority of Thailand, TDRI, Bangkok

Toyota, M (1996) 'The effects of tourism development on an Akha community: A Chiang Rai village case study' in M Parnwell (ed), *Uneven Development in Thailand*, Avebury, Hants, pp 226–241

Wood, Robert E (1980) 'International tourism and cultural change in Southeast Asia', *Economic Development and Cultural Change*, vol 28, no 31, pp561–81

WTO (World Tourism Organization) (1993) *Recommendations on Tourism Statistics*, Madrid

Chapter 6

South Africa's Domestic Tourism Sector: Promises and Problems

Eddie Koch and Peter John Massyn

Introduction

Since the election of a non-racist government in South Africa in 1994, the country has experienced a major growth in its tourism industry. It has, in fact, recently been portrayed as one of the world's fastest-growing tourist destinations (*The Economist*, 20 May 1995).

The country's highly visible role as a symbol of peaceful transition to democracy with the potential to create multi-ethnic harmony – the rainbow nation – has acted as a powerful generic marketing tool and magnet for large numbers of in-bound tourists. The result is that national and provincial governments have all become increasingly aware of the potential for tourism to contribute to economic growth and social reconstruction in the country. The central government has prepared a White Paper which explicitly recognizes the positive role that tourism can play in terms of promoting a peaceful and relatively prosperous transition from apartheid to democracy.

At the same time, there are indications of large-scale growth in the tourism sector of the economy. This is driven by increased demand, primarily from foreign tourism, and also by supply-side interventions on the part of local and international investors. The state has adopted a number of investment-harnessing programmes that are designed to attract foreign and local capital into parts of the country that, it is argued, have the natural and social resources to become internationally competitive tourism destinations. These programmes, known as spatial development initiatives (SDIs), form a key part of the South African government's macro-economic framework for economic growth, known as Growth Employment and Reconstruction (GEAR). They will be elaborated on later in this chapter.

A large number of foreign hotel chains today are operating in the major cities and in other parts of the country. While the hotel sector of the tourism industry was primarily locally owned and operated in the apartheid era, the lights of the Hyatt, Hilton, Best Western, Holiday Inn, Golden Tulip and other international brand names now light up the skyline of the country's major cities.

The tourism sector has also become a major site for investment by black empowerment consortiums that have mushroomed since the 1994 elections. Many of these are black-owned investment companies that are able to mobilize worker pension funds and other long-term savings to capitalize ventures in key sectors of the economy. They frequently also go into partnership with foreign companies to bid for investment opportunities as South Africa's economy opens up under the neo-liberal policies being promoted by GEAR. For example, the Congress of South African Trade Unions (COSATU), South Africa's biggest labour federation, has recently formed an investment company called Kipano ke Matla (Unity is Strength). The South African National Civic Organization (SANCO), a close ally of the African National Congress during the struggle against apartheid, has also formed an investment company. Both these organizations are now bidding against each other, each with foreign partners, to buy a chain of state-owned leisure resorts from a parastatal called Aventura, which is privatizing in terms of the government's macro-economic policies. The intense interest by organizations that once encouraged a boycott of South African tourism in order to weaken the apartheid state in direct investment in tourism plant is a barometer of the new-found fascination with tourism as a mechanism for social and economic development in the country. The same popular opinion is reflected in a wave of enthusiasm by rural people, previously excluded from the mainstream of the apartheid economy, in exploiting tourism as a form of business and entrepreneurship.

Domestic Tourism in South Africa

Whereas foreign tourism in South Africa has been growing at an increasing rate since the introduction of political reform and is the driving force behind the overall growth in tourism, relatively little is known about the country's domestic tourism sector. This is in line with research patterns in other countries with emerging domestic tourism markets.

Research carried out in the past has tended to focus on researching the attitudes of foreign tourists. This began to change in 1994 when the South African Tourism Board (SATOUR) conducted a survey among 2000 households of all the races inside South Africa, including questions pertaining to holiday and business travel (Kessel Feinstein Consulting, 1996, p9). Some of the more interesting findings of the first SATOUR survey were:

- South Africans generally favour a growing tourism industry as a means for generating jobs and economic growth.
- Some 8 million South Africans take at least one holiday (defined as being for one or more nights away from home) a year.
- The average duration of the holiday is seven days, shorter by one day than it was in 1992.
- The most popular provincial destinations are KwaZulu-Natal (25 per cent of respondents), Gauteng (16 per cent) and Western Cape (13 per cent).
- The average spent per trip is R1020 (about US$200) made up in the following ways: accommodation 25.4 per cent; food 21.4 per cent; transport 25.8 per cent; 'spending money' 27.4 per cent.
- An estimated 3 per cent of the population takes at least one business trip a year, spending on average R1073 (about US$215) per trip.
- Some 63 per cent of business trips are by car and 23 per cent by plane (ibid p9–10).

More detailed analysis of the domestic market is, however, a complex task since domestic movements are difficult to monitor and consist largely of day-trippers and people visiting friends and relatives.

The only really reliable way of measuring domestic tourism is through a large-scale household survey (the SATOUR survey has been criticized for being based on a relatively small sample of 2000 people).

However, it is clear that the domestic tourism market in South Africa – traditionally dominated by the white population with the greatest levels of wealth, mobility and access to amenities – has recently witnessed a dramatic change in the composition and nature of domestic tourism which is attributable to the ending of apartheid and an increase in prosperity among 'previously disadvantaged' social groups.

Table 6.1 summarizes the findings of a report released by Durban Metropolitan Council's Urban Strategy Department (*The Mercury*, 13 December 1996) which projects a 261 per cent increase in urban black South African tourists from 1986 to the year 2000 and a 473 per cent increase in rural black tourists over the same period. Although these figures are derived from a very low base, they reflect the rapidly changing nature of the domestic holiday market.

The Land Agricultural Policy Centre (LAPC) reported the following details on the subject:

> *The emergent class of tourists tend to have lower spending power and preferences towards gregarious types of entertainment experiences. They also consist of a higher proportion of day-trippers and VFRs (visiting friends and relatives). Existing tourism facilities are not geared to meet this demand, hence long-term investment is required. This could lead potentially to the creation of new employment opportunities in both the construction and operation of new facilities catering for this market'* (LAPC, 1997).

Table 6.1 *Composition and projected growth of the domestic holiday market*

Racial Breakdown	1990 (%)	2000 (%)	Total Growth 1986–2000 (%)
Whites	45	28	22
Indians	4	4	105
Coloured	10	10	143
Urban blacks	28	38	261
Rural blacks	12	20	473
Total number	6,552,000	12,014,000	83

Source: The Mercury, 13 December 1996, based on a report released by the City Council's Urban Strategy Department

More recent research confirms indications that the expected growth in the domestic tourism sector is not as extensive as was first predicted in the wake of the 1994 elections. The growth potential of domestic tourism is largely dependent on conditions in the national economy where growth is predicted at between 2 per cent and 3 per cent over the next decade.

According to some sources, the estimated 1995 earnings from tourism amounted to some R16 billion (about US$3.2 billion). By the year 2000, tourism could amount to R42 billion (about US$8.4 billion), representing 6 per cent of GDP. This prediction is based on an expectation that more than 70 per cent of income will derive from foreign tourism, assuming an average growth of 10 per cent in overseas arrivals between 1996 and 2000. These figures, if correct, indicate that the domestic sector will experience relatively stagnant growth compared to the foreign sector, despite all the problems associated with foreign tourism (G Muller Associates, 1998, Ch 2).

However, within this pattern it is clear that in the domestic sector there will be a significant growth in demand for appropriate forms of tourism plans from previously disadvantaged groups among the black, 'coloured' (mixed race) and Indian populations. There appears to be a spontaneous growth of accommodation facilities to cater for these segments of the domestic market. The plans by COSATU to purchase and convert the state-run Aventura resorts into working-class recreation and leisure destinations are also indicative of this demand. However, in general, there is little evidence of a coherent drive from the country's main tourism agencies to meet this demand.

Provincial Distribution of Domestic Tourists

Table 6.2 provides a breakdown of the percentage of domestic tourists visiting each province relative to their respective share of the total South African population. The major domestic holiday tourist destinations are KwaZulu-Natal, the Western Cape and Gauteng. However, Gauteng receives a small proportion of domestic tourists relative to its population size.

Table 6.2 *Provincial market breakdown (percentage)*

Province	% of all trips	% of total South African population
KwaZulu-Natal	24.6	20.6
Gauteng	16.0	21.5
Western Cape	12.9	10.3
North West	10.1	7.8
Eastern Cape	9.3	14.3
Northern Province	8.9	10.1
Mpumalanga	7.6	7.2
Orange Free State	6.6	7.2
Northern Cape	2.0	1.0

Source: SATOUR, 1995b

Domestic Tourist Motivations

Figure 6.1 provides a breakdown of the main domestic tourism purposes in 1994. Holidaymakers and VFRs each accounted for approximately two-fifths of the market, while business travel accounted for only 5 per cent.

The primary purpose of travel among Living Standards Super Group (LSSG) A respondents was holiday, whereas in LSSG B and LSSG C it was VFR.[1] This is not surprising given the greater spending power of the former group.

These figures suggest the following strategic indications:

- There is a relatively small conference and business segment in the domestic sector.
- Many of the emerging tourists prefer to visit friends and relatives, thus enhancing the informal sector but limiting demand in the formal sector of the tourism industry.
- The traditional and privileged segment of the domestic tourism market, which has probably been deracialized, retains the greatest spending power.

Expenditure Patterns

Table 6.3 provides a breakdown of the way in which domestic holiday expenditure is constituted according to LSSG. Domestic tourism expenditure is fairly evenly dispersed between accommodation, food, transport and spending money. Tourists from LSSG A spend a higher proportion of their total expenditure on accommodation than those from lower income groups. The highest spending category for LSSG B and C is transport, indicating a smaller expenditure on other goods, rather than absolute higher levels on transport. The projected grand

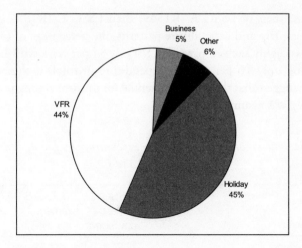

Figure 6.1 *The purpose of travel for domestic tourists*

Source: SATOUR 1996a, 1996b
Note: The 5 per cent of domestic tourists recorded as business travellers translates into a sample size of 20. Since this is too small to facilitate reliable quantitative evaluation of the employment generated through domestic tourism, it is restricted to the domestic holiday tourism market (which includes VFRs).

Table 6.3 *Breakdown of spending by LSSG for domestic tourism market (at 1997 prices)*

	LSSG A (%)	LSSG B (%)	LSSG C (%)	Total (%)	Average total per trip (1997 Rand)	Projected grand total (1997 rand)
Accommodation	26	11	16	25	R299	R4.4m
Food	21	17	24	21	R252	R3.7m
Transport	26	44	36	26	R304	R4.4m
Spending money	27	28	24	27	R324	R4.9m
Total	100	100	100	100	R1178	R17.6m

Note: 1) 1994 figures have been adjusted to allow for inflation to represent equivalent 1997 spending. 2) The projected grand total is calculated on the basis of the total number of trips recorded in the survey
Source: Calculated from SATOUR/Markinor Domestic Tourism Survey, 1995b

total provides an estimation of the economic contribution to the key tourism sectors generated by domestic tourism.

Table 6.4 provides a breakdown of the proportion of domestic tourism trips made by LSSG A, B and C. It is evident that a far higher proportion of people from LSSG A (established achievers) make domestic holiday trips than LSSG C (less privileged) and that the average expenditure per trip is also far higher for members of LSSG A (R1549) than LSSG C (R188). As a consequence of these trip and expenditure patterns, the percentage of total tourism expenditure is highly skewed towards LSSG A, 84 per cent, with LSSG B and C constituting only 16 per cent of expenditure in total. If these figures are reliable, they suggest that there is less potential for tourism among poorer groups than generally was assumed.[2]

Table 6.4 *Breakdown of domestic tourism expenditure by Living Standard Super Groups A, B and C*

	LSSG C (less privileged)	LSSG B (emergent market)	LSSG A (established achiever)
% of SA population	25%	41.5%	33.4%
% of all domestic tourist trips	9.7%	34%	56.3%
Average expenditure per tourist per trip	R188	R420	R1549
Average spending per person per annum	R36	R172	R1,309
Total expenditure (million)	R0.3m	R2.5m	R15.1m
Percentage of total tourism expenditure	2%	14%	84%

Source: Calculated from Markinor and SATOUR 1995a

Total Economic Contribution of Tourism in South Africa

Table 6.5 provides an estimation of the contribution of tourism to GDP in South Africa from 1992 to 1995 and predicts its contribution in 2000. In 1995, tourism was estimated to contribute around R 22.8 billion, constituting 4.9 per cent of GDP. The value of tourism has increased significantly in recent years and it is estimated that tourism's contribution to GDP could be close to 7 per cent by the year 2000.

Table 6.5 *Estimated economic contribution of South Africa's tourism industry*

	1992 (R bn)	1993 (R bn)	1994 (R bn)	1995 (R bn)	2000 (R bn)
Foreign tourism	4.4	5.4	6.9	8.9	29.7
Domestic tourism	8.4	10.3	12.4	13.9	22.8
Estimated total	12.8	15.7	19.3	22.8	52.5
Ratio of GDP	3.75%	4.09%	4.45%	4.9%	7%

Notes: 1) Estimates assume an inflation at an average of 7.5 per cent per annum between 1995–2000 and a growth rate in real terms of 2.5 per cent per annum (Kessel Feinstein Consulting, 1996). 2) Domestic tourism figures are based on results of the domestic household survey (SATOUR, 1995b)
Source: Calculated from SATOUR, 1996a, South African Reserve Bank, Kessel Feinstein (1996)

The figures quoted in the above table are actually an underestimation because they do not include capital expenditure in the tourism sector. According to the World Travel and Tourism Council (WTTC) (1996), tourism investment amounts to 21 per cent of the total contribution of tourism to the global GDP.

The WTTC estimated that tourism contributed 9.8 per cent of GDP for the Middle East/Africa in 1996. After subtraction of an assumed investment of 21 per cent, we estimate that in the Middle East/Africa region tourism (excluding capital expenditure) contributed 7.8 per cent to GDP. If we assume this average to be an achievable figure, this means that there is still a significant growth potential for the South African tourism industry. This potential is further highlighted by the fact that at a global level tourism ranks as the top foreign exchange earner, whereas in South Africa it is ranked fourth (SATOUR, 1996a).

The figures indicate that domestic tourism currently contributes more extensively to the national economy than does foreign tourism (R13.9 billion vs R8.9 billion in 1995) but that the ratio will change dramatically by the year 2000 (R22.8 billion vs R29.7 billion) despite the injection of new 'emerging' tourism classes into the domestic tourism market.

Economic Contribution of Domestic Holiday Tourism to South Africa

Based on the findings of the 1994 Domestic Tourism Survey, SATOUR estimated that some 17.3 million domestic holiday trips were undertaken in 1994, generating just over SAR19.5 billion in domestic expenditure (adjusted to 1997 price levels). It has been suggested that this figure is exaggerated. However, actual figures for 1997 are likely to be greater than this given that domestic tourism is perceived to be increasing.[3]

Table 6.6 demonstrates the proportional economic contribution of tourism to each province relative to the number of trips. Interestingly, both KwaZulu-Natal and the Western Cape receive a higher percentage of total expenditure – 32 per cent and 24 per cent respectively – than their share of trips would suggest. This is largely due to the socio-economic characteristics of tourists visiting these provinces.

The majority of the Western Cape's and KwaZulu-Natal's source markets come from LSSG A. The majority of Gauteng's source market comes from LSSG B and C and its percentage share of total expenditure is therefore smaller (6 per cent) than its percentage share of trips (16 per cent).

The figures shown in Table 6.6 suggest that the most popular provinces – KwaZulu Natal and Western Cape – are favoured by tourists from the more privileged classes. Gauteng province clearly displays a need to cater for travellers from the less privileged groups, notably the working classes who live in the industrial areas of this province.

Table 6.6 *Provincial market and LSSG breakdown (percentage)*

Province	% of all trips	% of total domestic tourism expenditure	LSSG A	LSSG B	LSSG C
KwaZulu-Natal	24.6	32.0	61.5	28.5	10.0
Gauteng	16.0	6.0	39.9	45.5	14.6
Western Cape	12.9	24.2	88.6	8.8	2.6
North West	10.1	6.7	38.7	47.0	14.3
Eastern Cape	9.3	9.7	53.9	36.5	9.6
Northern Province	8.9	5.0	40.7	48.6	10.6
Mpumalanga	7.6	6.4	54.8	31.3	13.9
Free State	6.6	5.0	61.5	35.5	3.0
Northern Cape	2.0	2.3	62.1	35.9	2.0

Source: Markinor and SATOUR, 1995a

Present Government Policies

The potential of tourism to play a major role in the reconstruction of South Africa and in the generation of employment is widely recognized. This has not always been the case; in the mid-1980s, tourism was perceived to be of minor economic importance. It was not officially recognized as a separate industry and was given scant attention by the government.

General Awareness of Tourism Potential in Southern Africa

The development of tourism – especially international tourism – has been identified as a priority by governments in the region as well as by the Southern Africa Development Community (SADC).

Key actors, including trade unions, grass-roots organizations, the private sector and NGOs, have taken on board the potential of tourism as a job creator, an earner of foreign exchange and a way of diversifying economies and reducing reliance on primary exports.

Beyond these benefits, many within the region also realize the role that tourism can play in reconstruction and development at the level of people and communities, as well as furthering regional cooperation and integration. Thus the SADC notes that: 'Tourism has the potential to become one of Southern Africa's largest industries.'

Action for Southern Africa (ACTSA) reported as follows:

Tourism also offers great scope for increased regional integration in Southern Africa. SADC has made a great deal of progress towards closer regional co-operation since it was set up in 1992. Both the rate of progress and future potential of the SADC have been enhanced by the joining of two new members with relatively strong economies and tourist industries – South Africa joined in 1994 and Mauritius joined in 1995 (ACTSA, 1997).

A SADC Tourism Protocol is being finalized. In August 1995 a new regionwide body was set up to help increase Southern Africa's share of the international tourism market – the Regional Tourism Organization of Southern Africa (RETOSA). RETOSA will have a direct role in policy-making and the marketing of the region.

South Africa's White Paper on Tourism

The new government of South Africa produced a White Paper on Tourism in July 1996. It notes: 'Tourism, perhaps more than any other sector, has the potential to achieve the objectives of the Reconstruction and Development Programme (RDP) of the new government' (DEAT, 1996, p4). 'Tourism development in South Africa has largely been a missed opportunity. Had its history been different, South Africa would probably have been one of the most visited places in the world' (ibid, p4). The paper points out that the South African tourism industry in the past has been protected from foreign competition, its domestic sector restricted to the needs of a small and homogeneous privileged class and its foreign sector limited by the pariah status of the apartheid state.

The paper goes on to suggest a number of ways in which this can be corrected. It proposes 'responsible tourism' as the guiding concept for tourism development and defines it in the following way:

> *Responsible tourism implies a pro-active approach by tourism industry partners to develop, market and manage the tourism industry in a responsible manner, so as to create a competitive advantage. Responsible tourism implies tourism industry responsibility to the* environment. . . *It also means responsibility of government and business to involve the local communities that are in close proximity to the tourism plant and attractions through the development of meaningful economic linkages. It implies the responsibility to respect, invest in and develop local cultures and to protect them from over-commercialisation and over-exploitation* (ibid, 19, emphasis original).

The paper argues that tourism, if managed in the correct way, brings development to rural areas and creates opportunities for previously neglected groups to enter the formal economy as new entrepreneurs. It also notes that tourism contributes to local livelihoods because, unlike extractive industries based on primary products, tourism is a 'final good'. Value is added inside the country and this can generate benefits locally, unlike industries based on primary exports which benefit foreign countries.

It notes that for tourism to ameliorate rather than contribute to environmental degradation it needs to make mandatory integrated environmental management procedures, encourage social and environmental audits, promote 'sustainable and responsible' consumption of water and energy in tourism plans, support mandatory environmental management practices in ecologically sensitive areas such as the coastal zone and wetlands, and ensure that the tourism plan does not deprive communities of access to coastal resources needed for their livelihoods.

The paper says that the government is committed to managing and conserving the cultural resources of South Africa:

> *The cultural environment includes much more than museums and unique archaeological sites. It also includes mission settlements, sites of slave occupation, urban space used for ritual purposes, rock art sites, rock formations and natural landscapes which have national and international cultural significance.*

In order for the tourism sector to contribute to the preservation of this heritage, the paper proposes the following guidelines:

- Cultural resources be managed to the 'negotiated benefit' of all interested parties within communities.
- Access to the management of cultural resources should be as broad as possible within specific communities.
- Planning for tourism development should include effective protection for, and sustainable utilization of, cultural resources (ibid, pp37–38).

The paper makes a strong plea for the South African government to work collaboratively with other countries in Southern Africa.

The paper notes simply that the government should 'stimulate the domestic tourism sector'. However, it pays no special analytical attention to domestic tourism and tends to emphasize the foreign sector as a source of growth.

GEAR and Spatial Development Initiatives

In addition to the White Paper, the national Departments of Trade and Industry, and Transport have initiated a number of spatial development initiatives (SDIs) in various parts of the country as part of the government's effort to implement its economic growth programme:

- To generate economic growth by making maximum use of the inherent but underutilized potential of the area. The key is for governments to maximize private sector involvement and to create an attractive and stable climate for investors to operate in.
- To maximize job creation by ensuring that the new industries being stimulated are competitive and have a long-term future in the region.
- To broaden ownership patterns in the regional economy.
- To ensure cooperation between all levels of governments in Southern Africa whose countries straddle the development corridors (DTI/DOT, 1998).

A number of SDIs are encouraging linkages between tourism and other sectors, including agriculture, particularly in the areas of services, cultural tourism, agriculture, building and construction, light manufacturing and crafts production. They aim to create clusters of economic activity around lead investment projects that will ignite regional economic growth in these formerly depressed areas.

Most of the SDIs have been planned on the basis of rigorous feasibility studies to assess new tourism development prospects in the area concerned. In general, they are based on a prediction that foreign demand for new tourism destinations will grow at an average of 10 per cent per annum, while growth in domestic tourism demand will shadow the relatively sluggish 3 per cent growth rate of the national economy.

Thus these tourism growth strategies and the specific tourism projects they are promoting tend to be geared towards foreign tourists. However, as we shall see later, many of these programmes are encouraging innovative forms of involvement by resident groups and local cultural workers in the new tourism projects.

World Heritage Sites

The Ministry of Environment Affairs and Tourism is also engaged in a process whereby applications are being made for a number of tourism and cultural destinations to be registered as world heritage sites in terms of the Convention Concerning the Protection of the World's Cultural and Natural Heritage.

Topping the list of candidates for World Heritage status since South Africa became the 150th member of the convention in October are Robben Island, the Greater St Lucia Wetland Park, Table Mountain and the Kruger National Park.

The strategy being followed by the Department of Environment Affairs and Tourism with regard to World Heritage Sites recognizes that the domestic and foreign tourism sectors will be enhanced in areas where World Heritage Sites exist as magnets for travellers. However, it appears that, as with the spatial development initiative strategy, the emphasis as far as tourism promotion is concerned is on the ability to attract foreign tourism.

Provincial Tourism Policies

In addition to the above, all the provincial governments in the country have adopted policies that are designed to encourage domestic and foreign tourism. In 1995, for example, the province of KwaZulu-Natal drafted a Strategic Framework for the Implementation of the Tourism Policy of KZN. This document lists a number of steps required to broaden the base of the province's tourism industry. These include: an evaluation of the province's tourism asset base, the creation of tourist development and marketing areas, identification of potential tourism nodes for development, and appropriate forms of tourism at each node.

But there appears to be little awareness of the need to clearly disaggregate the assessment of tourism demand into local and foreign segments and to plan accordingly. Policy documents produced by various agencies responsible for tourism planning in the province vary in terms of the emphasis they place on domestic or foreign tourism. The KZN Economic and Development Strategy places an emphasis on lower income groups, whereas officials in the provincial government continue to rely on international and high-income tourism as the main drivers of growth in this sector.

Culture and the Tourism Industry

Finally, the national Department of Arts, Culture, Science and Technology (DACST) has initiated a programme to link cultural activity to the tourism projects being developed in some of the spatial development initiatives.

A report, prepared by Mafisa (an agency dedicated to research and planning for community based tourism projects in southern Africa) for the Department of Arts, Culture, Science and Technology argues that the area surrounding tourism nodes in the SDI region of KwaZulu-Natal is extremely rich in cultural activities. These range from history, heritage, music, dance and craft manufacture to the rituals and traditions that are practised during the everyday lives of the region's residents. The report states:

> *If carefully planned the cultural resources embedded in the villages and towns of the area, could be used to add extra value to the tourism products being planned by the SDI – and at the same time provide residents with new business and development opportunities* (DACST, 1997).

As a result, the DACST has asked the national Cabinet to approve plans for the department to assist in the creation of a number of cultural projects that will improve the potential performance of the tourism sector in the region and, at the same time, enhance local cultural vitality.

As with the SDIs, the emphasis in this policy document is again on the potential for demand from the foreign sector, although there is a heavy focus on the potential for reconciliation and peace to be promoted by the cultural activities that can be stimulated by foreign demand. This theme will be elaborated later in the discussion.

Links with Growth Strategy and other Sectors of the Economy

A study for South Africa's Department of Labour, published by the Land and Agriculture Policy Centre, notes that the tourism industry is interlinked in a complex of ways with various business segments. The report analyses the breakdown of expenditure of foreign and domestic tourism in other sectors and demonstrates that the sectors that derive the most benefits from tourism are accommodation and transport, followed by restaurants and food retail outlets, and curios. All these are labour-intensive sectors, which suggests that it is in these sectors that the greatest tourism-related employment creation will occur.

The White Paper on tourism issued in June 1996 also recognizes the importance of linking tourism planning to other sectors of the economy:

> *Tourism can also play a strategic role in dynamising other sectors of the economy – the agricultural sector that feeds the tourism industry (driving the demand for new agricultural products and services such as organic agriculture and farm tourism); tourism also creates linkages with the manufacturing sectors (the supply of furniture and fittings, construction, linens, pots, pans, sun cream etc.) as well as crafts (wood-working, curios, fine art). Perhaps the most undeveloped economic link in the tourism industry in South Africa is the services sector (health services, entertainment, health and beauty, banking and insurance).*

We have also seen that the government's spatial development initiatives are designed specifically to promote these kinds of linkages. Official statistics do not, in general, distinguish between the impacts of the domestic and foreign sectors of the tourism industry on these linkages. Thus it is not possible from official statistics to disaggregate the relative importance of domestic over foreign tourism in this regard.

Impacts on Local Livelihoods

It is estimated that, in South Africa as a whole, 810,000 people are directly or indirectly employed in tourism, representing just over one in 20 economically

Table 6.7 *Tourism's contribution to employment, 1994*

Industrial sector	No of workers	% of total economically active
Manufactured goods	1,399,513	9.8
Tourism	810,000	5.6
Agriculture	982,616	6.9
Mining	613,584	4.3

Note: LAPC's estimate based on WTTC, CSS and SALDRU data
Source: CSS, SALDRU and WTTC

active people, including both formal and informal sector workers.[4] If the expected growth in tourism materializes, this could create up to 350,000 extra jobs.

Table 6.7 shows how this compares to employment in other major industrial sectors in 1994.

The Relative Contribution of Domestic and Foreign Tourism to Job Creation

Table 6.8 provides a breakdown of the amount of tourism-related employment generated in each province. The provinces with the highest share of tourism-related employment are Gauteng, Western Cape and KwaZulu-Natal, as they receive the largest share of tourism expenditure.

Since these provinces also report a proportionally higher usage of hotels, restaurants, shopping facilities, banking services and car rentals by foreign tourists, they are likely to enjoy a greater than proportional increase in tourism-related employment creation as tourism demand increases.

This is a vitally important set of statistics because it shows that, notwithstanding the relatively slow growth predicted in the domestic tourism market, this sector accounts for far more employment than foreign tourism in every province except Gauteng.

Accommodation accounts for a significant proportion of expenditure by foreign and domestic tourists. In 1995, foreign tourists spent an average of R1600, or 11 per cent of total expenditure, on accommodation (SATOUR, 1996a). Domestic tourists on average spend less than their foreign counterparts – R265 per trip. However, accommodation constitutes a higher proportion of expenditure – 26 per cent – since far less is spent on transport.

The LAPC notes that, in terms of domestic tourism, specific reference was made to a change in the socio-economic characteristics of this market, with a noted increase in black tourists, particularly in cheaper self-catering accommodation.

Table 6.8 *Total tourism-related employment, by province*

Province	Foreign Tourism (000s)	Domestic Tourism (000s)	Total (000s)
Gauteng	107	30	137
Western Cape	89	120	208
KwaZulu-Natal	67	158	226
Northern Cape	5	11	17
Eastern Cape	15	48	63
Orange Free State	5	25	29
Mpumalanga	15	32	47
Northern Province	8	25	33
North-West	5	33	38
Total	320	480	800

Source: Estimates based on SATOUR estimates of total value of tourism to each province, CSS provincial employment data, and LPAC's estimate of total tourism-related employment

In particular, informants in urban areas highlighted a growing subsection of black tourists who visit the city in large groups from outlying areas specifically to shop, spending an average of one night in 'cheap' accommodation. In addition, hotel managers in city centres reported an increase in the number of black business travellers frequenting their hotels.

Despite this increase in demand, the LAPC report indicates that employment numbers in existing accommodation establishments have remained fairly stable over the past five years:

> *In larger establishments with pools of permanent staff members, it is often the case that the increase in demand has been met by increases in the average weekly hours worked by the labour force. Moreover, in the larger establishments, there appears to be a trend towards contracting out services such as cleaning and security, effectively counteracting the increase in demand.*

Additional employment generated in emerging bed-and-breakfast facilities appears to be limited since relevant duties often fall in the realm of domestic staff who are already employed by the household. Thus the profits from these activities often accrue directly to the owners, generating little or no additional direct employment.

Self-catering establishments also provide limited employment opportunities since they require a low level of service input. Based on the limited information obtained through interviewing, it is estimated that the employment ratio in simple hotels and self-catering accommodation is approximately one 'regular' employee for every two to three rooms.

The provisional picture that emerges is thus one in which domestic tourism sustains a much larger number of jobs in the formal tourism sector than does foreign tourism. However, this appears not to be generating significant growth in employment figures, nor is it changing negative wage, race and gender inequalities.

The more positive impacts in regard to informal sector employment and managerial or plant ownership opportunities for previously disadvantaged groups appear to be in the domain of new plant and strategies predicated primarily for the foreign tourism sector.

Race and Gender

According to the LAPC's analysis of the data, tourism-related employment is dominated by black employees (49 per cent) with a smaller, yet significant, proportion of whites (32 per cent). Table 6.9 indicates that there has been little change in the racial composition of the workforce over the past ten years. Most noticeable is a small decline in the proportion of whites in tourism-related employment. The LAPC's report states: 'Consultation with employers in the tourism industry has suggested that black employees generally hold semi/ unskilled positions, while white employees are employed at higher paid managerial and administrative levels.'

Table 6.9 *Racial composition of permanent employment in tourism-related employment*

Year	White %	Coloured %	Asian %	Black %	Total %
1985	35.3	12.2	5.5	47.0	100
1990	33.5	13.6	5.5	47.4	100
1995	31.5	13.9	6.0	48.6	100

Note: These were calculated from statistics for 1985 and 1990 which included wholesale and retail trade, catering and accommodation services, while for 1995 wholesale and retail trade, hotels and restaurants were included.
Source: CSS, 1995 and 1996.

The LAPC argues that there is an almost equal split in the ratio of male/female employees in tourism. According to its report, gender composition varies considerably between the specific tourism sectors. The restaurant, hotel and entertainment, and wholesale and retail sectors are dominated by female employees, while transport and communication are male dominated.

This suggests considerable gender stereotyping of the activities undertaken, with maintenance and technical jobs being male dominated, and domestic-related positions being female dominated. Discussions with stakeholders in the tourism industry support this finding.

There is thus no evidence to suggest that the employment levels generated by the domestic tourism sector will result in a significant wage improvement for previously disadvantaged groups in the tourism sector.

Wage Levels

The following table from the LAPC report demonstrates that there are large racial discrepancies in income levels in tourism-related activities, with white employees earning on average three times more than their black counterparts. This is largely attributed to the predominance of black employees in low skilled positions. Thus, while the domestic tourism sector can be said to generate more employment than the foreign sector, there is no evidence that it places any upward pressure on wages in the tourism industry.

Table 6.10 *Average monthly salaries and wages, 1993*

Average income	White	Coloured	Asian	Black
R2083	R3452	R1480	R2111	R1145

Source: CSS, 1995 – Wholesale and Retail Trade, and Catering and Accommodation Services

The Informal Sector

The LAPC report demonstrates that in the informal sector – which accounts for a large proportion of self-employed workers – black females dominate in street vending activities, and black and coloured males dominate in the taxi industry. White and coloured males are the dominant self-employed group in the restaurant and hotel/entertainment sector (Table 6.11).

The LAPC notes that a significant proportion of tourism-related employment is found within the informal sector. This sector is expanding and will undoubtedly capitalize on the opportunities created by the increase in tourism.

Activity in the informal sector can be divided into four broad categories: trading and hawking, service industries, production and construction, and illegal activities. As with formal employment, it is difficult to estimate the proportion of the informal sector activity attributable to tourism: trading and hawking include the sale of curios and foodstuffs to tourists; production and construction

Table 6.11 *Racial and gender composition of the self-employed in tourism-related activities (% of total self-employed)*

Activity	African		Coloured		Indian		White		All	
	M	F	M	F	M	F*	M	F	M	F
Street hawkers	17	35	17	21	12	37	6	10	15	31
Taxi operators	12	0	8	–	2	–	–	–	9	0
Restaurant, hotel and entertainment	1	–	6	–	2	–	6	6	3	1

Note: *Sample size too small for conclusions to be drawn
Source: SALDRU (1994)

activities include the production of foodstuffs and curios; service industries include car-washing, car-watch and the taxi industry; and the illegal category includes drug-related commercial activity and prostitution.

As with the formal sector, skill requirements and income vary according to occupation, season, gender, experience and location. There are distinct gender divisions in the nature of employment and subsequent remuneration in the informal sector. Women tend to dominate the petty trading of food and curios and home-based piecework.

While this can be seen as a means of enabling women to develop small businesses and thereby facilitate both their integration into the wider economy and their active participation in the development process, international studies have shown that returns on hours worked tend to be very low. It is commonly accepted that petty trading, in particular, tends to provide a haven for older, less skilled and single or divorced women.

Wood (1996) provides an example of wage levels and the socio-economic characteristics of participants in informal curio manufacturing and trading activities in north-east KwaZulu-Natal. Detailed benefit-cost analysis, based on a survey of informal traders, found that craft markets typically generate low levels of remuneration but serve an important role in generating income in areas that are characterized by a distinct lack of waged employment. The study further confirmed that craft markets are predominantly the domain of women (94 per cent of participants) with low levels of education and formal training. Average weekly net revenue was estimated at R96 'in season' and R18 'out of season'. This translated into average implicit hourly wage rates of R2.8 in season and R0.7 out of season. However, income distribution among markets was highly skewed with a few individuals receiving a disproportionate amount of total revenue.

Interviews with key players involved in the establishment of cultural villages and craft markets indicate that foreign tourism generates more significant demand for local handicrafts than does domestic tourism. Package and coach tours are especially important in this regard, and make a significant difference to the level of income that can be generated for craft workers by tourism. In this sense, it can be suggested that foreign tourism has a greater beneficial impact on the informal sector activities related to tourism – specifically the manufacture and sale of curios and crafts – than does the domestic tourism sector.

Impact on Local Cultural Diversity and Lifestyles

Forms of Cultural Tourism in South Africa

Tourism enterprises in response to the escalating demand for 'cultural tourism' are growing in various parts of the country. These draw on indigenous history, music and dance, and other traditions including craft manufacture, rituals and customs that are practised during the everyday lives of local residents. With some exceptions, these projects have not been subjected to detailed scrutiny or monitoring. Nor has any major economic analysis been conducted to determine the financial performance and level of benefit that these deliver to resident peoples.

Impressionistic Evaluation

Impressions obtained from existing studies and media coverage are that these projects tend to stereotype the cultures being depicted, often because they are predominantly owned by outsiders in the mainstream tourism industry.

In one case, women working at a cultural village complained of having to behave like 'professional Ndebeles' while not earning enough to move out of the mud and zinc shacks they live in after work – housing structures very different from the brightly coloured indigenous homes at the cultural village.

The !Kung and !Khwe people from the Schmitsdrift community in the Northern Cape have also explicitly rejected the notion that Khoisan culture can be depicted in an authentic way. They stress that their culture is constantly adapting to new circumstances and prefer to talk of an oorkruisingskultuur (cross-over culture) rather than a static set of traditions.

There are, however, countervailing tendencies. The Shakaland project appears to have devised an effective solution to the problem of 'authenticity'. Hamilton's study indicates that aspects of rural Zulu culture are extremely well presented here. Participants and employees have a significant say over the way that their culture is presented. Much of the ritual and tradition is of use to academic anthropologists because of its level of authenticity.

Hamilton says much of this is achieved because Shakaland, instead of trying to present all Zulu culture, chooses to re-create the set of the film *Shaka Zulu*. By narrowing its scope, and by injecting an element of hyper-reality rather than claiming to complete authenticity, the managers of the projects are able to present the content in an accurate, sensitive and detailed way.

However, Hamilton makes the point that the depiction of Zulu traditions – while acknowledging that the culture is dynamic, fluid and changes in response to outside forces – is frozen into a rural and pastoral paradigm. Recent political tensions over the way in which debates over Zulu cultural weapons were injected into civic conflict in parts of KwaZulu-Natal and Gauteng are ignored, probably because they are too divisive and contentious (Hamilton, 1993, Ch 10).

Kessel Feinstein Consulting note a large growth in the accommodation sector outside formal hotels. These include holiday flats, guest-houses, hostels, various kinds of resorts. These developments open increasing opportunities for township and village residents.

For example, six villages on the border of the Kruger National Park, between the Letaba and Shingwedzi Rivers, have decided to allocate about 14,000 hectares of their land for wildlife. In return, the park will allow people who stay in lodges and guest-houses started by the villagers the same amount of land for game viewing. One of the major attractions of this plan is that tourists who come to Kruger will be the guests of rural people and will, therefore, be able to combine culture and wildlife into one experience.

At Rhodes village near Mount Frere in the Eastern Cape, local residents have opened their homes to tourists. They charge R165 a day for the visitors to experience day-to-day life. The visitors, mostly foreign, milk cows, feed chickens, fetch water and eat suppers made of umngqusho and umphokoqo.

The project has hosted small groups of tourists from Sweden and the US. It was initiated by an organization called Isinamva (isiXhosa for 'He who dances last dances best'), and replaces small enterprises that have failed in the village, such as sewing and a bakery. Isinamva also promotes primary healthcare and encourages people to make extensive use of their local herb, ubuhlungwa, which grows in abundance around Mount Frere and is known to cure stomach pains and other ailments.

Similar examples of local bed-and-breakfast accommodation where visitors can mix spontaneously with local residents exist in Mpumalanga, the Richtersveld in the Northern Cape, KwaZulu-Natal, Kosi Bay, the Ndumo Game Reserve in KwaZulu-Natal, and 42nd Hill near Ladysmith in KwaZulu-Natal.

Most have been subjected only to superficial journalistic treatment. But there is a general consensus that because they are controlled by the owners of the culture depicted, and because they allow for spontaneous interaction with residents during their daily lives, they avoid some of the stereotyping pitfalls that are inherent in the cultural village models. They epitomize the difference between re-creating a past culture and the presentation of an actual, living culture.

Relative Contribution of Domestic Tourism to Successful Cultural Projects

The cultural tourism industry has not been subjected to any serious analysis and there is an absolute lack of hard data to determine the motivation, demand and behaviour patterns of various segments of the tourism market with regard to these kinds of products. However, most informants involved in the cultural tourism industry indicated that the demand for sensitive and authentic exposure to local lifestyles derives primarily from foreign tourists, especially organized groups.

Bongani Lodge in the Mthethomusha Game Reserve, for example, reports that it sends a game-viewing vehicle every day to villages surrounding the reserve so that its guests can meet local people, eat their food and talk about their lifestyles. According to Bongani's general manager, Mark Taylor, the desire to meet local people becomes almost as important as game viewing in the list of people's motivations for visiting the area. The demand, though, is driven almost exclusively by foreign tourists, says Taylor.

There was almost unanimous consensus among the above informants that domestic tourists were not generally interested in most forms of cultural tourism. The informants indicated that this also applies to the new classes who have joined the 'emerging tourism market'. Mafisa is currently administering a questionnaire that will subject this conclusion to more rigorous scrutiny.

There are, however, significant countervailing tendencies. François Meyer, general manager of Shakaland, pointed out that domestic tourists who come to this complex as part of a conference group, for instance, end up exploring Zulu culture with a new degree of fascination, even though this was not their primary motive for visiting. He also points out that the centre, and the services provided there, are used extensively by local school groups.

The demand for various forms of cultural activity – apparently driven mainly by foreign tourists – has also generated some novel alliances between the formal tourism industry and local cultural workers. Taylor describes how his company helped to promote a local theatre group from the nearby township of Matsulu. Through professional support and training facilitated by the lodge, the theatre group was able to raise the standard and quality of its performances. The Matsulu Theatre Group now provides significant levels of income for its members and frequently travels around the country to perform at other lodges and hotels.

Interest in local history and culture has developed a similar quest for, and respect by, owners of formal tourism projects for the heritage of the area where they live. Bertus Bezuidenhout, general manager of Tau Lodge in North-West province, says his company is desperate to promote oral history, story-telling, theatre and music groups in the villages surrounding this lodge because there is such extensive demand from foreign guests. The Madikwe River Lodge in the same area is supporting plans to set up a heritage route through the area which will explore various phases of the region's history because of the demand being generated by foreign visitors.

Impact on National Reconciliation

Mafisa's preliminary research findings suggest that the tourism industry is not a significant source of national reconciliation for South Africans. Demand for cultural experiences appears to derive primarily from foreign visitors.

However, the above examples indicate that forms of cultural tourism which emerge to meet foreign demand can generate secondary impacts that result in increased respect among South Africans for aspects of local cultures they do not belong to. This is demonstrated in the emerging alliances between lodge managers and local cultural workers in various parts of the country. Cultural activities designed for foreign guests also interest local conference groups and organized groups of schoolchildren.

Foreign demand for cultural tourism has also generated another fascinating secondary effect on the prospects for national reconciliation. For most of the 1980s and early 1990s the province of KwaZulu-Natal was destabilized by a low-intensity civil war between supporters of the more militant African National Congress (ANC) and the traditionalist Inkatha Freedom Party.

One of the many reasons for this conflict, which claimed up to 20,000 lives, was a major split between the youth of the province, who supported the left-wing ideas of the ANC and its allies in the South African Communist Party, and traditional chiefs and elders who backed Inkatha because it respected their traditions and customs.

There is now evidence of a recent renaissance in Zulu cultural pride in the province, partly driven by renewed tourism interest and respect for these traditions. During the 1980s, culture and tradition was the site of political struggle and conflict. Some of the urban youth, including many who aligned themselves with the ANC, were dismissive of Zulu heritage, perceiving this as being tribal and backward. This sometimes provoked a backlash from traditional leaders and elders who saw their authority and culture as being threatened.

A number of informants have noted that since the decline in political sectarianism in the wake of the 1994 elections, there has been a revival of interest in Zulu history and patrimony. The Shembe Church, for example, is drawing increasing numbers of young people into its ranks where they practise a Christian form of religion fused with traditional dancing, dress and ritual.

New interest in the resistance offered by Zulu chiefs to British and Boer colonialism is also evident. Dance and theatre groups are incorporating traditional styles into their productions in a variety of ways. A number of informants pointed out that this cultural revival was helping to bridge the generation divide that fuelled much of the civil strife in KwaZulu-Natal during the 1980s and early 1990s. Said one informant:

> *The chiefs were perceived by some of the youth as being reactionary and uncivilized. Now the youth are beginning to meet with them and to talk about their common past. And the chiefs are including the youth in their* izimbizo *(councils) where they discuss development. A new culture of respect is emerging with this new alignment to tradition.*

Prompted by this revival, and in an attempt to consolidate it, the KwaZulu-Natal Tourism Authority has decided to make September a month of cultural activity and creativity. Various districts have been urged to organize cultural events, festivals and displays, specifically to enhance the tourism appeal of these regions.

Environmental Impacts

Green Consumers

Most of the informants interviewed as part of this study indicated that foreign tourists were more environmentally sensitive than their local counterparts. They said the 'green' sensitivities of European and North American visitors placed strong pressures on the owners of hotels, lodges and other tourism plant to adopt environmentally friendly policies. Waste management, energy and electricity supply, and the use of chemicals and cleaning agents are all being shaped by foreign sensitivity to these issues.

The need to prevent the overutilization and degradation of local heritage and natural sites was also being generated by foreign interest in this area. The application for World Heritage Site status was cited as an example where foreign interest was helping to maintain and conserve fragile ecological areas in South Africa (Jenny Bredenhan, Mike Fabricius).

Generally, the informants claimed that domestic tourists are less sensitive about these matters and that it is the foreign sector that is imposing pressures on the tourism industry to adopt environmentally friendly policies. Some inform- ants noted that older tourism establishments, set up to cater for the traditional domestic sector of the market in the apartheid area, had serious negative environmental impacts. They referred especially to large coastal resorts that had damaged large parts of the Western Cape and KwaZulu-Natal coastlines.

Political Economy: Role of the South African Green Movement

However, the above views deal with environmental issues in a narrow con- sumerist way. It can be argued that South African citizens have played a major role in shaping the political economy of the tourism industry in a much broader sense: through the pressures that a fairly powerful environmental movement have imposed to encourage ecologically friendly forms of tourism as an alternative to other more damaging forms of land use.

The example of St Lucia in KwaZulu-Natal is instructive. In 1994, after a protracted struggle by a powerful coalition of environmental and political organizations, the South African government announced that plans by Richards Bay Minerals to strip-mine the dunes for titanium and heavy minerals would be prohibited. What began as a two-sided battle between protection-minded environmentalists and industrial mining interests quickly widened to look at how either option would benefit the local population through economic development and employment creation. It was clear that the level of poverty and unemployment in the region meant that conservation of the environment could only be justified if economic development occurred at the same time.

Nature tourism was chosen as the alternative form of land use to develop the area, and thereby to create jobs and other benefits for the people who live in this economically depressed part of the country.

New Forms of Environmental Management

Various SDIs are also implementing wide-ranging strategic environmental management frameworks (SEMFs) as part of its implementation of the Greater St Lucia Wetland Park. Unlike conventional environmental impact studies, which are restricted to an assessment of the discrete impacts of individual projects, SEMFs are designed to assess the combined effect of various industrial and commercial activities on the entire ecology of a region. They allow the relevant government agency to consult widely with all parties who are likely to be affected by, and thus have anxieties about, proposed commercial developments. Environmental law in South Africa traditionally has been intrinsically restrictive and protectionist. Consequently, it does not enable the sustainable utilization of the natural environment to be maximized. The St Lucia example, however, indicates a recent paradigm shift regarding the relationship between environmental protection, new legislation and economic development. There is now widespread recognition of the potential to combine economic development with the sustainable utilization of the environment, often through various forms of nature-based tourism.

Thus it may be concluded that foreign tourism helps to generate the 'green' management of issues such as energy use and waste disposal in some sectors of the tourism industry. However, it has been shown that domestic forces have helped to create a major change in the country's political economy, one that favours environmentally sensitive forms of tourism over more extractive and damaging industries in some parts of the country.

Although this pressure derived primarily from the country's green movement rather than from domestic travellers, it does indicate a strong commitment on the part of South Africans in general to create a responsible and sustainable tourism industry as an integral part of the country's reconstruction drive.

Final Remarks and Issues for Further Inquiry

The domestic sector of South Africa's tourism industry is, like those in other parts of the world, seriously under-researched. This chapter shows that most of the key policy interventions and development programmes around tourism as a form of growth focus primarily on the strategic advantages of foreign tourism.

The negative aspects of foreign tourism have apparently not resulted in any significant examination of the extent to which the domestic sector can offset some of the classic problems that derive from over-dependence on foreign demand.

This chapter represents an initial attempt to examine the strategic importance of domestic tourism in South Africa's growth strategy. The following provisional conclusions were based on an interrogation of existing (and inadequate) data and on a limited set of interviews with key players in the tourism industry.

Available data indicate that domestic tourism currently contributes more extensively to the national economy than does foreign tourism, but that the ratio will change dramatically in the early years of the 21st century despite the injection of 'emerging' tourism classes into the domestic tourism market. It is predicted that the domestic tourism sector will experience a sluggish growth rate of about 3 per cent, while foreign tourism to South Africa will grow at a more vibrant rate of approximately 10 per cent. However, existing (and scanty) evidence suggests that the growth area in domestic tourism derives from the entry of previously disadvantaged groups into the industry as consumers. There is some evidence that suggests a spontaneous response to this increased domestic demand in the form of new guest-houses and informal forms of accommodation. The Congress of South African Trade Unions has also devised plans to create a network of working-class resorts to meet this demand. The province of KwaZulu-Natal – one of the most popular destinations for domestic tourists – would appear to be the only province with some programme to cater for the emerging domestic market by designing plans to create accommodation for the lower end of the domestic tourism sector. However, most policy and investment strategies in the tourism sector remain predicated on the foreign sector, which is generally perceived to be more lucrative and buoyant.

In regard to domestic tourists' motivations and preferences, statistics compiled by the South African Tourism Board suggest that there is a relatively small conference and business segment in the domestic sector (although the sample on which this conclusion is based was too small to be significant). Many of the emerging tourists prefer to visit friends and relatives, thus enhancing the informal sector but limiting demand in the formal sector of the tourism industry. The traditional and privileged segment of the domestic tourism market, which has probably been deracialized, retains the greatest spending power. Apart from KwaZulu-Natal, other most favoured destinations are the Western Cape, Gauteng and the Kruger National Park.

SATOUR statistics suggest that the percentage of total tourism expenditure is highly skewed towards 'established achievers' (LSSG A) with 84 per cent, while the emergent market and disadvantaged groups (LSSG B and C) together constitute only 16 per cent of total expenditure. If these figures are reliable, they suggest that there is less potential for tourism among poorer groups than was generally assumed.

Various organs of the South African state have devised policy positions and strategic interventions that are designed to enhance the ability of the tourism sector to contribute to post-apartheid economic growth and reconstruction. There is a stated intention from most countries in southern Africa to use tourism as a means for promoting regional co-operation and stability. These programmes and policies stress the need for responsible tourism, community involvement, changes in the structure of the economy in favour of previously excluded groups, and environmental sensitivity. However, most of the policies and interventions are skewed in favour of the foreign sector with little analysis and strategic importance placed on the domestic sector. There appears to be little awareness of the need to disaggregate the assessment of tourism demand into local and foreign segments and to plan accordingly. Only the KwaZulu-Natal Economic and Development Strategy seems to place a particular emphasis on lower income domestic tourism as a source of travellers for new developments in the province.

It is estimated that the tourism industry employs 1 in every 20 workers in South Africa. Employment figures indicate that in every province except Gauteng, the domestic tourism sector accounts for by far the largest number of jobs in the sector. These important statistics highlight the folly of neglecting the domestic tourism market. However, the current strategic value of domestic tourism in terms of contributing to local livelihoods through wage employment is reduced, as the formal accommodation sector appears not to be generating significant growth in employment figures, due mainly to its tendency to contract out services. Nor does it appear to be changing negative wage, race and gender inequalities.

The more positive impacts with regard to informal sector employment, and managerial and plant ownership opportunities for previously disadvantaged groups, appear to be in the domain of new plant and strategies predicated primarily on the foreign tourism sector.

The tourism sector has significant linkages with other sectors of the economy and promotes growth within them. Available data are not disaggregated sufficiently or are not extensive enough to determine the relative contribution of the domestic and foreign sectors to this ripple effect. However, it is clear that new growth strategies have a deliberate intent to promote these linkages and are based primarily on the perceived strategic growth in the foreign sector, as it is regarded as the fraction of the market where more opportunities lie for both the informal sector, and the managerial and plant ownership for previously disadvantaged groups. It would also appear that foreign tourists account for growth in the informal curio and craft markets, which are an important source of employment for unemployed and single women.

The cultural tourism industry has not been subjected to any serious analysis and there is an absolute lack of hard data to determine the motivation, demand and behaviour patterns of various segments of the domestic tourism market with regard to these kinds of products. Most informants involved in the cultural tourism industry indicated that the demand for sensitive and authentic exposure to local lifestyles derives primarily from foreign tourists, especially organized groups. This demand has generated some novel alliances between the formal tourism industry and local cultural workers. New and vibrant cultural products have emerged and they afford the opportunity for specific segments of the domestic market – mainly conference groups and school tours – to explore other cultures of their country. There is some evidence that foreign interest in South African cultures is generating new-found respect among the youth for the traditions of their elders. This is helping the generation conflict that contributed to the civil strife that destabilized many parts of South Africa in the 1980s and early 1990s. This 'healing' role of cultural tourism is especially evident in KwaZulu-Natal.

On the environmental front, it appears that foreign tourism helps to gene-rate the 'green' management of issues such as energy use and waste disposal in some sectors of the South African tourism industry. Domestic forces have helped to create a major change in the country's political economy, one that favours environmentally sensitive forms of tourism over more extractive and damaging industries in some parts of the country. This is evident in the case of St Lucia where there are extensive plans to promote a sustainable tourism industry instead of extractive mining as a way of creating jobs and alleviating poverty.

Notes

1   LSSG A refers to *established achievers*: urbanized, live in metropolitan areas, own their own homes, tend to have tertiary education and have an average monthly income of R4571.
    LSSG B refers to the *emergent market*: urban, mainly non-metropolitan, black and literate; over half have some high school education; blue-collar employed; average household monthly income R1059.
    LSSG C refers to the *less privileged*; mainly rural, young black adults or black adults over 50; 60 per cent have never been to school or have only received some primary education; mainly unemployed; students or retired; average monthly household income R557.
2   It needs to be said, however, that the survey did not focus on day trips. Lower income groups could spend most of their income on day trips. No detailed research is available, however, to confirm this.
3   The only other estimate of domestic expenditure is provided by Kessel Feinstein who provide a very low estimate of domestic tourism at a value of only 2.6 billion for domestic tourism expenditure. Since Kessel Feinstein were not prepared to discuss the methodology used in deriving these estimates, their estimate could not be used with confidence in the LAPC report.

4   The number of people employed in tourism in South Africa has been calculated by applying a weighting of 1.14 to the proportion of GDP constituted
by tourism (4.9 per cent) to calculate the percentage of totally economically
active employed by tourism (5.6 per cent). Total tourism employment
figures have been calculated by applying this percentage to CSS employment
data. The weighting of 1.14 is derived from WTTC estimates of relative
contributions of tourism to GDP and employment globally.

References

Books and Papers

Action for Southern Africa (ACTSA) (1997) *People-first tourism: The Vision
from Southern Africa and the Role of the United Kingdom*

Central Statistical Services (CSS) (1995) *Annual Report on Tourism Data*, Pretoria

Central Statistical Services (CSS) (1996) *Annual Report on Tourism Data*, Pretoria

Department of Arts, Culture, Science and Technology (DACST) (1997)
*Cultural Tourism in South Africa: Papers Presented at a Conference of the
Department of Arts, Culture, Science and Technology* (uncorrected proof)

Department of Environmental Affairs and Tourism (DEAT) (1996) *White Paper
on Development and Promotion of Tourism in South Africa*

Department of Trade and Industry (DTI) and Department of Transport (DOT),
various consultants' reports on tourism-led projects in the Lubombo SDI
region

The Economist (1995) 20 May

Hamilton, C (1993) *Authoring Shaka: Models, Metaphors and Historiography*,
PhD to Johns Hopkins University

Kessel Feinstein Consulting (1996) *Tourism Talk Southern Africa*

Land Agricultural Policy Centre (LAPC) (1997) *Employment Strategy for the
Tourism Sector*, unpublished report prepared for the Department of Labour

The Mercury (1996) 13 December

G Muller Associates (1998) *KwaZulu-Natal Lubombo Spatial Development
Initiative: Framework Planning For Tourism Development*

South Africa Labour and Development Research Unit (SALDRU) (1994) *South
Africans Rich and Poor: Baseline Household Statistics*

South African Tourism Board (SATOUR) (1995a) *summer survey*

SATOUR (1995b) *The South African Domestic Tourism Market*, March

SATOUR (1996a) *The South African Foreign Tourism Market, Some Useful Facts
and Figures*, April

SATOUR (1996b) *International Travel to South Africa, Summary Findings*,
released 15 March

Wood, E (1996) *An Economic Assessment of Local Community Craft Markets near Protected Areas in KwaZulu-Natal, South Africa*, Masters in Environmental and Resource Economics, University College London

World Travel and Tourism Council (WTTC) (1996) *Travel News Network*

Interviews and Personal Communication

Bertus Bezuidenhout, General Manager of Tau Lodge

Jenny Bredenhan, Chief Executive, Mpumalanga Tourism Authority

Mike Fabricius, Director for Tourism in the Department of Environment Affairs and Tourism

Paul Jourdaan, verbal presentation on Spatial Development Initiative at a workshop at the Development Bank of Southern Africa, 10 February 1998

François Meyer, General Manager of Shakaland

Shaun Swaney, General Manager of Madikwe River Lodge

Mark Taylor, General Manager of Bongani Lodge

Chapter 7

The Survival Ethic and the Development of Tourism in Nigeria

Abdul Raufu Mustapha

Introduction

Nigeria has enormous tourism potential, particularly for domestic tourism. It has the largest population in Africa and one of the largest pools of educated middle-class professionals in sub-Saharan Africa. In the 1970s, vast resources were expended on extending national infrastructure such as roads, hotels and telecommunications. The country also has a varied flora and fauna, along with cultural, geological and archaeological resources worth developing for tourism purposes. This combination of natural and infrastructural resources, and a sizeable potential market ought to have led to an accelerated development of both international and domestic tourism. In reality, however, the potential has not been realized; this chapter seeks to explain some of the reasons for this dismal performance.

The development of modern tourism is closely related to the elaboration of a leisure ethic associated with the boom in industrial capitalism and the welfare state in post-Second World War Europe and North America. In Nigeria, particularly since the mid-1980s, this leisure ethic is noted more for its absence. In the face of crushing economic conditions, the dominant ethic is the struggle to make ends meet – the survival ethic. Sustained economic and political crises have led to the collapse of social and economic infrastructure, forcing the majority of the economically active into the quest for personal or familial survival. Within this context, the development of tourism has been severely impaired.

The dismal state of tourism since the 1980s represents a reversal of trends in the 1960s and 1970s when significant advances were made in the promotion of domestic and international tourism. With the onset of the economic crisis, most Nigerian middle-class professionals were unable to take a holiday abroad, something that had become a common practice in the 1970s. Worse still, they could not afford to take holidays within Nigeria either. At the same time, sustained political and economic crises have generated large-scale social tension, violent crime and insecurity, all of which have contributed to make the country a most unattractive destination for tourists. These reversals in the development of Nigerian tourism reflect changes in the economic, political and social climate, and their effects on real incomes, infrastructural maintenance and development, and public security.

These issues will be addressed in this chapter. The subsequent two sections will describe the natural and current state of some of the major tourism sites in Nigerias and the development of tourism policy since the 1960s. This will be followed by an examination of conceptual issues relating to the distinctions between international, regional and domestic tourism. The chapter will then look at the patterns of development in domestic and regional tourism with subsequent sections returning to the theme of economic and political adversity, and their impact on the development of tourism. The final section will contain a few concluding ideas. The final section will contain a few concluding ideas.

Some of the Major Tourist Sites in Nigeria

Most literature on tourism in Nigeria is of the journalistic or promotional kind and displays a tendency to exaggerate the natural and cultural tourism potential of the country. Dubious climatic claims often go hand-in-hand with question- able historical claims. For example, Okorafor (1995, p11) states:

> *In terms of endowment with exquisite natural tourist attractions, Nigeria ranks amongst the most favoured nations on earth. The 923,768 square kilometres which constitute the country's land and inland water mass present to the connoisseur of nature a pageant of beauty and visual entertainment which make some of the popular world tourist destinations fade into commonness.*

In the same vein, some old canons used in the British Army East African campaign of 1918 have been presented as important items of military history. Nigeria is often presented as a country with everything to offer tourists (Friday, 1997). These exaggerated claims are partly the result of over-enthusiastic and nationalistic business promotion, but also reflect the fact that tourism resources are not well researched and classified. Still, the country does possess a number of valuable tourist sites with some potential. There are about 29 national parks and game reserves, 60 museums, 25 scheduled sites recognized for their archaeological or historical importance, and 13 tourist villages, centres and complexes in the country. Many Nigerian cities have a bustling life, interesting old quarters, markets and historical artefacts that give an idea of African cultural conditions and historical trajectory. There are also about 1500 annual festivals, as well as prehistoric rock paintings, geological formations and bird sanctuaries with tourism potential. Many of these tourist sites have attracted both international and domestic tourists. The most important of these sites are the Yankari National Park in Bauchi State, the Kainji Lake National Park in Niger State, the Mambilla Tourist Centre in Taraba State, Obudu Cattle Ranch in Cross River State, the National Museum and the National Arts Theatre in Lagos, Ikogosi Warm Springs in Osun State, Oguta Lake Resort in Imo State, Arugungu Fishing Festival in Kebbi State, the Jos Wildlife Park and Museum complex and the Lekki/Badagry Beach complex on the coastal strip of Lagos State.

Yankari National Park is arguably the jewel in the crown of Nigerian tourist sites. It comprises 2244 square kilometres of woodland and within it lie the Wikki Warm Springs. It is about 115 kilometres from the provincial capital of Bauchi on the scenic road to the Benue Valley. It was established in 1956 by the colonial administration as a game preservation unit and opened for commercial operations in 1962. It was run by the regional and state governments until 1991 when it was turned into a federally controlled national park. It has 110 chalets, largely in a run-down condition. The road in the immediate approaches to the park is also in a deplorable condition. The pressure of population in the area has meant increased human interference with the flora and fauna. The park administration lacks the basic tools and resources to function properly. As a consequence, basic facilities like electricity and communications are inadequate. Still, Yankari continues to attract both foreign and domestic tourists and there are plans on the drawing board for its refurbishment. The Kainji Lake National Park was established to take advantage of Lake Kainji which was formed when the first hydroelectric project was established in the country. It has facilities for wildlife tourism, fishing and boat cruises. It was established in 1976 and comprises of 5341 square kilometres of bushland and lake. Like the Yankari National Park, Kainji also suffers from dilapidated facilities and poaching. It is less easily accessible compared to Yankari.

The Mambilla Tourist Centre is located on a high plateau on the border with Cameroon. The plateau has a semi-temperate climate and has beautiful undulating hills. Its scenic beauty is further complemented by the Barup Waterfall. It also has the Gashaka Game Reserve which is reputed to have unique and rare species of birds and animals. There is also a Gorilla Camp within easy reach of the Tourist Centre. However, road connection to the plateau is poor and hazardous, and the facilities at the centre need serious upgrading. Obudu Cattle Ranch is another semi-temperate resort near the southern sections of the Nigeria–Cameroon border. It has been described as a place of exquisitely beautiful grasslands, deep valleys and waterfalls (Nason, 1991). It is very close to the Oban Forest Reserve which contains virgin rainforest, lowland gorillas and forest elephants. Like the other tourist resorts, its facilities are in dire need of refurbishment. The National Museum at Onikan in Lagos contains over 5000 items of archaeological, historical and cultural significance dating back to the Nok culture in central Nigeria in 500BC. It also holds exhibits on the slave trade and the advent of Christianity. It has a unique restaurant, constructed on traditional lines and serving delicious local cuisine and drinks. It is, surrounded, however, by the chaotic traffic and urban hustling of Lagos and some of its facilities are run-down due to the lack of resources and managerial problems. The National Theatre in Lagos houses the most dynamic of contemporary Nigerian drama, music and dance. It is also the most important venue for the screening and promotion of Nigerian films.

The Argungu Fishing Festival in north-western Nigeria dates back to the 16th century. Since 1939, the festival has expanded to include traditional boxing and wrestling, archery, a motor rally, an agricultural show and traditional dancing. In the 1970s it was a major attraction in Nigeria and participants and tourists also came from the neighbouring Niger Republic. Facilities have been provided at Argungu and at Sokoto to cater for visitors. The Jos Wildlife Park is situated in the pleasant hills outside the cosmopolitan city of Jos in north-central Nigeria. It is an enclosure of 8 square kilometres containing hills, streams and different types of vegetation. It has 43 kilometres of safari tracks passing by animal and bird enclosures. Also in the Jos area are the Mado Tourist Village, a museum, a zoo, the Museum of Nigerian Architecture and a number of waterfalls. Jos is a major tourist destination in Nigeria on account of its scenic beauty, its cool climate and its proximity to Yankari.

The Lekki Beach and Badagry Beach in Lagos State are beautiful sandy stretches with numerous palm trees swaying in the sea breeze. They provide relief to the 8 million inhabitants of the bustling and chaotic metropolis of Lagos. Facilities provided at Lekki, to the east of Lagos, are extremely rudimentary and the Lagos State Government, the UNDP and private investors have plans to invest in tourism facilities there. Badagry Beach is to the west of Lagos and a number of private investments have already taken place in the area, particularly the Whispering Palms Resort at Iworo. Similar ventures, equally targeted at the Lagos cosmopolitan market, can be found at Aivojeh Compound towards the Seme border and at Saad, on the Idiroko Road. Whispering Palms is the most popular of these resorts and was established in 1986 to provide a peaceful retreat from the hectic urban life of Lagos. It caters to both day-trippers and longer staying residents.

Primary data for this chapter were collected from a number of tourist sites: Yankari National Park, the Bauchi State Museum and the Abubakar Tafawa Balewa Tourist Complex (ATBTC), the Whispering Palms Complex and the

Tourist Camp in the ancient northern city of Kano which caters largely for trans-Saharan tourists. These site-specific data are often more accurate than the official tourism figures generated by governmental organizations.

Development of Tourism Policy

The development of modern tourism in Nigeria dates from the period following the Second World War when Nigeria started to receive a trickle of European tourists and adventurers. After Independence in 1960, an ad hoc committee was established by the federal government to look into the viability of promoting tourism. As a result, in 1962 a non-profit organization was established called the Nigerian Tourism Association. This association was to develop tourism facilities and encourage both domestic and international tourism. The association received government subvention and was supervised by the Ministry of Trade. It was composed of public and private companies directly related to tourism: the hotel industry, the national railways, the national airline and the Elder Dempster Shipping Line which was dominant on the sea route from Europe to British West Africa. By 1964 it was felt that direct government involvement in tourism was necessary for the development of the industry. To this end, the Nigerian Tourism Company was registered with a share capital of £350,000. Both the Association and the Company remained in an uneasy coexistence for much of the 1960s and the 1970s (Okorafor, 1995). Between 1962 and 1972, official figures indicate that tourist arrivals increased by over 800 per cent, as shown by Table 7.1.

Table 7.1 *Nigeria: Tourist arrivals 1962–1996*

Year	Arrivals
1962	6120
1972	49,368
1982	216,477
1992	272,000
1996	822,000

Sources: Nigerian Tourism Development Corporation (NTDC); Federal Establishment Department; Okorafor (1995) and private communications from NTDC

In relative terms, by 1972 tourism had hardly taken off in Nigeria. Africa's share of global arrivals in that year was 3.4 million or 1.8 per cent (WTO, 1979), and within this paltry African performance, Nigeria's share was a barely noticeable 1.5 per cent. Between 1967 and 1970, Nigeria fought a civil war which disrupted the orderly development of the economy and the tourism sector; international visitors could hardly be expected to flock to a country at war and one that was represented in the popular consciousness by images of starving Biafran orphans.

The end of the civil war in 1970 was followed by the oil boom which swelled government coffers with petro-dollars. This led to vastly increased resources for social and infrastructural development in different parts of the country, and for raising general income levels and living standards. The Udoji Salary Review Commission in the early 1970s massively increased public sector incomes and allowances and this had an immediate knock-on effect on private sector remuneration as well. The 1970s therefore saw the Nigerian salaried classes awash with enormous disposable income which went to the purchase of consumer durables from cars to refrigerators. There was also the increased pursuit of leisure activities, including foreign trips as tourists. Since the 1940s, large numbers of Nigerian youth have been going to Britain for schooling, returning at the end of their studies; many of them have also been going purely for pleasure. This was a symbol of considerable social prestige. Such was the influx of middle-class Nigerians to the United Kingdom for holidays in the 1970s that the Nigerian Naira was quoted on London Bureau de Change operations and was acceptable currency in markets like the Petticoat Lane Market in London, frequented by Nigerian tourists.

The end of the war also unleashed a nationalistic fervour which soon led to campaigns aimed at Nigerians, seeking to encourage them to take their holidays at home and to discover their own country. It was claimed that this would save foreign exchange and, above all, encourage national awareness and national cohesion. Some leaders like General Obasanjo took their holidays on the Mambila Plateau with much publicity. The promotion of domestic tourism became a political issue associated with national cohesion and national pride. Other developments of the 1970s encouraged this trend towards domestic tourism; increased incomes for the working classes and the lower middle class encouraged more extensive travelling within the country, while the reduction of the working week from six to five days increased the possibility for weekend leisure pursuits. The standardization of the pump-head price of petrol across the country effectively meant the subsidization of petrol consumption by the state.

Furthermore, the post-war period saw the enactment of a maiden legislation on tourism. Decree No 54 of 1976 established the Nigerian Tourist Board with the objective of encouraging Nigerians to spend their holidays in the country and increase the amount of foreign visitors as well. The decree also sought to encourage the provision of tourism facilities in different parts of the country. The erstwhile Nigerian Tourist Association was wound down and its resources were transferred to the new board which was also empowered to establish the National Travel Bureau as a profit-making enterprise to organize package tours in the country. State-level Tourism Committees were also set up to advise and assist the board. The board was financed by the federal government and run as a government parastatal. This resulted in a bureaucratized organization and a lethargic work ethic – characteristic of most sections of the bureaucracy – which undermined the efficient running of the organization. Another government legislation also established the Kainji Lake National Park.

Another post-war catalyst for increased tourist activity was the second World Black and African Festival of Arts and Culture, Festac 77, which was staged between January and February 1977. Although the motive for this extravagant event was the drive to enhance Nigeria's standing in the world as a major centre of black and African affairs, its effect on tourism was enormous. Large-scale infrastructural developments were undertaken in places like Lagos and Kaduna. Hotels, airports and similar facilities were constructed or upgraded. Thousands of visitors also came into the country on account of the festivities. The third National Development Plan, 1975–80, also included for the first time a specific allocation for tourism development. Of the ₦120 million earmarked, each of the then 19 existing states was given a grant of ₦1 million in 1978 for tourism development, particularly for the construction of tourism villages and camps to cater for local and foreign visitors. Subsequently, most of the states could not account for these grants, but a few used the resources to establish or modernize ventures, some of which are still in use today: the Yankari Game Reserve, the Hotel Presidential in Port Harcourt in the Rivers State, the Arugungu Fishing Festival, the Ikogosi Warm Springs and the Mado Tourist Village in the salubrious surroundings of Jos.

By the late 1980s tourism had been established as a sector of the national economy requiring encouragement. In May 1987 a National Hotel Classification committee was established to encourage improved standards in the hotel industry. Also in 1987 a Tourism Expo was held in Lagos with the aim of encouraging local businesses to invest in tourism-related ventures and to sensitize the general public to the opportunities for domestic tourism in the country. Although a stated objective of all these policy initiatives was the encouragement of domestic tourism in the face of the annual 'pilgrimages' to Britain by the Nigerian middle classes, the real thrust of the policy remained the encouragement of international tourism to Nigeria. Domestic tourism remained a powerful nationalistic ideology all the same. As a result of increased government attention, tourist arrivals to Nigeria increased sharply from the mid-1970s as shown by Table 7.1. Importantly, however, in 1988, Nigeria received 341,000 international tourists, positioning it eighth in the African league with only 2.7 per cent of the regional total (Okorafor, 1995,84).

It is important, however, to situate this increased attention for tourism within the general dynamic of the Nigerian political economy in the 1970s and 1980s. From 1970, proceeds from crude oil exports became increasingly prominent in the Nigerian economy. The source of foreign exchange for the economy increasingly shifted from agriculture to oil exports, which accounted for about 90 per cent of all foreign exchange earnings. At the same time, increased petro-dollar resources were put into an expanded bureaucracy, defence, education and the construction of roads and communication facilities. Very little concrete attention was paid to other sources of generating foreign exchange such as agriculture and tourism. For most of this period, agriculture, which provided the livelihoods of about 70 per cent of the population, was allocated only about 5 per cent of the total capital expenditure. Tourism, which had a lower socio-economic profile, received much less. Therefore, increased attention to tourism at the policy level was hardly matched by any sustained investment in the sector relative to other social and economic sectors. This lack of determined commitment, even when policy and institutional initiatives on tourism were being carried out, was a major inhibiting factor that affected the industry.

In 1990, further governmental initiatives on tourism development were unfolded. The Federal Ministry of Trade was transformed into the Federal Ministry of Trade and Tourism. A Tourism Department was established within the new ministry to cater specifically to tourism-related matters. In 1992 the ministry was renamed the Ministry of Commerce and Tourism and to this day that is the governmental institutional format for tourism management at both the federal and state levels. Also in 1990 the National Tourism Policy was launched by the then military Vice-President Aikhomu, signifying a heightened level of policy, if not practical, intervention. Numerous international organizations, including the UNDP and the WTO, were invited to the fanfare. Under the policy, the Federal Ministry of Commerce and Tourism has overall responsibility for policy initiation, research, planning, monitoring, coordination and the funding of national level tourism infrastructure. The ministry also sets standards and acts as a regulatory body for tourism establishments.

The policy also highlighted three basic areas for the development of tourism in Nigeria: objectives, guidelines and strategies. The objectives, which reflected continued practical interest in international, rather than domestic or regional tourism development, included: the need for an increased inflow of foreign exchange through the promotion of international tourism; the encouragement of the even development of tourism-based ventures in all parts of the country; the acceleration of rural–urban integration through infrastructural provisions for rural tourist sites; the fostering of national unity through the promotion of domestic tourism; the encouragement of private sector participation in tourism development; and the preservation of national cultural heritage and historical monuments.

The guidelines for achieving the objectives were: the development of incentive packages for the attraction of foreign and domestic investments into the sector; identifying viable tourist sites through cooperative action between the three tiers of government in the country; promotion of a conducive environment for foreign tourists in Nigeria; establishing effective coordinating organs for the planning, development, promotion and marketing of tourism. The strategies for achieving the guidelines included: infrastructural development at tourist sites; simplified land-tenure management to make it easier for land allocations for tourism development; giving tourism a 'preferred sector' status, as is the case with agriculture, so that private investors can be encouraged or 'pushed' into the sector; the use of cheap credits and tax holidays to encourage investment.

The National Tourism Policy was high on good intentions and low on concrete measures or achievements. Conceptually, it reflected a retreat from the nationalistic premises of promoting domestic tourism. Its major thrust was to see the tourism sector as a major source of foreign exchange; from about 1982, the slump in the world market price of crude petroleum had seriously eroded Nigeria's foreign exchange earnings. Furthermore, in 1986 Nigeria embarked on a structural adjustment programme that has all but choked off middle-class incomes and the associated internal demand for foreign and domestic tourism. The domestic market for tourism shrank, leading to an increased emphasis on the international component. The policy initiatives should therefore be understood against this background of the withdrawal of middle-class and other salaried classes from leisure pursuits and tourism.

The policy's main outcome was increased bureaucratization without an accompanying improvement in management efficiency in the coordinating institutions of the government. Equally important was the fact that the macro-political, economic and security climate in the country continued to exert a negative influence on tourism arrivals. Nevertheless, government policy interventions continued. In 1991 the National Tourism Policy Forum was established to act as a think-tank for tourism development. Also in 1991 a study commissioned by the federal government on tourism development was published. As a result of the recommendations contained therein, the government promulgated Decree No 81 of 1992 which is the current operative law governing tourism management in Nigeria. The decree abolished the Nigerian Tourist Board and in its place established the Nigerian Tourism Development Corporation (NTDC). The NTDC is presented as a commercially oriented parastatal with responsibility for the promotion, marketing and dissemination of tourism information.

One reason why the translation of policy into reality has proved very difficult is the division of powers under the Nigerian federal constitution and the practical consequences for tourism management deriving therefrom. Right from 1960, tourism has always been on the exclusive legislative list reserved for the central government. This has meant the pre-eminence of the Federal Ministry of Commerce and Tourism and its parastatals in all tourism matters. Yet the majority of tourist sites are located in rural areas in the states, removed from the immediate reach of federal bureaucrats. As a result, a series of 'trusteeship' arrangements have developed between the three tiers of government – federal, state and local government – with respect to the actual management of tourism resources. In theory, the federal ministry coordinates the activities of the state ministries. These state ministries implement policies and directives from the federal ministry. However, they are able to initiate some projects on their own since Decree No 81 of 1992 has converted state tourism boards from mere committees to statutory boards. Local governments are expected to establish tourism committees that will, among other things, maintain museums and monuments under their jurisdiction.

In practice, however, inefficient management and ambiguities characterize the relationship between the three tiers of tourism management. Museums and monuments are managed by the Federal Commission for Museums and Monuments. Yet local governments are expected to fund and maintain these museums run ostensibly by federal level officers. Predictably, the cash-strapped local governments do not pay serious attention to this important duty. Between 1993 and 1998, 95 cultural objects were stolen from six museums in the country, while customs officials seized 275 antiques from illegal exporters (Yaro Gella, 1998 [Director-General, Commission of Museums and Monuments]). Similarly, the NTDC is weakly linked to the state tourism boards, leading to serious problems of lack of coordination. Its zonal offices are too poorly staffed and resourced to carry out effective coordination. Despite all these problems, tourist arrivals into Nigeria are set to continue to rise in the 1990s, as indicated in Table 7.1.

The figures provided so far in this chapter are, at best, tentative. Official statistics in Nigeria are notorious for their unreliability and tourism figures are no exception. And there is every reason to doubt the accuracy of some of the figures; in fact, it is not unusual to come across a different set of figures for the same period. The suggestion that 822,000 foreign tourists came to Nigeria in 1996 is highly debatable. Micro-level data, collected at the level of the tourist enterprise, are often much more reliable. Nevertheless, a number of swings and ebbs are noticeable in Table 7.1. The dip in the number of arrivals in 1966 is no doubt reflective of increased anxiety associated with the first military coup of January 1966 which overthrew the civilian regime of the First Republic. Continued tension related to the civil war might be responsible for the dip in 1969. On the other hand, the jump in the number of arrivals in 1972, which continued into the 1970s, must be associated with increased economic and infrastructural resources associated with the oil boom period from 1970. The dip in the number of arrivals in 1982 also correlates with the advent of economic adversity and the adoption of the policy of economic austerity. The dips in 1984 and 1990 reflect two incidences in military incursions into Nigerian public life: the 31 December 1983 coup which overthrew the Second Republic (1979–1983), and the infamous Orkar coup of early 1990, which not only sought to remove the incumbent dictator, Babangida, but also announced the partition of the country.

Despite all the policy developments, the contribution of tourism to the GDP has been consistently low; Central Bank of Nigeria figures for the hotel and restaurant sector – the nearest to tourism – indicate that the sector contributed only 0.56 per cent of the GDP in 1989, 0.53 per cent in 1990, 0.51 per cent in 1991, and 0.50 per cent in both 1992 and 1993 (CBN, 1994, p78). However, between 1990 and 1996, tourism receipts were said to have risen from US$25 million to US$85 million.

Tourism in Nigeria: Conceptual Issues

The original conception behind Nigerian tourism policy in the 1960s was the notion that tourists were people from the developed countries of the North visiting sites of natural, historical or cultural significance. In the 1970s, however, this conception was altered to incorporate Nigerian tourists in Europe and Nigerian domestic tourism. However, the ambiguous commitment to domestic tourism did not make for the rapid development of the sector. In the first place, despite official political commitment, its development continued to meet with middle-class resistance. They continued to indulge in the more prestigious travel to Europe. More importantly, the tourism industry in the country did not develop a coherent definition of the 'domestic tourist' or consistent policies aimed at that market.

Some tourism professionals claim that travelling for leisure or recreation is alien to most Nigerian cultures (Okorafor, 1995, p25). Accordingly, a tourism board manager classified 'domestic tourism' under a number of sub-headings which tend to demote the leisure principle as a primary motivation: visiting friends and relatives; commerce; sports; religious; and health (Executive Secretary, Kano State Tourism Board, personal communication). This formulation neglects the fact that, whatever the traditional legitimacy of the leisure ethic, there has emerged a substantial middle class of salaried workers, professionals and business persons who have taken to leisure travels, particularly to Britain and other European centres. These classes have obviously embraced the leisure ethic even if the roots of it are not to be seen in traditional cultural norms. Secondly, we may also challenge the claim that traditional Nigerian cultures have no conception of travelling except for familial, pecuniary or religious purposes. In many traditional cultures the transition into adulthood is often marked by random travels to face odds and acquire maturity and experience. This phenomenon of random travelling has been well captured in a number of novels such as D O Fagunwa's *My Sojourn in the Forest of Daemons* and Cyprian Ekwensi's *The Passport of Mallam Illya*. Admittedly, these random travels do not quite amount to an affirmation of the leisure ethic through tourism, but they do suggest that traditional attitudes and conceptions on the issue may be much more flexible and accommodative.

Another thorny issue in defining domestic tourism in Nigeria relates to the length of stay of the domestic tourist at the tourism venue. According to the World Tourism Organization, the minimum stay away from home should be 24 hours, while the maximum should not exceed 12 months (Ghimire, 1997, p4). Most of the officially classified domestic tourism in Nigeria would normally be day trips of less than 24 hours' duration. The definition of domestic tourism remains problematic and its quantification is a task that is yet to be properly undertaken. Most figures for domestic tourists tend to include both day-trippers and those staying for at least 24 hours. On the other hand, VFRs (tourists visiting friends and relations) are hardly enumerated as they rarely come into contact with institutions or organizations interested in collating tourism statistics. There is also the question of what constitutes the 'domestic'? Nigerian hotels and tourist establishments often record the nationality of their visitors rather than where the visitors come from. As a consequence, many foreigners normally resident in Nigeria are not recorded as 'domestic' tourists but simply as 'foreigners'. The data collection system does not therefore distinguish between foreign 'arrivals' and foreign 'residents'. If anything, there is the implicit supposition that all foreigners are 'arrivals', a point which is clearly untrue.

These conceptual qualifications notwithstanding, domestic tourism is an important aspect of the tourism industry in Nigeria. The NTDC acknowledges that 'domestic tourism activities have, from the available data, been taking place on a higher index than international tourism in the country' (personal communication), but it also points out the lack of institutional and managerial capacity, particularly at grass-roots levels, to monitor and evaluate the volumes of traffic involved. The micro-level data used in this chapter relate specifically to those aspects of domestic tourism that have been officially recorded at the tourist sites.

Domestic and Regional Tourism in Nigeria

What is the possible and realistic level of domestic tourism in Nigeria? What are the problems involved in any assessment of this subsector? Okorafor (1995, p2) asserts that 'the numerical dominance of domestic tourism is beyond question' in Nigeria. Citing data for arrivals at the Yankari Game Reserve in 1992, he suggests that only about 26 per cent of visitors were international tourists, the rest being made up of domestic tourists. His overly optimistic perspective fails to situate properly trends in domestic tourism within the consequences of the negative socio-economic issues that have affected middle-class incomes since the introduction of the Structural Adjustment Programme (SAP) in 1986.

The Extent of Domestic Tourism in Nigeria

In 1976, 79 per cent of all visitors to Yankari were non-Nigerians, prompting the conclusion that Nigerians were not interested in domestic tourism (Helleiner, 1977). Twenty years on, in 1996, Nigerian visitors to Yankari were 77 per cent of the total.

Table 7.2 *Tourist arrivals: Yankari National Park – January–December 1996*

Country	Numbers	Country	Numbers
Australia	64	Israel	12
Austria	6	Italy	36
Bangladesh	3	Japan	5
Belarus	9	Jordan	10
Belgium	3	Lebanon	110
Brazil	5	Netherlands	145
Britain	305	New Zealand	85
Bulgaria	42	Niger	2
Cameroon	2	Nigeria	8401
Canada	51	Norway	16
China	79	Pakistan	43
Croatia	4	Poland	16
Cuba	2	Portugal	3
Cyprus	4	Romania	5
Denmark	96	Sierra Leone	46
Egypt	6	South Korea	22
France	129	Spain	11
Germany	369	Sri Lanka	15
Ghana	2	Sweden	5
Guinea	16	Switzerland	65
Hungary	45	Turkey	6
India	257	USA	321
Ireland	76	Yugoslavia	4
		Total	10,959

Source: NTDC (personal communication)

Figures from the nearby ATBTC and from the Bauchi State Museum show an even higher proportion of 90 per cent of domestic tourists in the region, as figures for 1988 to 1994 in Tables 7.3 and 7.4 indicate.

The number of visitors to the Whispering Palms Resort between July and August 1997 amounts to 457 adults and 381 children, of which it is roughly estimated that half are Nigerian, the rest being largely made up of American and Indian residents in Lagos (Whispering Palms Records).

The final set of data comes from the Kano State Tourist Camp in Kano which caters for trans-Saharan travellers from Europe as well as local visitors.

Table 7.3 *Tourist arrivals: ATBT Complex, 1988–1994*

Year	No of Nigerians	No of foreigners	Total
1988	7121	149	7270
1989	9027	2	9029
1990	7283	166	7449
1991	6138	61	6199
1992	6833	8	6841
1993	6511	83	6594
1994	4101	57	4158
Total	47,014	526	47,540

Source: NTDC (personal communication)

Table 7.4 *Tourist arrivals: Bauchi State Museum, June 1988–May 1994*

Year	No of Nigerians	No of foreigners	Total
1988	3089	93	3182
1989	4018	273	4291
1990	3785	256	4041
1991	2637	116	2753
1992	2027	87	2114
1993	1603	50	1653
1994	942	28	970
Total	18,101	903	19,004

Source: NTDC (personal communication)

Table 7.5 *Tourist arrivals: Kano State Tourist Camp, 1994*

Month	No of Nigerians	No of foreigners
January	194	291
February	196	169
March	115	161
April	150	193
May	127	345
June	175	90
July	452	192
August	158	60
September	170	28
October	862	121
November	586	264
December	589	211
Total	3774	2125

Source: Kano State Tourism Board Records

Figures from these five tourism sites are fairly representative of the situation in the other sites in the country and a number of conclusions can be drawn from them. Firstly, for a country with an estimated population of 104 million in 1997, the absolute and relative level of tourism, both domestic and foreign, is quite low. However, as pointed out earlier, many components of domestic tourism remain unrecorded. Secondly, within this low level, the level of domestic tourism is relatively high, rising from about 50 per cent in the case of Whispering Palms to over 90 per cent at the Bauchi State Museum. Most tourism establishments, including popular sites like the Jos Museum, the Jos Wild Life Park, the Obudu Cattle Ranch and the Kainji National Park, would fall within this continuum. Only annual festivals, such as the Arugungu Fishing Festival, the Lekki Beach Carnival and the Ovia Osese Festival in Ogori/Magongo in Kogi State, are likely to attract much higher proportions and numbers of domestic tourists.

Social Base of Domestic Tourism

Different social groups tend to patronize different segments of the domestic tourism industry. At the top end, visitors to rural-based tourist sites which require long-distance travel and extended stay, such as the Whispering Palms Resort, Yankari and Kainji National Parks, Obudu Cattle Ranch and the big hotels in the urban centres, are likely to be in the upper reaches of the professional, bureaucratic and mercantile groups. Many are likely to be high-ranking bureaucrats with formal and informal access to state resources with which to support a lifestyle that still encompasses leisure pursuits. Others are likely to be high-flying business persons who are in a position to cushion themselves from the harsh economic conditions that are prevalent in the country. A third segment is likely to be made up of foreign nationals who are resident in Nigeria and working in the diplomatic community or in the organized private sector. The motivation of these groups is relaxation. Their expectation is likely to be the need to get away from the stressful situation of their work places, in particular, and the urban environment, in general. These groups are also the segment of Nigerian society that still travels to European and North American destinations for holidays; some of them also venture into regional tourism, particularly to Benin Republic, Togo, Ghana and the Ivory Coast. It is a very tiny social category.

The bulk of middle-class professionals – and students of higher institutions – had the same tastes and tourism orientation as the upper segment for most of the 1970s. The major difference, however, was that this group was also very interested in the potential for shopping at their tourism destination. Since the mid-1980s, this group has increasingly been integrated into the ranks of the 'new poor', and has been pushed out of the tourist market. Most of its members are currently concerned with survival rather than leisure. This is the largest potential market for domestic tourism, but it has been crippled by economic adversity. In the current situation, however, some members of this group, at best, may be periodic day-trippers to tourist sites located in their immediate localities. This would principally involve run-down urban-based sites, such as the Jos Wildlife Park and the various museums and zoos in the country.

Further down the social hierarchy, the lower segments of the salaried classes, operators in the lower reaches of the informal sector, secondary school students and the unemployed were likely, right up to the early 1980s, to travel to their natal homes or to visit relatives in far-flung rural or urban centres, particularly during religious festivals, annual holidays or during school holidays. A Hausa proverb, valid for most other Nigerian societies, states that kinship is located in one's legs, implying that you need to travel around to your kin in order to oil the ties of kinship. The railway system was a particularly popular and cheap mode of transportation for this segment of Nigerian society. Since the mid-1980s, this group has also faced severe restrictions to its capacity to travel around the country. It is symbolic of the 'grounding' of this category of Nigerians that the railway system virtually ground to a halt from the mid-1980s. Since then, the escalating costs of road transport (see Table 7.9) have meant reduced travels or no travel at all. In the current situation, this group also patronizes the same urban-based tourist sites as the bulk of the professional classes, but on a much more restricted basis; they are likely to visit such sites only on public holidays and religious festivals.

The most important determinant of domestic tourism in Nigeria is therefore the economic and political entitlement of the different social groups involved. In a sense, the current Nigerian situation is the inverse of the situation in post-Second World War Western Europe where increasing prosperity and the welfare state meant that more sections of society could indulge in leisure pursuits. In Nigeria, the centralization of state resources under military dictatorship, the corrupt dispensation of these resources to a select few, and the resulting economic adversity and adjustment policies since the mid-1980s have been constricting the potential social basis of any sort of tourism and tending to limit it to a minuscule group of the economically strong or politically well connected. The rest of society are restricted to day trips or no leisure at all.

The Extent of Regional Tourism in Nigeria

Figures on tourist arrivals to the Yankari National Park in 1996 (Table 7.2) suggest that tourists from the West African subregion made up only 0.6 per cent of total arrivals. Although there are no comparable figures from other sites, my suspicion is that the figures from such sites are not likely to be any different. It would therefore seem that regional tourism is extremely low in Nigeria. One reason for this low level of uptake is the very negative opinion of Nigeria by many members of the middle classes of neighbouring countries.

They tend to perceive Nigeria as a chaotic place with little security of life and property. However, if we move the analysis away from tourist sites and look at the wider dynamic of interaction between Nigeria and her neighbours, then we observe intricate networks of commercial and social interaction that must increase the level of regional tourism. Apart from the Economic Community of West African States (ECOWAS) treaty, which has led to officially sanctioned movements of people and goods in the subregion, Nigeria is also at the hub of a series of parallel market activities that span the countries of Western and Central Africa (Hashim and Meagher, 1997). There is therefore considerable movement of people to and from Nigeria from these countries, as Table 7.6 indicates.

Table 7.6 *Selected statistics of persons arriving and departing from Nigeria, by nationality, 1987–1990*

Selected countries	1987		1988		1989		1990	
	arrivals	departures	arrivals	departures	arrivals	departures	arrivals	departures
All countries	186,346	217,047	147,810	376,240	275,264	687,689	208,743	395,076
American	6851	4507	7882	8136	22,004	20,939	15,040	16,599
British	14,545	10,054	12,384	13,811	9346	11,602	22,397	25,511
West German	5827	3690	6176	6025	10,855	13,982	3668	6367
French	6445	4237	7260	6351	10,462	15,150	9654	10,199
Nigerian	61,266	191,958	955	221,794	n/a	362,658	1487	179,589
ECOWAS tourists	41,221	26,034	50,109	53,262	98,506	108,109	77,724	78,146

Source: Federal Office of Statistics, 1996, pp5–6

There are a number of important points suggested by Table 7.6 and I shall return to some of them in due course. We can, note, however, the importance of ECOWAS persons in the flow of human traffic to and from Nigeria. Persons from ECOWAS made up 22 per cent of all arriving persons in 1987, 34 per cent in 1988, 36 per cent in 1989 and 37 per cent in 1990. These figures are clearly at odds with a figure of just 0.6 per cent for tourist arrivals, particularly if we consider that 'travel relating to trade and occupational activities might obviously contain some elements of tourism' (Ghimire, 1997, p5). The least that can be said is that the potential for increased regional tourism exists. We are not likely to know the full extent of regional tourism in Nigeria until the conceptual and logistic problems of tourism data collection are sorted out. The UNDP is reported to be assisting the NTDC in establishing a logistic system for data collection. On the conceptual front, there seems to be a continuing reliance on WTO definitions without any effort to establish their correspondence to local realities.

The Social and Environmental Impacts of Tourism

The low levels of international, regional and domestic tourism relative to the population of the country mean that the social and environmental impact of tourism-related activities is negligible. Most domestic tourists, particularly the VFR category, fit into existing networks of familial and communal relationships that are constitutive of contemporary Nigerian life. For example, most tourists from southern Nigeria visiting relatives in the northern half of the country are likely to reside in the sabon gari (tr. new town), or 'strangers' quarters' in which most southern immigrants in northern cities reside. This segregated nature of residence in northern cities was imposed by British colonialism and was very different from the dynamic of the social geography of the area in the pre-colonial period. Although this pattern is now breaking down as a result of demographic and social changes, it is still of sufficient relevance and continues to condition social contact and conflict between domestic tourists in northern cities and the indigenous communities. The same situation applies in southern Nigeria, with northern immigrants – and domestic tourists – likely to be found in the sabo quarters of southern cities. Among middle-class immigrants and tourists, however, there is a wider flexibility of residence and encounter, but this has not posed any social problems.

The social impact of regional tourists is very similar to that of domestic tourists. Most regional tourists are likely to go to areas with which they have had long-standing pre-colonial and colonial connections. Most regional tourists from the Sahelian countries of Niger, Chad and the northern part of Cameroon are likely to visit the northern parts of Nigeria where they have existing supportive networks. Similarly, most visitors from the coastal parts of Ghana, Benin Republic and the Ivory Coast are equally likely to go to the south-western parts of the country. One important exception to this pattern is Lagos, which seems to draw visitors from all parts of Nigeria and from various parts of the West African region. Except in periods of drought when large numbers of people flood into Nigeria from the Sahelian countries, there is little conflict between visitors from the West African subregion and their Nigerian hosts. The expulsion of half a million Ghanaians from Nigeria in the early 1980s was a result of government policy and not a reflection of conflict between hosts and immigrants at the societal level.

The social impact of international tourism is more consciously felt, even if the numbers are low. The major point of anxiety, particularly in the Moslem northern parts of the country, is the perception that some tourists from Western countries are too 'scantily' dressed. Backpackers, in particular, are often seen as objects of curiosity. These international tourists are, however, too few to cause serious concern. Even by local reckoning, foreign films and music, rather than tourists, are seen as the main vehicles for the transmission of Western cultural values and tastes, and the corrosion of local values.

The environmental impact of tourism is often indirect, being contained within the much wider conflict between demographic pressure and environmental protection policy. There is a general tension between the environmental policy of the reservation of forests, wildlife, wetlands and woodland, and the resource and economic demands of nomadic pastoralists and expanding population in many parts of Nigeria. This tension usually expresses itself in poaching, illegal tree-felling and encroachment into reserved places. Because rural tourist sites are often located at such reserved places, there is sometimes a conflict between the demands of the local and nomadic populations and the demands of effective tourism management. A prime example is the Yankari National Park where poachers and local farmers invade the reserved area, threatening both the wildlife and vegetation; bush-burning, for hunting and farm clearance, is not uncommon in the park which still contains substantial local communities within it. The central problem is, however, not the tourism policy as such, but lies with the long-standing tensions within colonial and post-colonial environmental policy. Indeed, a thriving tourism sector may provide profitable opportunities for local communities and reduce the latent conflict over resource claims.

The Survival Ethic and Domestic Tourism in Nigeria

By the 1970s, the leisure ethic had taken hold in Nigeria, with holidays in Britain, Europe and America becoming a major status symbol among the middle classes. Among the mercantile classes of the Moslem north, pilgrimages to Mecca became very pronounced. As mentioned above, various Nigerian governments and other institutions began to realize the enormous economic and socio-political potential of redirecting this budding tourism from foreign destinations to domestic ones. Over the years, many specific programmes have been developed to redirect the middle classes into domestic tourism. For example, the federal government launched the operation 'Know Your Country' in the 1970s, targeted at the youth; a youth camp was built at Jos, along with a museum of Nigerian architecture featuring architectural designs from all parts of the country. Some private organizations, such as the Sheraton Hotel in the new federal capital of Abuja, also developed package tours in conjunction with some private airlines to get Nigerians to visit and explore their new capital territory.

One result of this promotion of domestic tourism is the rise in the domestic component of tourism, as shown above. But relative to the population size and the available potential, this domestic tourism remains stymied. The central reason for this lack of progress, as indicated above, is not the lack of a leisure ethic embracing tourism, but increasing economic adversity from the mid-1980s. In 1986 Nigeria embraced a structural adjustment programme that led to a 99 per cent depreciation of the naira relative to the US dollar between 1986 and 1998. Such was the devastating impact of the economic crisis and the subsequent structural adjustment programme on salaried incomes that, by 1987, real wages at the lower rungs of the public sector were worth only 37 per cent of their 1975 value; middle-level civil servants earned only the equivalent of 20 per cent of their 1975 wages (Meagher and Yunusa, 1996, p2). The very middle class that pioneered the expansion of both domestic and international tourism has been virtually decimated in the process. Many lost their means of livelihood, while those still in employment found their salaries inadequate as a living wage. Survival strategies proliferated even among the middle classes (Mustapha, 1991) and the survival ethic became the central organizing principle of daily existence. As a result of this intensified economic pressure, the leisure ethic, including both outbound and domestic tourism, has become a thing of the past for the vast majority of the population.

Apart from the economic crisis, Nigeria has also faced a major political crisis since the annulment of the presidential elections of 1993 and the ascendancy of the repressive Abacha junta which led the country into a pariah status because of its crackdown on human rights in the country. The combination of long-run economic adversity and the political crisis has led to serious deterioration in the socio-economic conditions in the country. A wide range of social infrastructure has virtually collapsed. Fuel, electricity, water and telecommunications are becoming more difficult to access by the day. Violent crime and politically motivated violence have become endemic. The resultant tension in the country has not been conducive to the development of both international and domestic tourism. Although Table 7.1 claims that international arrival figures have continued to rise, it is common knowledge that many foreigners avoid going to Nigeria under the current circumstances. For example, the US State Department has formally warned:

> ... *U.S. citizens of the dangers of travelling to Nigeria. Violent crime, practiced by persons in police and military uniforms, as well as by ordinary criminals, is an acute problem. Harassment and shake-downs of Nigerians and foreigners alike by uniformed personnel and others occur frequently throughout the country ...*
> ... *Violent crime affecting foreigners is an extremely serious problem, especially in Lagos and the southern half of the country. Visitors, as well as resident Americans, report widespread armed muggings, assaults, burglary, carjackings and extortion, often involving violence. ... Reports of armed robberies in broad daylight on rural roads in the northern half of the country appear to be increasing. ... Pickpockets and confidence artists, some posing as local immigration and other government officials, are especially common at Murtala Muhammed Airport...* (US State Department, 1996).

Government statistics confirm some of this gloomy assessment. Figures for crimes reported to the police are falling for most crimes, but not for armed robbery, as Table 7.7 indicates. Similarly, Table 7.6 (above) shows that from about 1989 more people have been leaving Nigeria than are arriving in the country; in particular, Nigerians have been deserting their country in droves. Clearly, for many people, even the prospect of survival is proving difficult.

Table 7.7 *Armed robbery cases reported to the police in Nigeria, 1981–1995*

Year	No of Cases
1981	1747
1982	1310
1983	1430
1984	1415
1985	1195
1992	1568
1993	1975
1994	2044
1995	2109

Sources: Okorafor, 1995, p52; Federal Office of Statistics, 1996

These general comments can be further substantiated with a wide array of economic and social statistics showing the deteriorating situation in Nigeria during the last decade. It is also possible to illustrate some of the consequences on tourism-related sectors of the economy. Firstly, we can see the vastly declining real wages of the middle class, as illustrated by Table 7.8:

Table 7.8 *Annual salaries of an average level senior lecturer, 1982–1994*

Year	Salary	
	Naira	US$
1982	13,100	23,500
1986	13,100	2,620
1989	17,736	1478
1993	52,800	1218
1994	52,800	754

Source: adapted from Bangura, 1993, p3

And this sharp decline in real wages is against the background of serious inflationary pressures, as shown by Table 7.9.

Table 7.9 *Composite consumer price index in Nigeria, 1985–1995*
(1985=100)

Year	All items	Food	Accommodation, fuel and light	Transport	Other services	Rec, ed, cu and e
1986	105.4	100.1	140.6	118.2	136.3	–
1987	116.1	108.7	146.6	133.8	165.9	–
1988	181.2	195.3	138.7	151.2	142.5	165.7
1989	272.7	298.1	181.0	247.4	193.9	228.2
1990	293.2	308.0	217.0	291.3	231.5	263.1
1991	330.9	345.9	226.3	314.5	287.3	307.1
1992	478.4	506.8	298.3	440.7	412.2	405.9
1993	751.9	800.2	612.7	706.3	629.2	654.7
1994	1180.7	1174.6	1056.7	1532.0	1114.9	1236.2
1995	2040.4	2021.1	1845.0	2374.3	1960.4	2154.3

Note: Rec, ed, cu and e stands for recreation, education, culture and entertainment
Source: Central Bank of Nigeria, 1995, p144

Even the higher echelons of the middle classes, like university academics and other professionals who had enjoyed frequent holidays in Europe in the 1970s and would have been obvious targets in the development of domestic tourism, found themselves facing escalating costs of subsistence with diminishing real wages. Lower sections of the middle and salaried classes were worst hit. In 1997, the cost of an average room per night, minus food and other incidentals, in a very modest hotel in the provincial backwaters town of Lokoja on the confluence of the Niger and Benue Rivers was about ₦600. This is 10 per cent of the monthly take-home pay of some of the best paid academics in the Nigerian university system. On the other hand, should this hypothetical academic decide to take a holiday at the new federal capital in Abuja and stay at the Sheraton Hotel there, he/she must be prepared to pay a nightly rate of ₦7600 per room with a nightly deposit of ₦11,500. These are 127 per cent and 192 per cent of his/her monthly take-home pay respectively. In the current circumstance, hotel occupancy levels are sustained by patronage from governmental bodies and the organized private sector. Within the tourism industry itself, declining real wages and cheap labour strategies have led to poor standards and lack of efficiency; the survival strategies of staff in tourism establishments often lead to a lack of professionalism.

Of course, the conflation of statistics on day-trippers and those who stay for at least 24 hours makes it difficult to see the consequences of the price and income relationships on official domestic tourism figures. In reality, however, Nigerian academics and other professionals, many of whom used to go to Europe on holidays in the 1970s with their families, now find themselves unable to go on holidays in Nigeria itself. According to Okorafor (1995, p46):

> *Although many Nigerian families take children to recreation parks on Public Holidays, the number of families which can afford the expense of tours away from home is now very limited. The opulent minority in the country have a predilection for overseas tours. The down-turn in the Nigerian economy has therefore had a devastating impact on domestic tourism.*

The contraction of potential domestic tourism which is inherent in the socio-economic situation in the country is further illustrated by Table 7.10 which contains aggregate data on domestic air transportation in the country. Although these figures are not directly related to the levels of domestic tourism, their potential implications must be enormous since, everything being equal, tourism-related traffic will tend to fall at the same, or a higher, rate compared to travels motivated by business or social considerations.

Table 7.10   *Volume of domestic air transportation in Nigeria, 1985–1995*

Year	No of passengers (000s)
1985	1548
1986	1334
1987	1064
1988	781
1989	549
1990	624
1991	556
1992	415
1993	198
1994	349
1995	355

Source: CBN, 1995, p154

The official aggregate data for international tourist arrivals (see Table 7.1) suggest that tourism levels have been rising through the 1990s. At the same time, more reliable micro-level data from tourist sites suggest that the domestic component of tourism is rising. If both positions are true, then domestic figures should be rising even faster than the international figures. This is clearly not the case and the figures in Table 7.1 should therefore be treated with due scepticism. The more likely situation is that tourism numbers, minus day-trippers, are contracting in general, as Table 7.11 suggests. And the reason is not the lack of a leisure ethic in the country, but the unrelenting demands of survival.

Table 7.11 *Annual number of visitors at Yankari National Park,*
1985–1996

Year	No of visitors
1985	36,000
1991	22,000
1992	19,490
1996	10,946

Source: Yankari National Park records

Conclusion

Tourism development in Nigeria is beset by a number of crucial problems. Some of these are internal to the tourism sector, while others relate more directly to the wider national socio-political dynamic. At the level of the industry, there is the problem of lack of adequate finance both in public and private sector ventures. The collapse of the social infrastructure has meant that facilities like water, electricity and telecommunications, which ought to be municipal concerns, now have to be provided for by each hotel or tourism facility. The financial, technical and managerial demands of the situation are enormous. Then there is the problem of the over-bureaucratization of public sector ventures like hotels and tourism-related governmental organizations. Associated with this is the low level of skills and lack of professionalism among most catering and tourism staff in many ventures. Finance, infrastructure, managerial capacity and technical professionalism are therefore the most serious problems within the tourism industry. The industry also needs to confront the problem of information dissemination both in Nigeria and abroad, and that of setting and monitoring standards. Then there is the problem of data collection and research. Further research may investigate prevailing local attitudes to domestic tourism and their relationship to the levels of participation in the industry. Other potential research themes may include the classification of tourism resources and the clarification of conceptual and logistical problems related to data collection.

Within the wider socio-political context, tourism development is constrained by a very hostile economic and political climate. In 1997, the management of the macro-economy led to severe shortages of petroleum products for months on end and prolonged electricity blackouts in many parts of the country. At the same time, heightened political tension, and even political violence, have generated considerable anxiety in the country. In 1994, hundreds of thousands of Nigerians fled from their homes to their natal regions because of fears of political violence; the death, in detention, of Bashorun MKO Abiola in July 1998 led to three days of rioting and ethnic killings in many cities in the south-west of the country. Then there is the culture of impunity within the security forces guarding the highways, airports and other such vital public facilities. This has tended to frighten many tourists, domestic or foreign, from venturing about or into the country. Outrages by marauding bands of armed robbers are a daily occurrence in many Nigerian cities and on public highways; in July 1993, the fatal shooting of two policemen and an American tourist arriving at the Murtala Mohammed International Airport in Lagos led to the American government advising its citizens to avoid using the airport. In 1997 and 1998, inter-communal clashes continued, claiming lives in many parts of the country, including the historical/cultural centre of Ife. There is also the political anxiety generated by the dubious programmes of transition to democracy, first under General Babangida and then under the late General Abacha; in April and May 1998, pro-democracy agitators clashed with govern-ment forces in many cities in the south-west of the country, leading to at least 11 deaths. In aesthetic terms, many Nigerian cities continue to be eyesores of the most atrocious proportions.

The National Tourism Policy launched in 1990 seems to be pointing the industry in the right direction. Furthermore, in the 1998 budget, the federal government also promised to privatize its holdings in the leisure sector, a move that will address the problem of over-bureaucratization and lack of managerial goals and efficiency. Under normal circumstances, operators within the industry would be expected to take advantage of these governmental initiatives and improve their own efficiency and levels of operation. Unfortunately, things are far from normal in the current situation in Nigeria. Falling incomes and rising costs make it very difficult to develop the potential for domestic tourism. At the same time, a crumbling infrastructure, criminal and political violence, and general insecurity make it difficult to develop regional and international tourism potentials. There are indications, however, that the post-Abacha regimes are beginning to address these macro political and economic problems. While it is too early in the day to be sure about the military's intentions, it is obvious that such macro-level reforms are extremely vital if Nigeria's tourism potential is to be realized.

References

Bangura, Y (1993) *Intellectuals, Economic Reform and Social Change: Constraints and Opportunities in the Formation of a Nigerian Technocracy*, International Symposium on Hidden Actors of Development: Intellectuals, Technocrats and Social Change in the Third World, University of Leiden

Central Bank of Nigeria (CBN) (1994) *Annual Report and Statement of Accounts for the Year Ended 31st December 1993*, Lagos

Central Bank of Nigeria (CBN) (1995) *Statistical Bulletin*, vol 6, no 2, December

Federal Office of Statistics (FOS) (1996) *Facts and Figures About Nigeria*, Lagos

Friday, E (1997) *Kogi State Tourist Guide Book*, Kogi State Tourism Board, Lokoja

Ghimire, K (1997) *Emerging Mass Tourism in the South*, DP 85, UNRISD, Geneva

Hashim, Y and K Meagher (1997) *Cross-Border Trade and the Parallel Currency Market: The Parallel Organization of Trade and Finance in the Context of Structural Adjustment. A Case Study of Kano, Nigeria*, research report for the Nordiskafrikainstidtutet, Uppsala, May

Helleiner, F M (1977) 'Geographical origins of visitors to Yankari Game Reserve', in O. Adejuyigbe and F M Helliner (eds), *Proceedings of the 20th Annual Geographical Conference of the Nigerian Geographical Association*, University of Ife, Ile-Ife, March

Meagher, K and M Yunusa (1996) *Passing the Buck: Structural Adjustment and the Nigerian Urban Informal Sector*, Discussion Paper No 75, UNRISD, Geneva, May

Mustapha, A R (1991) *Structural Adjustment and Multiple Modes of Social Livelihood in Nigeria*, Discussion Paper No 26, UNRISD, Geneva

Nason, I (1991) *Enjoy Nigeria*, Spectrum Books, Ibadan

Okorafor, Charles (1995) *Tourism in Nigeria: Progress, Problems and Prospects*, African Educational Services, Owerri

US State Department (1996) *Nigeria – Consular Information Sheet*, Washington, DC, 25 November.

WTO (1979) *Tourism Compendium*, Lagos

Yaro Gella (1998) Xinhua News Agency, 19 May

Chapter 8

Domestic Tourism in India

Nina Rao and K T Suresh

Tourism Policy in India

At the very outset it is important to identify what we consider to be the key dimensions of appropriate tourism development for India, a country located in South Asia, that is considered one of the least developed nations in the world, and yet is a regional economic power in its own right. India also has a large population, of whom 70 per cent live in rural areas and 40 per cent live below the poverty line. Is the purpose of a tourism policy to help our planners and policy-makers to 'attain broader and environmental goals' when determining the priority given to domestic or international tourism? To attain broader and environmental goals involves three crucial dimensions of tourism development, which are equally applicable whether we are discussing the option of international or domestic tourism, or both.

1 Whether formal or informal, spontaneous or planned, tourism development is a process that proceeds through a number of stages and is driven by several variables. The most important variables are demand, supply and capability. How tourism has developed at any destination is therefore a reflection of the tourism process not only for the destination but for the nation as well.

2 The term 'development' indicates that the tourism process should result in 'outputs'. The output or product of tourism activity is reflected in the course of action to be followed by a destination to allow for the realization of regional or national goals in the face of competitive pressure. This dimension is therefore concerned with the content of tourism, and the objectives or the goals for which it is being promoted.

3 The 'broader and environmental goals' indicate that policies relate to and reflect varying contexts in the developmental process. It needs to be mentioned that India is a very heterogeneous country in terms of levels of development, nationalities and cultures, and factors of endowment for tourism activity. The context of tourism activity would often defy the logic of broader and environmental goals.

We have seen that domestic tourism in its three phases, traditional (pilgrimage, fairs and festivals), historical (pleasure and leisure activities of the nobility) and the colonial period, was driven by a motivation that went beyond demand and supply, although the propensity to travel was related to the capability, or purchasing power, of those involved in tourism activity. In all its stages of development the state subsidized the traveller with limited means (Ministry of Tourism, 1997).

In the colonial period, the British imposed the pattern of the development of tourism that they were familiar with at home. Rural hamlets in the hills were turned into urban settlements, popularly known as hill stations, and beach tourism as well as sports and adventure were developed with an infrastructure of small hotels, circuit houses and rest houses, as well as the hospitality of the rulers of the princely states who maintained game reserves for their hunting pleasure.

However, it is only in the post-colonial period that national and regional goals have been set for tourism development. These goals have been primarily economic. Tourism was advocated for developing countries to help them to overcome poverty and to catch up with the developed countries. It was also thought that tourism would help new nations to develop a national identity. Since economic development was linked to foreign exchange earnings, domestic tourism growth has been spontaneous up to a certain level, until the decade of the 1960s when the state began to invest in tourism infrastructure and services. Today states that have been lagging in the developmental process or sections of the population that have been marginalized in the process of the shift to a modern industrial state are being offered the opportunity to earn an income from tourism, in a planned initiative by the state government, the private sector supported by national and foreign capital, as well as local investment. This process has led to a greater segmentation of the domestic tourist market and the emergence of new products and new destinations.

The second issue that should be noted is that there is so far no uniform definition of tourism, and this is a problem that is not adequately understood by policy-makers or the public. In 1979, the National Working Group on Domestic Tourism recognized this problem and decided to use several methodologies to collect data and then, by a process of elimination, evolved a definition of a domestic tourist (Department of Tourism, 1979 and 1994).

The need was for a definition that the state governments could use easily without creating an elaborate organization in the early stages of the statistical process, since most developing countries have a problem with trained manpower. This problem is now being addressed by the WTO, which has set up the process of developing Satellite Accounting Systems that would help the countries concerned to collect reliable and comparable data on tourism activity and performance (WTO, 1998). The need for such data is to ensure more purposeful and effective planning of facilities for domestic and international tourists. Thus, a data base has been an important objective, since resources for tourism development have not only been scarce, but committing resources for tourism has also been problematic when agricultural and infrastructural demands were being made on the economic system of newly independent India.

The working group suggested that data should be collected by the card method (which included the registration card provided by accommodation units as well as information collected from sightseers travelling on conducted tours or tourist taxis or other modes of transport), supported by a survey to be undertaken every five years either by the Department of Tourism or the state government, through their own resources or by hiring a private agency. Registration at accommodation units continues to be the main source for data on domestic tourism.

Broadly, we will define tourism for the purpose of research on domestic tourism movement and activity as the study of the activity and behaviour of people away from their usual habitat, involving the services of an industry to cater to their needs while they are travelling, and the social, economic, ecological and cultural impact on the community of residents at the destination(s) they visit. This definition again assumes that tourism services can be termed an 'industry' even though there is a great deal of divergence, even a low level of integration, in the collection of businesses that provide travel- and traveller-related services. Some researchers have preferred to view tourism as a system since the quality of an experience depends on the interdependence of many services. For a system to function effectively much will depend on the manner in which tourism is handled at the destination and on the business ethic and culture of the providers of the services. In Asian countries where cultural and lifestyle differences are very significant, this factor becomes extremely important in balancing the goals of the different role players in the tourism process, activity and context.

Since India lacks a set of objectives, internal similarities (Smith, 1989, p163), the tourism process has grown unevenly. For example, the level of economic development of the metropolitan cities of India is much higher than that of other regional cities and towns, and the difference is more significant between rural and urban centres. There are differences in the level of development of the regions in which the process of industrialization has a longer history, and between the plains and the mountain areas. Areas developed by tradition and colonialism have a higher tourism awareness and activity in comparison with the newer destinations. Ignoring these differences, and often with the stated objective of overcoming them, the tourism policy in India has concentrated on international circuit tourism, linking countries or multiple destinations within a country, resulting in an ethnocentric market-led 'institutionalization' of tourism activity. Similarly the metropolitan economic and cultural hegemony in tourism development has led to the demand for global quality standards like resorts, hospitality activities and travel organizations in the sphere of domestic tourism as well. This is in sharp contrast to the diversity of resources, their exploitation and the richness of local cultures that demand a need-led developmental process rather than a market-led process favoured by the policy-makers (Krippendorf, 1987; Poon, 1989).

In the Asian region public control of the tourism industry, since private sector resources had been insufficient, was both politically and economically correct. Governments, according to Richter (Richter, 1989), had five policy options: public versus private tourism development; domestic versus international tourism; quality versus mass tourism; centralization versus decentralization; and integrated versus enclave tourism. These choices were necessitated by the resource crunch as well as the ideological imperatives of the political and economic system of newly independent countries in the Asian region. In India we have a mix of private and public involvement. Airlines, railways and some hotel facilities are government owned, while travel services are privately owned. Government is seen as an agency of encouragement and competition. Secondly, since India has a federal political system, there is a division of tasks between the federal government and the state government. The latter concentrates on facilities for domestic tourists. Today there is a renewed policy debate in India as structural adjustment programmes turn South Asian economies into export-led economies and this implies that international tourism has to be privileged. This process will increase enclave tourism and will undermine the process of decentralization that is natural in a federal political system.

Two factors have set off the tourism debate in the Asian region. The first is the rapid economic growth and restructuring in the region triggered by the reform process. The second is the active involvement of the government in tourism planning and the expansion of tourism activity beyond traditional destinations. The role of the public sector in the superstructure of tourism is being questioned, and economists and planners are pushing the privatization model. There is, however, no clear 'high road' to tourism development in developing countries and policies have to be sensitive to the consequences of tourism for the region, the community and its resources (Go and Jenkins, 1997).

In the South Asia region there is a slow dismantling of political barriers, as a result of which the broad pattern of present as well as prospective travel is over relatively short-distance domestic travel. Travel to neighbouring countries is not a viable alternative as in other regions. In India this process is different and domestic tourism is often substituted by long-haul international tourism since we do not have good political relations with our neighbours. In many of the frontier states we also have the problem of separatist and militant movements disrupting daily life. With a GNP of US$272 and a population of 860 million, the WTTC had estimated a potential market of 9 million outbound Indian tourists by the year 2000, although the outbound tourists numbered just over 3.2 million in 1997 (WTTC, 1996). India has already become a major market for Mauritius and Singapore, not only in numbers but also in expenditure. Domestic tourism accounts for 83 per cent of all worldwide movements (Go and Jenkins, 1997), yet domestic tourism is more difficult to measure because such tourists do not cross borders or exchange money and there are few regular records of domestic tourists (Department of Tourism, 1979).

In India, a domestic tourist is a person who travels within the country to a place other than the place of residence and stays in hotels or other accommodation establishments or in dharamashalas, sarais, musafirkhanas, agra-shalas, choultries, etc (classified as Indian-style accommodation) for a duration of not less than 24 hours and not more than 6 months, for the following purposes: pleasure (holiday, leisure, sports); pilgrimage, religious and social functions; business conferences and meetings; study and health. Excluded from the count are persons arriving to take up an occupation, or establishing more or less permanent residence, or persons visiting their home town on leave or for a short visit to friends and relatives, or attending social or religious functions, at which times they do not use commercial facilities. Foreign residents in India are also excluded (Department of Tourism, 1994).

In India, tourism was a part of the agenda for national integration and economic development at the time of independence. The Sargent Committee had identified tourism as a developmental activity. However, it was not until 1967 that a Ministry of Tourism and Civil Aviation was set up to coordinate the policy options and to implement tourism programmes in the country. China and India are said to lead in domestic tourism with 600 million and 100 million nationals participating in tourism activity in 1996 (Lew and Yu, 1995). However, the promotion of domestic tourism is not a priority in many Asian countries, and India is no exception. This shift away from domestic tourism has come in the wake of the economic reforms that the Indian government had launched since the beginning of the decade of the 1990s. Our previous policy statement of 1982 had put domestic tourism and national integration as a top priority to legitimize the financial involvement of the government in providing services and facilities for tourists.

A new tourism policy was placed before the cabinet in June 1997. With the installation of a BJP-led coalition government in March 1998, the tourism policy was given a new thrust on paper, to support the development of pilgrim sites and to realize the commitment made to tourism in their National Agenda for Governance. Unlike the National Action Plan (NAP) of 1992 which functioned as the tourism policy for raising India's share of the international market to 1 per cent, the new policy will need to look at the issue of selective developmental needs, as well as the demands of a wide section of domestic travellers (*The Pioneer*, 1997a). The policy has indicated proper coordination between Panchayat Raj (local self-government bodies), institutions, NGOs and local youth in creating facilities at places of domestic tourist interest, while central government investment ought to be concentrated in the area of integrating infrastructure. It also discusses the issue of congestion at selected destinations, as well as environmental pressures at overexposed destinations. The draft points out that tourism was never given the importance it deserved, resulting in the neglect of the sector in the post-independence years. The new BJP government has given a commitment to tourism, but has allocated a mere 110 crores[1] to tourism in the current year (1998).

The first tourism policy was announced in the sixth plan period in 1982, specifying developmental objectives and an action plan based on the travel circuit concept. In the seventh plan, tourism was accorded industrial status and in 1988 the National Committee on Tourism recommended a package of incentives for the accelerated growth of tourism. A Tourism Finance Corporation was set up to encourage investment in tourism. A tourism synergy programme was evolved on the basis of the NAP in 1993, which was modified into a national strategy for the development of tourism in 1996 to implement the concept of special tourism areas and the intensive development of selected circuits and destinations (Ministry of Tourism, 1992). While these deliberations have been paying lip-service to domestic tourism, resources have been concentrated and budgetary support has been given primarily for the growth of international arrivals.

The reason that domestic tourism has been neglected in practice, but talked about as a priority, is that the logic for earning hard currencies by encouraging foreign tourists has remained high among international bodies, like the WTO. And this logic has tended to override the concern of communities for income and employment opportunities. Since separatist movements and militant action in the border states became significant in the 1980s, tourism was seen as a unifying force in a period of political and constitutional crisis. The basis of these movements had been the frustration of the educated youth who had remained unemployed and the developmental needs of regions that since independence had not been given their due share of resources and investment. The separatist movement in Kashmir valley is an example. The civil strife and the militancy in the north-east is also related to the demand for development.

Tourism, it was thought, would be a good way of understanding the aspirations and viewpoints of others and would help in nation building. The Youth Hostel movement was therefore to be supported to allow youth to participate in tourism activity, along with adventure and camping activities. Hand-loom and handicraft activities were to help rural artisans to access urban markets. The National Committee on Tourism recommended that anti-poverty and area development plans should be integrated with tourism development. Backward areas should be seen as areas with high tourism potential. INTACH (Indian National Trust for Culture and Heritage), an NGO, has been involved in such activity since its inception in the 1980s.

The NAP had stated that facilities for domestic tourists, especially the budget segment, would be strengthened and expanded through central assistance to state governments for investment in tented camps and paying-guest accommodation. Incentives would be provided to the travel trade if their turnover reflected the domestic business. It was noted that pilgrim flows formed an important part of domestic tourism and infrastructure and facilities needed upgrading at pilgrim centres. The central government would set up a fund of Rs^2 5 crore for accommodation, wayside facilities and transport at important pilgrim centres. Data on the Amarnath Yatra and Vaishno Devi (both in Jammu and Kashmir), Tirupati and the sites of the Kumbh Mela (held once every 12 years at Haridwar, Nasik and Ujjain) indicate that all these locations have exceeded their carrying capacities and management of numbers has become critical to their survival (Ministry of Tourism, undated). Pilgrims have been staggered, held back, often faced the rods of security forces and shrines have been shut down to allow the rest of the staff to perform rituals, and yet the numbers keep increasing every year.

Craft villages have also to be set up in all the states. Similarly fairs, like the Sonepur Cattle Fair or Pushkar, and festivals, like the Dussehra at Mysore and Kullu, are to receive financial assistance for development. The Department of Culture, the Archaeological Survey of India and the Zonal cultural centres are to be assisted in promoting son et lumière shows, craft bazaars and food plazas as well as cultural evenings. Most of these ideas, wherever they have been developed, have focused exclusively on the seasonal and destinational mix of the international tourist rather than the domestic tourist, and the pricing is also beyond the means of the domestic tourist. The practice of enclosing and ticketing has often appropriated a local festival, like the one at Khajuraho, and turned it into an international tourism product.

The Indian Association of Tour Operators' (IATO) list of aims states as number one 'to promote national integration, international welfare and good will', and this is a good indication of the focus given to the role of tourism in creating an Indian identity. They organized a business session on domestic tourism at their annual convention in 1996, where it was seen that state tourism officials were very enthusiastic about the possibilities of domestic tourism since it was more attuned to India's cultures and problems, as well as exhibiting an increasing ability to pay. Market research has estimated that 2 million Indians earn a monthly salary/income of Rs30,000 and above, which makes the domestic market as attractive as the budget international traveller (*The Pioneer*, 1997c). They have made a commitment to offer off-season package holidays to domestic tourists at resorts and destinations which have been developed for the foreign tourist. This possibility is linked to the concept of a dual tariff, reflecting the purchasing power of the rupee vis-à-vis the dollar for tourism services. The rupee has been devalued significantly, and Indian tourists are unable to pay the same tariffs as international tourists since their salaries have not grown at the same rate. This debate is dividing different sections of the travel trade, with the tour operators supporting the 'fair trade' stand of the international customer and the accommodation units fighting for higher occupancy by lowering rupee tariffs for the domestic business.

The regulatory policies of the government have always been tourist centred since they view success in terms of numbers and foreign exchange earnings. There is pressure on the Department of Tourism to bring in tourism legislation to ensure 'transparency' as consumer protection laws in the West claim to have done. The travel trade is, however, resistant to regulation since the small operator is still vulnerable to economic collapse and very strongly controlled by the big operators. The latter have much greater access to government departments and their views are reflected in the direction of policy and regulation. The large operators control market forces and the role of the small enterprise, which benefits the local community, is yet to be given adequate importance.

The Indian Railways, with the Leave Travel Concession (LTC) and the special trains, both high cost and holiday specials, have played a significant role in enhancing the number of domestic tourists, which is constantly growing. Indian Airlines and Air India also offer LTC fares between mid-April and the end of July on domestic sectors. There is a demand from the Himalayan states to extend the LTC fare to their region and not only on the metro routes as at present, which their travel trade feels is important in making the Himalayan region accessible to the holidaymaker.

The FHRAI (Federation of Hotel and Restaurant Associations of India) has also committed to the creation of budget facilities for domestic tourists to avail of state incentives and central funding. Hotels offer attractive packages from 1 April to 30 September, the off-season for international tourists. India has a long summer vacation during which the domestic traveller looks for holiday options. With a large increase in double-income families, these packages are considered cost effective. The value add-ons offer new opportunities to the domestic tourist for whom the hotel becomes the destination. It is a fact that the destinations on offer are either too hot or have too much rain at the time of the year when domestic offers are made. However, the customers have the rare chance of sampling a five-star lifestyle. These offers are as popular with budget tourists from abroad. The FHRAI is also keen to avail of the incentives being offered for three-star and lower categories of hotels, as well as investment in hotels in hill areas and other backward regions of the country, particularly heritage properties. For the promotion of domestic tourism, hotels located in remote or backward regions have been offering rupee tariffs to domestic travellers to maintain year-long business, since international tourism is highly seasonal and not very significant in numbers.

Examples of offers for the summer season of 1997 indicate the emphasis of the private sector in the domestic market. Three-night/two-day packages from the Oberoi group range from Rs3775 for Agra to Rs12,000 for Bangalore; suites are available for Rs17,000 and deluxe villas for Rs20,000. The package includes two-way transfers, a welcome drink, two children under 12 accommodated free and the use of facilities like the health club as well as a sightseeing trip. Food credit of Rs1550 per couple is given. The Taj Group is offering packages from Rs7000 to Rs19,550. In comparison, the ITDC (public sector) is offering packages from Rs1444 to Rs3333 (*The Pioneer*, 1997b).

The Travel Agents Association of India (TAAI) has also pledged its support to domestic tourism since the NAP offers incentives for promoting domestic tourism which should contribute 25 per cent of the revenues of the travel trade. However, under pressure from the hotel lobby, which has resisted the expenditure tax levied by state and central governments on tariffs above Rs1200 per night, the travel trade has also been subjected to a 5 per cent service tax (Hariharan, 1997; Business Times Bureau, 1997), which is an attempt by government to regulate trade practices and make them more transparent. The BJP government has now suspended the service tax for two years in response to IATO and TAAI pressure (*Times of India*, 1997).

Dimensions of Domestic Tourism in India

The success of these policies can be measured by the data available with the Department of Tourism. Domestic tourism surveys are generally not published since they are for the use of the state and central governments in planning their investments. However, a pilot study on domestic tourism to 22 destinations estimated that tourist traffic in 1981 was 5.5 million and, if extended to 1000 destinations favoured by domestic tourists, it was estimated at 14 million. The figure for 1991 increases to 82.7 million and, for 1995, to 135 million. These estimates are based on the coverage of 3 metropolitan cities, 3 business centres, 5 hill stations, 2 beach resorts, 6 pilgrim centres and 3 historical cities.[3] If we consider Agra, a premier tourist destination, we have an interesting picture of the importance of domestic tourism. Some 7 million domestic tourists visited the city of the Taj in 1996, while foreign visitors numbered 1.4 million (*Economic Times*, 1997a).

The plan outlays for the Ministry/Department of Tourism (actual expenditure) in the eighth plan (1992–1996) show that actual expenditure on tourism development was Rs794.1 million in 1992–1993, Rs855 million in 1993–1994, Rs1035 million in 1994–1995 and Rs1107 million in 1995–1996. The assistance to the states was Rs209.2 million, which reduced to Rs105.4 million in 1995. The Tourism Finance Corporation released (March 1995) an amount of Rs7546.9 million. Of this Rs6200 million went to the three- four- and five-star categories of hotels (Department of Tourism, 1994). These figures indicate that domestic tourism in India is a low-cost investment opportunity to the economy with high productivity. Yet standards and costs to the domestic tourist remain beyond the means of most urban dwellers and are far from satisfactory. Facilities also remain concentrated at particular locations. For instance, at hill stations like Manali, Shimla and Mussorie, it is clear that tourist traffic needs regulation. Mining, felling of trees and concrete structures have destroyed the environment of the three premier hill stations. The rush of tourists has begun to pose problems for the police, the municipality, transport management, parking and waste-disposal agencies, and disrupts the life of the residents who are not offering accommodation or other services to tourists. The tourist trade, however, rakes in profits.

The Department of Tourism has proposed an investment of Rs31,350 crores over the next four years since tourism has provided employment to 7.8 million (provisional estimate) in 1994. Earnings from domestic tourism are estimated to be double or three times that of international tourism, which were Rs7365.61 crores in 1994. Estimating earnings from domestic tourism remains a problem since state governments do not have the means to collect such data. An ESCAP (*Tourism Review*, 1992) study estimates this figure at Rs18,000 crore (*Economic Times*, 1996). However, the path to tourism development is paved with grave environmental impacts like car exhaust, rubbish (solid waste and plastic bags) at sanctuaries, lakes, hill stations and monuments.

The geographical concentration of investment triggers a chain of consequences leading to inflation of real-estate costs, price rises and changes in land use and traditional access to common land and resources. Paddy-fields in Kerala, being promoted as 'God's own country' and 'A woman of substance', are fast disappearing in the real estate boom. Agricultural land is the easiest to develop (*Economic Times*, 1997b). At wild life sanctuaries and lakes like the Dal in Srinagar, there is a massive displacement programme, funded by the World Bank, for the relocation of thousands of families to promote environmental tourism.

In 1985–1986, 37 prominent tourist centres accounted for 70 per cent of tourist activity, and today the figure for the same destinations stands at 67 per cent. According to ESCAP:

> *Tourism has been developed in an unplanned and unco-ordinated manner. Where planning exists it is loosely enforced, defeating the objective of the planning exercise. . . In some countries tourism has been accorded top priority in terms of marketing, but virtually none in terms of management, leading to widespread deterioration of the product* (Economic Times, 1996).

For India the solution lies in directing investment to other potential centres of tourism activity. This calls for a change in the approach to the assessment of demand for tourism products and services so that fresh investment takes place at new locations. As long as demand assessment is based on international tourists and first-class domestic tourists, the mass of middle-level and low-cost demand will continue to put pressure on the established destinations.

Benefits of Domestic Tourism

Domestic tourism is usually the predecessor of international tourism since it helps to create tourism awareness and tourism culture that can sustain international tourism in the long term. In India it received very little attention until 1980. This is because no study of the discretionary income of Indian people had been made. We did not have a tradition of leisure travel. Pilgrimages and visits to fairs and festivals for commercial and religious reasons had been the predominant motivation. It is also true that domestic tourism was ignored because it competed for facilities and services with international tourists and these were in short supply. The majority of domestic tourists are individual or independent travellers, and a few of the higher income groups are only now beginning to use travel services for transport and accommodation. The increase in paid holidays with leave travel concessions by rail, road and air has subsidized domestic travel. The marketing and organization of domestic tourism services have become very recently part of the function of the travel trade in India. The trade has given attention to the domestic tourist only after years of continuing crisis in the field of international tourism, where flows are controlled by international agencies and governments that issue unfavourable travel advisories to discourage tourism to India.

Domestic tourism has other advantages. It helps to sustain demand for tourism when overseas visitor arrivals show seasonal variations. The failure of the Visit India Year 1991, due to the Gulf War, turned the attention of policy-makers and the industry towards the role of domestic tourism. It helps to conserve foreign exchange by encouraging Indians to see their own country rather than travelling abroad. However, the high-spending domestic tourists find the product and quality of tourism in India below their expectations. It helps to expand investment and transfer resources from richer to poorer areas and enables local people to benefit from government investment in tourism infrastructure, particularly transport and communication, which bring in information and access to new products and the growth of the tertiary sector. For instance, the introduction of air services and electricity after 1974 changed the quality of life in Leh town. In a period of economic recession, domestic tourism protects the occupancy of accommodation and other services as tourists from overseas decline. It is also not vulnerable to bad publicity, internal security problems and poor infrastructure. In a competitive environment, where the Asia Pacific region is promoting very similar products, domestic tourists can sustain tourism development. It should be promoted because it meets the recreational needs of the resident population and helps to create awareness about the natural resources of the country and their conservation.

Domestic tourism is, however, very segmented. In India, it has developed along two paths. The older pattern centres on traditional festivals and pilgrimages to Hindu, Buddhist, Muslim, Sikh and Parsi shrines, as well as the shrines of saints and holy men. The second pattern of domestic tourism began in the colonial period, which involved the retreat to the hills in the hot season. This type of excursion attracted the British, the princes and upper-class Indians. Government rest houses, privately owned hotels and second homes provided accommodation, and surface transport was also developed to make such destinations accessible. After Independence, government policies have supported domestic travel, although in a passive way. They have promoted tourism from information offices, low-cost accommodation and sightseeing tours, to state tourism development corporations and low-cost transport, to leave travel concession schemes. Domestic tourists demand both first-class as well as low-cost facilities. Tourism policy in India has been unable to decide between these two options and has now settled for the first-class tourist, although it claims not to ignore the needs of the budget tourist in its incentive programmes. The choices that policy-makers entertain will have political and economic consequences, and the ambivalence of our policy indicates that we are not yet certain of the role that tourism is to play in our political and economic life.

It should also be pointed out that travel within national boundaries helps the infrastructure to develop and the tourism industry to expand and upgrade its services. Tourism can penetrate to where local communities can service the tourist and become tourists themselves because domestic tourists share similar standards in tourism facilities. Such movement can remove barriers and the feeling of difference and otherness, while bringing the distant and the unfamiliar into the range of understanding and recognition as a part of our heritage and cultural resources. New ideas, practices, cuisine, textiles and crafts can become new cultural symbols of unification through new territorial and cultural perspectives.

Holidays for domestic tourists often come at the same time and are celebrated in the same way. Paid holidays have encouraged the domestic tourist to extend the range of holiday activity beyond the home environment. Thus, domestic demand does not depend on external factors and benefits local manpower, the distribution of development and income, and gives a thrust to local craft and industry, both cottage and processing. It also helps agriculture to diversify its products to provide for the tourist. Off-season vegetable farming in the hill regions for sale to hotels and to markets in the foothills has grown out of tourism demand for certain types of cuisine. This has improved the

Table 8.1 *Domestic and foreign tourist arrivals*

States	1994			1995			1996		
	Domestic	Foreign	Total	Domestic	Foreign	Total	Domestic	Foreign	Total
Andhra Pradesh	32,846,914	48,720	32,895,634	39,317,707	84,092	39,401,799	33,450,743	63,652	33,514,395
Arunachal Pradesh	2222	0	2222	2266	0	2266	2263	0	2263
Assam	17,649	350	17,999	16,026	479	16,505	14,443	1000	15,443
Bihar	8,454,457	45,543	8500,000	8539,001	49,186	8,588,187	9,392,901	52,973	9,445,874
Goa	849,404	210,191	1,059,595	878,487	229,218	1,107,705	887,983	232,359	1,120,342
Gujarat	55,494	6001	61,495	57,303	3005	60,308	64,478	6581	71,059
Haryana	306,559	1284	307,843	311,535	2222	313,757	281,648	1763	283,411
Himachal Pradesh	1,720,616	51,824	1,772,440	1,563,690	47,903	1,611,593	1,615,878	50,230	1,666,108
Jammu and Kashmir	3,745,425	24,683	3,770,108	4,098,043	20,589	4,118,632	4,459,444	22,628	4,482,072
Karnataka	5,946,542	46,654	5,993,196	4,467,515	59,991	4,527,506	4,546,714	64,788	4,611,502
Kerala	1,284,375	104,568	1,388,943	3,857,603	142,972	4,000,575	4,243,363	185,863	4,429,226
Madhya Pradesh	7,032,125	75,673	7,107,798	6,583,461	91,934	6,675,395	7,241,807	99,012	7,340,819
Maharashtra	5,496,197	786,921	6,283,118	6,155,740	881,351	7,037,091	6,771,314	949,215	7,720,529
Manipur	80,122	559	80,681	84,613	288	84,901	86,959	218	87,177
Meghalaya	154,977	577	155,554	144,529	1172	145,701	135,906	1604	137,510
Mizoram	20,356	115	20,471	18,420	119	18,539	23,534	90	23,624
Nagaland	11,108	194	11,302	13,800	39	13,839	13,420	54	13,474
Orissa	2,594,992	26,024	2,621,016	2,697,165	28,231	2,725,396	2,773,245	34,303	2,807,548
Punjab	322,208	5309	327,517	328,652	5415	334,067	361,517	5831	367,348
Rajasthan	4,699,886	436,801	5,136,687	5,258,862	534,749	5,793,611	5,726,441	560,946	6,287,387
Sikkim	92,435	7132	99,567	98,555	5866	104,421	108,410	6901	115,311
Tamil Nadu	16,025,594	496,721	16,522,315	17,214,953	585,751	17,800,704	18,207,666	613,982	18,821,648
Tripura	203,746	0	203,746	192,881	0	192,881	206,232	2	206,234

Uttar Pradesh	28,840,000	571,000	29,411,000	30,704,000	617,000	31,321,000	33,774,400	664,509	34,438,909
West Bengal	4,330,172	163,208	4,493,380	4,377,407	181,489	4,558,896	4,448,938	183,330	4,632,268
Andaman and Nicobar	46,125	3798	49,923	58,629	3849	62,478	61,780	5796	67,576
Chandigarh	403,226	8246	411,472	410,777	8559	419,336	423,927	9017	432,944
Daman and Diu	51,871	3341	55,212	67,068	3682	70,750	73,774	3965	77,739
Delhi	1,154,868	892,007	2,046,875	1,270,354	1,007,967	2,278,321	1,397,389	1,113,803	2,511,192
Dadra and Nagar Haveli	0	0	0	0	0	0	0	0	0
Lakshdweep	2885	1743	4628	4038	664	4702	4441	715	5156
Pondichery	324,105	11,029	335,134	336,090	11,697	347,787	369,699	12,597	382,296
Total	127,116,655	4,030,216	131,146,871	139,129,170	4,609,479	143,738,649	141,170,657	4,947,727	146,118,384

Source: Department of Tourism, 1997

food security of communities where consumption was well below the average nutritional level.

Domestic Tourism Destinations and New Products

The prime tourist destinations identified by the ministry are:

- Bombay, Delhi, Madras (metro tourism).
- Amritsar, Bangalore, Guwahati (business tourism).
- Darjeeling, Nainital, Ooty, Shimla and Srinagar (hill stations).
- Goa and Kanya Kumari (beach resorts).
- Gaya, Haridwar, Mathura, Puri, Rameshwaram and Varanasi (pilgrim centres).
- Agra, Aurangabad and Jaipur (historical sites).

Industrial sources have added:

- Calcutta (metro).
- Chandigarh, Cochin, Hyderabad, and Bhopal (business centres).
- Leh, Kullu-Manali, Mussorie (hill stations).
- Trivandrum-Kovalam (beach resort).
- Patna, Konark, Bhubaneshwar, Lucknow, Madurai (pilgrim centres).
- Jaisalmer, Jodhpur, Khajuraho, Udaipur (historical sites).

The National Action Plan has identified the following circuits and destinations for intensive development:

- Kullu-Manali Leh (a circuit that covers Himachal Pradesh, and Jammu and Kashmir).
- Gwalior–Shivpuri–Orcha–Khajuraho (covers historical sites in Madhya Pradesh).
- Bagdogra–Sikkim–Darjeeling–Kalimpong (covers the hill region of West Bengal).
- Bhubaneshwar–Puri Konark (covers the pilgrim circuit of Orissa).
- Hyderabad–Nagarjunasagar–Tirupati (combines historical and pilgrim sites in Andhra Pradesh).
- Madras–Mamallapuram–Pondicherry (covers metro, historical site and beaches in Tamil Nadu).
- Rishikesh–Gangotri–Badrinath (pilgrim circuit in Uttar Pradesh).
- Indore–Ujjain–Maheshwar–Omkeshwar–Mandu (combines historical and pilgrim centres of Madhya Pradesh).

- Jaisalmer–Jodhpur–Bikaner–Barmer (covers desert and historical sites in Rajasthan).
- 20 Buddhist centres have been identified for tourism in Uttar Pradesh.

All these destinations indicate congestion and concentration of facilities for tourists in India. It is interesting to note that the destinations identified by the private sector show the most negative impacts of tourism on society, culture and environment as well as on issues of changes in land use. The NAP list seeks to elevate popular domestic tourism destinations to the level of international standards. It includes destinations to be developed as holiday centres:

- Lakshadweep islands (Kerala).
- Andaman Islands (Union Territory).
- Solang Nallah (Manali).
- Bekal Beach (Kerala).
- Muttukadu Beach (Tamil Nadu).
- Pong Dam (Kangra–Himachal Pradesh).

As domestic travel in India has expanded, television programmes on travel have started to cater to this demand. Market surveys have shown that increasing income translates quite rapidly into increasing travel. Three popular programmes are 'Namaste India' on Zee, 'Off the Beaten Path' on Star and 'Indian Holiday' on Sony. 'Namaste India' has focused on the well-known destinations; 'Off the Beaten Track' promotes youth and alternative tourism activities, and 'Indian Holiday' tries to locate new destinations for explorers. None of these programmes has shown a destination outside the listing given above.

All national dailies are also promoting domestic tourism by regular travel pages which highlight tourism and development issues, generally reflecting the promotional perspective of the tourism industry. Sunday papers carry profiles of destinations, activities and seasonal getaways, as well as weekend breaks that are becoming popular with the elite segments of metro city populations.

Many of these destinations are now gasping for breath with their carrying capacity having been exceeded. Many sites are now closing their doors on one day of the week or raising entry fees to control the number of visitors. For example, the Taj Mahal is closed on a Monday. Entry fees are Rs100 between 6 and 8 am and Rs15 between 8 am and 6 pm.

New Destinations

The golden triangle (Delhi–Agra–Jaipur) has been the primary product for domestic and international travellers. The Department of Tourism is now looking for an alternative to decongest the northern states where tourism services

214 The Native Tourist

and infrastructure are well developed. The north eastern states, hidden from exposure because of poor accessibility and political strife, are to be promoted as the green triangle in an attempt to bring development to Assam, Arunachal Pradesh, Tripura, Meghalaya and Nagaland. The prime minister's office has set up a task force for the region with the specific task of formulating a tourism policy. With a budget of Rs16 million (10 per cent of the tourism budget) the task force is to develop tourism projects keeping in mind the infrastructural constraints. Domestic tourism is to be promoted to create a tourism conscious-ness before promoting the product to international tourists. In 1996, 5 lakh[4] domestic visitors came to the region for ecotourism and the number is expected to grow by 10–15 per cent in the next few years (Bhatia, 1997). To keep numbers down, the Government wants to keep this region as a high-spending tourist product. The suggested figure is US$200 per night. It is also proposed to put a ceiling on the number of days a tourist can spend in the region and also to use a gateway air service to be backed up by road and, where possible, rail transport. Adventure tourism is another product to be developed. Rock-climbing, para-gliding, and trekking are other areas of investment. Cottage and tented accommodation are also being developed (*Indian Express*, 1997).

Goa, which had been the premier destination for domestic and international tourists, has also seen a decline in the last year due to congestion and over-development. Domestic arrivals were down by 2 per cent and international visitors were down by 5 per cent. The charter tourist is now landing in Goa and making for Kerala, the new destination to be promoted. The major reason is crowding on the beaches, expensive accommodation, unhygienic food, and no control over the drug trade and other illegal activities (Suresh and Babu, 1997). Another reason could be a shift in the tourism policy with new products that include highways, golf courses, offshore casinos, water sports, adventure tourism and heritage tourism. Such a policy excludes the domestic first-class tourists who make up 80 per cent of the tourists visiting Goa. Such develop-ments are being resisted by Goans.

Kerala offers private cruises through backwaters, fishing camps on the rivers, gourmet vacations on spice plantations, horseback tented vacations in the Nilgiris, private safari holidays with the royal family, hiking and golf. The cost of such customized vacations is between Rs4,500 and 6,000 per person per night. Such products are being planned for the high-spending domestic tourists who would otherwise visit Malaysia, Thailand or Singapore, as well as for overseas visitors.

As cities decay, the hill stations, which numbered about 80 urban settle-ments between the elevation of 4000 and 8000 feet at the end of colonial rule, are also congested beyond repair. The Uttar Pradesh Department of Tourism is to initiate massive development work to upgrade tourism in the hills. This is to include the widening of roads, parking space, accommodation and medical facilities, as well as electrification along the major trekking and pilgrim routes.

Thirteen locations have been identified in the Garhwal region for the setting up of budget accommodation. Plans are also being developed for bus stations, waiting-rooms and public toilets. Central government has provided 108 crores to the state for such improvements. Part of the budget includes the improvement of the water supply to tourism destinations and the regeneration of lakes.

The environmental pollution caused by the expansion of tourism facilities has led to the melting of the Pindari glacier, which will have many consequences for agriculture in the Uttar Kashi region. The judiciary has ordered the state Department of Tourism to demolish completely the tourism camps from the meadows to rejuvenate the glacier. The new investments could lead to more such disasters.

A five-day river cruise is being offered, covering the distance between Allahabad and Varanasi on the sacred Ganges. The package comes at Rs10,000 per person. For a larger group the cost comes down to Rs6500. Using motorized country boats, the cruise promotes the life on the river, which is quite different from that on the hinterland. White-water rafting is another popular activity with domestic tourists. Even pilgrims are taking to this adventure sport which is very popular in the Shivpuri–Haridwar stretch of the Ganges. The three-day camping-rafting excursion comes for anything between Rs1500 and 3500 per person.

The state government has allocated 20 crores for an Agra heritage fund, and motels-cum-tourist lodges at 20 Buddhist centres in Bundelkhand region at a cost of 175 crores. The private sector will·be given special incentives to participate in these projects as well as to set up amusement/adventure parks in the hills (*Asian Age*, 1997).

Himachal Pradesh, traditionally a summer retreat, is promoting winter sports and ecotourism. Twelve districts are to develop new tourist products like trout fishing and skiing, apart from the beauty of the scenery and old temples. Water sports, adventure sports and health resorts are also to be developed. Heritage and ethnic villages and film studios are also being planned, as well as a tourist train to be called Nature on Wheels. The state has infrastructural problems like frequent landslides, transport and telecommunication bottlenecks, and an electricity shortage. Some 240 projects worth Rs175 crores to create medium-scale resorts and amusement parks are being implemented. The estimated 60 lakh domestic tourists who visit the state are primarily pilgrims. Fairs and festivals are being developed for them, and tourists can hire state government helicopters to reach the less accessible places. The average charter cost for a six-seater in the region is Rs25,000.

Amusement parks and water parks are also a popular destination for domestic tourists. Nicco Ventures (Calcutta) and Essel (Bombay) are leaders in this activity, although they are still to break even after the large investment they have made in Calcutta and Bombay. Delhi is also likely to see such development in the Haryana tourism belt. Appu Ghar, the first amusement park in the exhibition complex at Delhi, is to be turned into a water park by the end of the year and will be open to members only. For a landlocked city, a water park is likely to attract Delhites. Investment in the organized sector is already Rs400 crores. For children in the 9–17 age group, Discovery Outbound Camps situated in the Kumaon region near Delhi are also a new summer option, offering outdoor activities and knowledge of flora and fauna. These packages come at Rs5500 per child. If a major activity like photography or aero modelling is chosen, there is an extra cost.

Honeymoon tourism is being promoted by all states as newly wed Indian couples have adopted this cultural practice from Western influences encouraged by media promotions and exposure. Dating destinations are also springing up around metro cities where young couples can go for a meal in privacy.

The biggest business in domestic tourism today is the time-share resort. A time-share is the sale of a unit of time (one week, two weeks or a month) to an individual for the stay and use of the facilities at a resort developed by a promoter. This sale is for a period of time, a lease, for 99 years. The unit is sold for one property but can be exchanged on a reciprocal basis for another property, either within the country or abroad. Sterling, in a joint venture with RCI, offers 12 domestic and unlimited international exchanges abroad. However, the time-share concept has developed a bad name in India during its 15 years in operation. Real-estate developers saw it as an easy way to make quick money. The price for a week varied from Rs50,000 to Rs3 lakhs according to the price of accommodation chosen. The Dalmias pioneered the concept and, along with Ansals and Sterling, they are the market leaders, claiming 70,000 members with 12 operational resorts. The Welcome, Taj and Oberoi Groups are also studying this market. Small operators are also entering the business. There are 45 operators in North India and 75 operators in South India. RCI already claims 1-lakh members in India in four years of operations. The low credibility of the business is due to the fact that there are very few norms that rule the time-share business in India and the customer never gets to see the promoter fulfil the promise made at the time of the sale. The entry of the Hutchinson Trust Company and the setting up of a regulatory body might make this segment highly significant in the near future (Hariharan, 1998; *The Hindu*, 1998).

Off-season packages are being offered by more than 2000 hotels located in popular hill resorts in a major private initiative to promote destinations jointly. Overcrowding during the summer season has come down from 2 months to 45 days because tourists are facing hardships in getting accommodation they can afford. If this trend continues, many hill resorts will have to close, because their viability depends on the summer business. This may be a blessing for the residents. Real-estate prices have come down because of overcapacity, which had been estimated on the basis of high tariffs and high occupancy. The off-season tariff includes attractions like cultural, educational and personality development programmes during the monsoon and winter seasons. Pollution control, the environment and better quality in the off-season are also highlighted. Hoteliers have eliminated undercutting and agreed to enforce uniform commissions to tour operators, as well as creating easy access to bookings.

However, the only area which has not been given special consideration are special facilities for single women tourists. For a large number of women travelling alone, being mistaken for a hooker inhibits them from sitting in a lobby or having a drink in the bar or eating alone in a restaurant. Some five-star hotels in the metros keep a set of rooms for single women. Rooms near elevators on certain floors are booked for women. Only regular staff are allowed in for room service. Phone calls are not routed without confirmation from the guest. Special facilities, like full-length mirrors and cosmetics, are also being introduced. The Maurya Group assigns a guest care officer to every single woman who checks in. Some hotels are creating smaller lobbies for single women, which includes a bar and sitting area. Hotel bills can also be presented in these special lobbies. However, a women who travels alone by air or overnight bus or by train is not so safe. Handling heavy luggage, being assigned a berth with male passengers, warding off unwanted attention from co-passengers and arriving at odd hours of the night are problems for single women travellers that have not received adequate attention. Safety and sexual harassment remain a major concern as more and more single women are travelling. Policy-makers have not given adequate attention to this issue. However, some enterprising women in Delhi have started a women-only tourist guesthouse as an experiment, but this caters primarily for Western women tourists. Indian women still prefer to travel in pairs or groups to create an atmosphere of security around them.

Bekal Tourism Project

Tourism authorities are moving ahead with the mega Bekal Tourism Project in spite of people's protests. The authorities boast of converting the region of Bekal, located in the northernmost rural coastal district of Kasaragod in Keralam, into Asia's largest beach tourism resort, consisting of 6500 resort units by the year 2011 (N Salim & Associates, 1995a). The total plan outlay for this project is estimated at Rs24,694,000 (ibid, 5–22 to 5–23). Four fishing panchayats (local government) would be wiped out completely by the time of the completion of this project. In every respect these fishing villages are the most sustainable, with fishing, fish-related trade, agriculture, coconut plantations and tobacco cultivation.

The average population density in rural Keralam is 747 persons per square kilometre, but in the tourism development area it is 1159 persons per square kilometre. The work participation rate for Keralam is 32.05 per cent but that of Kasaragod district is 33.25 per cent. Women directly employed in fishing-related activities in the state average 1.7 per cent only. But in Kasaragod district coast it is 29.6 per cent. The per capita fish consumption is higher than the national average in this region (N Salim & Associates, 1995b).

Unlike in other parts of the state where cropped area is being decimated due to urbanization, Kasaragod district has the unique feature of having increased the gross cropped area from 135,000ha to 143,000ha in the last five years (ibid, 2–26 to 2–29). The tourism industry requires 462ha of land for its construction activities alone in this fertile land. It also proposes an airport, buffer-land zones and an exclusive zone for railways and roads ranging from 500 metres to 20 metres on either side and even talks about sealed roads!

By the time this project is completed in 2011, its water demand will be 47 million litres per day. Some 80 per cent of this will end up as waste water, which means that 38 million litres per day will have to be treated for reuse. This resort will produce 58 tons of solid waste every day. There will be 6400 streetlights alone in this project (N. Salim & Associates, 1995b). This is envisaged in a state where even during the monsoon period, power cuts and load-shedding are a routine affair (*Business Line*, 1998).

The arrogance of the state and tourism authorities is that this mammoth project does not have a master plan to date or else it is kept as a secret document. One techno-economic feasibility study and a tourism-led urban structure plan had been prepared at the cost of Rs55 lakhs. This project would grossly violate all coastal regulation zone rules since resorts are planned at 200 metres high tide line and on the banks of backwater and riversides. Repeated requests from local communities for a proper hearing from their side had been made into sham hearings by the authorities. Repeated pleas from intellectuals, environmentalists and other groups to put a stop to this disastrous project are scorned both by the earlier Congress and the present Marxist ministries (Suresh, 1996). This project is also highly objectionable since it would come under the special tourism area (STA) under which Bekal Development Authority had been constituted. This would supersede the powers of existing local panchayats. There is no clarity concerning the powers vested in the STA or Bekal Development Authority.

The indigenous fishing community of Kasaragod is one of the last remaining communities along the Keralam coast with traditional fishing techniques. They abhor overfishing and adhere to more sustainable harvesting practices. The community still practises the traditional sea courts where the community heads assemble at the place of worship every day, and hear and decide on issues within the community. Despite these traditions, the government of Keralam has already started acquiring land under dubious public purpose. Some 38 acres of land have already been acquired and the second phase of acquisition has begun. The actual plan of tourism authorities is to buy land at the cheapest price and to sell the same to both the private and multinational hotel industry. Local people and groups in Keralam and outside were under the belief that the government and tourism department would at least wait until the completion of the court proceedings, but this has proved wrong. Land acquisition and selling Bekal at international tourism fairs has already started, without basic respect for the people and the environment.

Orissa Special Tourism Area

The 3300 acres of area near Puri beach followed the decision of the government of India to develop special tourism areas in selected parts of the country. Orissa is one of three such ambitious projects, the other two being located in Bekal beach of Kerala and Ratnagiri of Maharashtra. Among these, the Puri project is supposed to be the most comprehensive project in the country.

The Infrastructural Development Corporation of Orissa Limited (IDCO), which is involved in development of the facilities, has invited bids from the national and international consultants and developers. There were 34 respondents. Among them, 9 are bidders and the rest are consultants. The bidders are The Taj Group, Malwala-Vitala, Hyderabad-based Sujana, Khelgaon Resorts from Delhi, AVK of Chandhigarh, Suman Motels, Unitele Genesellegahal from New Delhi and Malaysia-based Chase Perdhana, which has an Indian owner. These groups have applied for setting up four- and five-star hotels. Those who asked for land are the Oberoi, KNBL Hotel Corporation, Patilson and Arachanian of Patna. Others are consultants (Patnaik, 1998).

Out of the 3300 acres of the project area, 2600 are privately owned and the remaining 700 belong to the government. Even these 2600 acres of land are encroached by a number of planters who develop cassurina and cashew plantations and sell the wood in the town and nearby areas. The Temple Trust of Lord Jagannath Temple that owns the area, and the chairman of the trust, the local district magistrate who coordinates the project work, do not seem to have raised any objections (ibid).

But there is a catch. A private family of 50 who own around 2600 acres, previously belonging to the government, has already won a case in the lower court, thanks to the consolidation officer who intervened on their behalf. The family, who are priests or pandas of the area, have considerable differences with the other members of the tribe, but the government was shortly hopeful of settling the issue amicably and starting the project.

The special tourism area will have an 18-hole golf course, four- and five-star hotels, budget hotels, resorts, time-share apartments, a water-sports complex and a helicopter pad. A craft village is also to be included. The land acquisition process has already been initiated, and government and bureaucracy are determined to do something.

Conclusion

Some issues that have been raised with regard to domestic tourism need to be discussed since they have not featured in tourism research. Some questions relate to the type of new domestic tourists, the regions from which they originate and their demand for quality services and global leisure activities. First-class tourists are generally from metropolitan cities or business centres. The regions that lead in domestic tourism on an all-India basis are Gujarat, West Bengal, Maharashtra and the national capital region. Bengalis have a specific travel season, the Durga Puja vacation, while the others travel north in the summer and south in the winter. Travel tends to concentrate on neighbouring states. Sightseeing forms the major interest, but many domestic tourists are increasingly interested in active tourism like adventure sports and trekking.

A strong motivation for tourists from states with alcohol prohibition is to travel to 'wet' destinations to be able to drink without restriction. For North Indian tourists, drinking forms an important leisure activity and they are becoming a menace in the hill stations which can be accessed in a couple of hours from the neighbouring states. Eve teasing (the teasing and pestering of women after drinking) has become a tourism-related activity. The awareness of adventure-oriented tourists is increasing, and the television programme 'Living on the Edge' has taken up tourism-related environmental issues for discussion. In general, domestic tourists, being temporary visitors, are not concerned with environmental or socio-economic impacts unless their level of education and travel experience is high. In our personal observation, a great number of domestic tourists do not repeat a destination, so they are unable to evaluate the degradation that tourism activity has caused.

Planners and policy-makers have not discussed either the environmental or socio-economic impacts in their research, or the issue of tourism and prostitution. India has had a long tradition of pilgrimage tourism, and most temples and shrines in the south have a tradition of the devadasi, or temple dancer. This tradition deteriorated into temple prostitution, with the result that social reformers and women's organizations took up the fight against the devadasis, without understanding the system or how it was corrupted. Devadasis were looked upon as fallen women, and the approach of the reformers was to rehabilitate them, outside the social pale, in much the same way as India's National Commission for Women targeted prostitutes in the red light districts of the metro cities. An example of the link between domestic tourism and prostitution is apparent in the world-renowned pilgrim centre of Mahabalipuram, which has been selected as one of the travel circuits for international tourism development. The authorities are now trying to clean up the prostitution rackets flourishing in the town. The special grade town of Panchayat has clamped down on prostitution by closing down identified brothels and the people involved in the brothels have been forced out of the town. Brothel

operators have been identified as 'outsiders'. Children have been warned by local youth and voluntary organizations who are on guard against child prostitution. The issue is seen as a law and order problem which can be handled by what we might call strong-arm tactics or treated as a menace, rather than seeing the social links between tourism and prostitution. This is an area that requires proper research and direction. It also requires an educational campaign with tourists to encourage them to see the implications of such tourist activity on women and children at the destination. Hotels in tourist destinations and resorts have also encouraged prostitution, in covert ways, to promote a destination. The representation of women who belong to a class lower than that of the tourist, and are therefore seen as objects of pleasure, is responsible for the demand for prostitution at destinations. On the other hand, the tourist is represented as rich and powerful and becomes desirable for women who are unable to fulfil their aspirations, both social and economic.

The economic magnitude of tourism has not been evaluated. Now that the government proposes a 5 per cent service tax on the travel trade, we may have a more realistic evaluation of the earnings from tourism. There is no doubt that local entrepreneurship has been given an investment opportunity, but this remains restricted to the local asset holder and rich members of the community. Other social groups are on the margins of the service industry since they do not have capital for investment. In domestic tourism, both domestic and international services, the tourist/server ratio is low (10:1) and HRD is not given importance since trained personnel will demand higher wages (Sharma, 1997). It is clear that domestic tourists' services do not maintain high standards and do not pay high wages. The weaker sections also face all the disadvantages of tourism development, like alienation from land and assets, price rises, the appropriation of local resources, particularly water and electricity, and free recreational opportunities.

Government deregulation in real-estate and construction has brought investors to beaches, mountains, deserts, forts and palaces to cater to domestic and foreign tourists. For the investor, the term 'hotel' includes motels, wayside amenities, hill and desert resorts, heritage properties and tourist complexes. Tourism-related industry includes domestic airports, golf courses, amusement parks, ropeways, water-sports complexes, wildlife, adventure and cultural activities, food and craft-training institutes, convention and seminar units, and organizers. Restrictions on imports for essential goods have also been liberalized. Hotels can import up to 2.5 per cent of their total foreign exchange earnings and recreational bodies up to 10 per cent. These imports are at a concessional rate of customs duty. This is an indication of the trend in investment in tourism-related business, which is likely to leave a very small space for the local entrepreneur.

Western-style consumerism has displaced the role of women as presenters and organizers of culture and ritual, and their cottage industry has been transformed from items of use value to items of souvenir interest. This has undermined their status as well as their economic autonomy as they become dependent on goods produced in the all-India market. The outflow of income to the manufacturing centres often creates distress for artisan communities. Perhaps the most significant shift has been the food dependency created by tourism consumption and the demonstration effect on the local population. This change is also evident in the dress and moral values as well as social relations between different members of the community and between generations. The understanding between different cultures of a nation can only be better when elites do not see their travel destinations as different, exotic entities; when one culture does not evaluate another from within its own value system. India is a multinational state and the issue of culture has depended very much on elite perceptions since they have controlled the political and economic system. New nation nationalism has also institutionalized regional cultural practices and cultural statements to create an Indian identity, and this process of showcasing culture has been visualized by elite perceptions. The festivals of India are an example of such perceptions, which have selected the highly visual, dramatic and presentable aspects of local cultural practices, and the same attitude is reflected in state-level festivals like Kerala's Elephant March. Consequently, there has been an alienation of the natural context of culture and the process of commodification has been the direct result of promoting tourism. As other subgroups and subcultures are creating their own space in the political system, there may be a change in the perceptions of other national cultures.

The heritage movement, centring on objects, people, buildings and sites, is subject to interpretation (Smith and Eddington, 1992). The ideology of the presenter and the receiver can often be radically different from historical objectivity. A good example is the Ayodhya crisis, where the forces of Hindu nationalism, led by the BJP, brought down a 15th century mosque (one of its kind in the town) built by Babar, the founder of the Moghul dynasty that ruled India from the 16th century until the advent of colonialism, because it was believed that it was built on the ruins of the birth place of Lord Rama, a popular Hindu God. Apart from the ideological reasons for the destruction of the Babri Masjid, it is a sad fact that Ayodhya, which is an ancient city that had monuments from all periods of the history of Indian civilization, lost this mosque which was the only monument from the 15th century.

The question of heritage is therefore not one that all can agree upon. The economic possibilities of heritage sites can be exploitative and the heritage industry frequently ignores the preservation and conservation needs for economic gains. Tourism goes beyond authenticity to create highly visual images based on recycled myths or pure invention. Different sections of society view the historical past in different ways. At different time periods a social crisis prompts a different interpretation of the cultural ethos of the people, their landscape, language and way of life. The modern concept of heritage is that with the intervention of the cultural statement desired, a period can be

reproduced in the present to act as a back-drop to modern tourist demand. This is believed to enhance national pride and identity, as well as to encourage tourism. We in India have made use of our feudal past in restoring old palaces, forts and havelis (a country or town house) and transforming them into hotels for tourists, but this is a manufactured heritage which is not representative of the way of life in the period that the building represents, but caters to the demand of the Westernized customer for a certain type of reconstruction to create the image of India as a land of maharajas while providing modern comforts for the privileged elite, both domestic and international.

A similar form of commercialization can also be observed at traditional pilgrim sites, where people flock for individual gains and benefits, and therefore demand a range of facilities that fit their status. The pilgrimage is no longer undertaken for the social prestige it confers on the pilgrim but for the private boon conferred on the visitor.

Domestic tourism does transform traditional resource use patterns, but not to the same degree as international tourism because it does not follow an enclave type of development. The gap between a large number of domestic tourists and the mass of the resident population tends to be less. The volume of consumption tends to be less and the impacts can be contained. However, as the high-spending domestic tourist begins to imitate the foreign tourists, there is not much difference in the impact of such tourism. We have to stress that even though domestic tourism is not encouraged by the government and the industry, in a country like India the numbers are so significant that unless domestic tourists are redistributed to the new destinations there is no way in which the environmental, social and economic impacts can be controlled. Domestic tourism also requires regulation, awareness and education to ensure that the negative impacts of tourism can be reversed. For example, domestic tourists consider wildlife sanctuaries picnic spots. The jungle is a new resort. Since the jungle lodge owners use domestic tourists to fill their rooms, they do not insist on the observation of environmental and jungle rules and regulations.

There has been a great emphasis, in the recent past, on human resource development (HDR). The WTO has been in the forefront of developing training programmes for developing countries to train the workforce to deliver international standards in tourism services. The WTO has also devised training programmes for tourism administrators, to streamline the approach to tourism development and marketing and promotion (WTO and University of Surrey, 1996). Ten Indian universities are running travel and tourism programmes that reflect this mainstream approach.

HRD begins at the school level, with a tourism or vocational option for the senior secondary student. The matriculated student has the option of a food craft institute, to teach basic skills in catering and in front office management. These are followed by undergraduate programmes, delivered through both formal and distance education programmes. These are then dovetailed into masters programmes, which are parallel to management programmes and meet the requirement of the executive category. Companies have now set up in-house HRD programmes since they find that the tourism education programme within the formal system does not meet their needs. The travel trade is critical of the kind of tourism education being provided in the system (Khan, 1997).

The pressure to standardize services and their delivery systems is likely to make the Indian tourist product a poor imitation of that which is available in the West. The HRD system being developed will make us lose our cultural input into the product. We will neither be able to imitate the West, because the service provider and trainee do not understand the cultural context of the tourist and do not share the lifestyle or expectations. Procedures can be learnt but not attitudes, which grow out of life experiences. For domestic tourism services, the providers are not willing to bear the cost and prefer the unskilled, and more docile and low-paid staff. High-spending tourists, for whom the Western style of services is an attraction, are dissatisfied with such services.

The intervention that is required is therefore to reverse the process of globalization that is taking place in the consumption of goods and services, lifestyles and aspirations. The drive for such change is coming from the new economic thinking and the need to educate all tourists is now becoming apparent. Tourism activists are organizing such campaigns to educate not only the tourists, but also the residents, the tourism industry and policy-makers on the need for such changes. Any argument for carrying capacity is meaningless without such education.

Domestic tourism has economic advantages because it represents activities, amenities and facilities that can be provided without straining the resources of the destination. It also represents a meaningful interaction between the leisure and recreational attitudes of both residents and visitors. However, as domestic tourism gets into the organized sector, tourism tends to transform, looks for external investments and world-class facilities because the organized sector depends on international tourism for its big profits. This creates cultural dependencies as well as economic pretensions which the credit card economy and the time-share movement are encouraging amongst the middle class in India. Once this transformation takes place, travel experience changes from being one of learning and cultural exchange to one of self-centred pleasure.

To link sustainable tourism, particularly domestic tourism, to numbers is to look at the tourism in development debate purely from the vantage point of the market economy, a model that is almost Darwinian in its implications, for the joy of being a traveller would then be open only to the 'fittest' tourist. The definition of fitness is also controlled by the industry, which does not consider social opportunities and social costs as being the determinants, but profitability, growth and expansion as symbols of economic efficiency. Data on tourism are presented for the ten top destinations, the ten top earners, and the ten top

value-for-money destinations, all of which then act as push factors for the competition between destinations. New destinations and new products compete on novelty values and risk factors, or the cost and expenditure values, for their status rankings. This is often described as allocentric or psychographic tourist profiling. Given that the WTO, affiliated governments, international agencies and industry are pushing for privatization in the tourism sector, it seems unlikely that a sustainable model of tourism is likely to emerge.

However, the possibility of domestic tourism being a sustainable alternative to mass international tourism is higher. Even though there is a lack of sufficient research, NGO studies have looked at domestic tourism impacts and suggested the decentralization of decision-making to determine the size of a project and the type of tourism to be developed, as well as the manner in which the economic benefits of tourism can be more evenly distributed (*Tourism in Focus*, 1994; Kaushik, 1993). This can only be worked out if we have an open mind on the question of the market economy. The argument that there is no alternative to market forces as the engines of development is an ideological argument, and it can be countered only when case studies indicating the destructive force of such a developmental model, which is heavily dependent on international and national money power, are popularized. The social and anthropological impacts of beach tourism and ecotourism should also be made known to the consumers who will be sensitized by the process of 'counter' information from below.

Several initiatives have already been put in place in India. The Indian National Trust for Culture and Heritage had funded several area development plans which seek to integrate tourism into the developmental needs of the destinations. These plans have covered the Kullu Valley, Ladakh, Varanasi, Panchmari, Chanderi and Ujjain. These plans have developed a methodology which can be further adapted. NGO organizations have also taken up eco-development plans at Kanha and Rajaji National Park where the issue of displacement of traditional communities and their rights to forest produce are being studied to improve the methodology of socio-economic planning for change. Both these experiences have shown that the bureaucratic structure of government institutions is not people-centred. The important lesson to be learnt from this experience is that planning in itself cannot accomplish change; it has to be a process in which the beneficiaries have to evaluate the changes and choose alternatives because their livelihood and lifestyle are under threat. These initiatives are being undertaken all over India, but especially by the NGO sector. State governments are also funding such studies since they have a resource constraint and would like to ensure that money invested will optimize benefits. Such research is the result of the sensitization of the government and the NGO sector through the struggles of concerned people, citizen groups and local government bodies to ensure that the tourism impacts that they have to live with beyond the tourist season do not extract a heavy cost (INTACH, 1989, 1990, 1992 and 1995).

There are certain social costs that come with tourism development that are, however, extremely destructive and need urgent redress. For issues like changes in land use, child prostitution, the burden on women at tourist destinations, the transformation of agriculture, etc, there is no longer the time to build a consensus. Local people have to determine their future, even where it goes against national resource planning. This is being demonstrated at projects like Tehri and Narmada. The tourism projects being resisted are at Bekal, Puri, Sindhudurg and Muttukadu (Bellaigue, 1995). These are all identified and designated special tourism areas (Government of India, 1994). A special tourism area is like an export promotion zone, where the investor, primarily the foreign investor in the case of a tourism project, will get single window clearance for the project. This involves the dilution of local and state laws and regulations, as well as diversion of resources that were being used by residents and traditional economic practices. This displacement and disempowerment, through the creation of international tourism enclaves, threatens the economic, political and social fabric of the nation. There is great resistance to this concept, which the government is seeking to overcome through the Tourism Awareness Programme (TAP) being spearheaded in India by PATA, WTTC and WTO. The success of local intervention will determine how the future of tourism will emerge.

Notes

1   1 crore = 10 million rupees.
2   In October 1998, US$1 = Indian rupees (Rs) 42.
3   Results of a survey conducted by the Department of Tourism, the Ministry of Tourism and the government of India.
4   1 lakh = 100,000.

References

Asian Age (1997) 'UP divided into 5 tourist sectors', Bangalore, 15 May
Bellaigue, C (1995) 'Packaged confusion', *India Today*, 28 February, pp187–192
Bhatia, Gauri (1997) 'And now a green triangle for tourists', *Indian Express*, New Delhi, 15 March
Business Line (1998) 'KSEB functioning to be revamped', Bangalore, 28 July
Business Times Bureau (1997) 'Hotel industry seeks tax rationalisation', *Times of India*, Mumbai, 21 January
Department of Tourism, Ministry of Tourism – Government of India (1979) *Report of the Working Group on Domestic Tourism*, Delhi
Department of Tourism, Ministry of Tourism – Government of India (1994) *India – Tourist Statistics 1994*, Delhi

Department of Tourism, Ministry of Tourism – Government of India (1997)
   India – Tourist Statistics 1997, Delhi
Economic Times (1996) Delhi, 17 November
Economic Times (1997a) Delhi, 11 May
Economic Times (1997b) Delhi, 25 May
Go, F M and L C Jenkins (eds) (1997) *Tourism and Economic Development in
   Asia and Australia*, Cassell, London
Government of India (1994) *Proceedings of the Rajya Sabha Question Hour*,
   Unstarred Question No 2299 – Answered on 11.8.1994 by Shri Ghulam
   Nabi Azad, The Minister for Civil Aviation and Tourism
Hariharan, Bagyalakshmi (1997) 'Recession hits Bangalore star hotels', *Business
   Line*, Bangalore, 5 September
Hariharan, Bagyalakshmi (1998) 'Resorts association sets up Consumer Redress
   Forum', *Business Line*, Bangalore, 8 May
The Hindu (1998) 'Body to promote timeshare and holiday ownership', 4
   October
Indian Express (1997) Delhi, 14 March
Indian National Trust for Culture and Heritage (INTACH) (1989) *Leh
   Development Plan*, Delhi
Indian National Trust for Culture and Heritage (INTACH) (1990) *Kullu-
   Manali Development Plan*, Delhi
Indian National Trust for Culture and Heritage (INTACH) (1992) *Ujjain
   Development Plan and Heritage Zone*, Delhi
Indian National Trust for Culture and Heritage (INTACH) (1995) *Panchmari
   Tourism Development Plan*, Delhi
Kaushik, Shubendhu (1993) *Towards a Tourism Strategy in Spit*, EQUATIONS,
   Bangalore
Khan, M N (1997) 'Human resource development, Training and upgradation
   in tourism industry', in *Proceedings of the South South-East Asian Convention
   on Tourism*, Hyderabad
Krippendorf, J (1987) *The Holiday-Makers: Understanding the Impact of Leisure
   and Travel*, Vera Andrassy, trans, Heinemann, London
Lew, Alan L and Lawrence Yu (eds) (1995) *Tourism in China*, Westview Press,
   Oxford
Ministry of Tourism, Government of India (1992) *National Action Plan for
   Tourism*, Delhi
Ministry of Tourism, Government of India (1997) *Draft National Tourism Policy*,
   Delhi
Ministry of Tourism, Government of India (undated) Statistics on Domestic
   Tourism in the Department of Tourism
Patnaik, R L (1998) 'Special area tourism development', *Express Hotelier and
   Caterer*, vol 1, no 49, Bombay, 7 September
The Pioneer (1997a) Delhi, 7 May

The Pioneer (1997b) Delhi, 24 May

The Pioneer (1997c) Delhi, 15 June

Poon, A (1989) 'Competitive strategy for a new tourism management', in C Cooper (ed), *Progress in Tourism Recreation and Hospitality Management*, vol 1, Belhaven, London

Richter, Linda (1989) 'Tourism policy in South Asia', *Annals of Tourism Research*, vol 3, no 3

N Salim & Associates (1995a) *Bekal Tourism – Tourism Led Urban Structure Plan*, vol I, Calicut

N Salim & Associates (1995b) *Bekal Tourism – Techno Economic Feasibility & Tourism Led Urban Structure Plan*, vol II, Calicut

Sharma, Ashish (1997) 'The untapped potential', *The Pioneer*, 19 October

Smith, V L and W R Eddington (1992) *Tourism Alternatives: Potentials and Problems in the Development of Tourism*, University of Pennsylvania Press, Philadelphia

Smith, L Valene (ed) (1989) *Hosts and Guests: The Anthropology of Tourism*, 2nd edition, University of Pennsylvania Press, Philadelphia

Suresh K T (ed) (1996) 'Bekal why?', *An EQUATIONS Dossier on the Bekal Special Tourism Area Project 1996*, EQUATIONS, Bangalore

Suresh K T and Hari Babu (1997) 'Development and sustenance of coastal tourism in India', in *Proceedings of the South South-east Asian Convention on Tourism*, Hyderabad

Times of India (1997) 'HC issues notice to centre on service tax for tour operators', Bangalore, 6 November

Tourism in Focus (1994) 'Bekal zoned for tourism urbanisation', summer issue, no 12

Tourism Review (1992) 'Tourism and development in least developed countries', no 11, Bangkok, ESCAP, United Nations

World Tourism Organization (WTO) (1998) *Tourism Satellite Account (Draft 4)*, WTO, Madrid, July

World Tourism Organization and University of Surrey (1996) *Educating the Educators in Tourism: A Manual of Tourism and Hospitality Education*

World Travel and Tourism Council (1996) *WTTC 1996/7 Travel & Tourism Report*

Index

Thailand
'Amazing Thailand' campaign 131–2, 137
American tourists 112
Association of Thai Tour Operators
(ATTO) 119
Bangkok 115, 116, 120
carrying capacity of tourism 122–8
Chiang Mai 121–2, 124
cultural impacts of tourism 128–30, 138
destinations 115, 116
development planning 132–5
Doi Inthanon National Park 124, 126–7
Doi Suthep National Park 126–7
domestic tourism 7, 10, 113–18
drug problems 129
economic impacts of tourism 120–1
ecotourism 125–8
environmental impacts 123–5, 136,
137–8, 139n4
Environmental Quality Act (1992) 125
evaluation of tourism resources 122–3
history of tourism 112–13, 130–1
impacts of tourism 110–12
international tourism 109–10, 112–13
Khao Yai national park 18, 113–14,
126–7
Kho Samui 124–5
litter 127, 136
motivations of domestic tourists 115–18
Nakhon Ratchasima 115
national park system 126–7
outbound tourism 118–20
Pattaya 112, 124
Phuket 120
regional tourists 111–12
religious tourism 8
second homes 113–14
sectoral planning 134–5
sex tourism 112
sustainability of tourism 111, 137–8
'Thais Tour Thailand' campaign 119, 131,
137
Tourism Authority of Thailand (TAT)
119, 126, 131, 138, 139n4
Tourism Organization of Thailand (TOT)
112

tourism policies 23, 130–8
training courses 135
trekking impacts 129–30
time-share resorts, India 216
toilet facilities, China 98
Tourism Concern 3
tourism indicators, Mexico 34–5
tourism policies
Brazil 59–63
China 95–8
domestic tourism 21–4
India 198–206
Mexico 36–8
Nigeria 176–82
South Africa 150–5
Thailand 23, 130–8
training courses, Thailand 135
transport
India 205
Mexico 33
trekking, Thailand 129–30

United Nations Educational, Scientific and
Cultural Organization (UNESCO),
domestic tourism 3, 28n3
urbanization, Brazil 68–9

visiting friends and relatives (VFRs) 16,
32–3, 39–40, 116

waste disposal, tourism impacts 20–1, 41, 127
women
impacts of tourism 19–20
South Africa 158, 160
travelling alone 217
see also prostitution
World Conference on Tourism, Manila
(1980) 21
World Heritage Sites, South Africa 153, 165
World Tourism Organization (WTO)
domestic tourism 3–4, 28n3, 55
Satellite Accounting Systems 200
tourist figures 1–2, 11–12
training programmes 223
World Travel and Tourism Council (WTTC)
149, 202